THEN AND NOW

1799–1974

AUSTRALIA
The Law Book Company Ltd.
Sydney : Melbourne : Brisbane

CANADA AND U.S.A.
The Carswell Company Ltd.
Agincourt, Ontario

INDIA
N. M. Tripathi Private Ltd.
Bombay

ISRAEL
Steimatzky's Agency Ltd.
Jerusalem : Tel Aviv : Haifa

MALAYSIA : SINGAPORE : BRUNEI
Malayan Law Journal (Pte.) Ltd.
Singapore

NEW ZEALAND
Sweet and Maxwell (N.Z.) Ltd.
Wellington

PAKISTAN
Pakistan Law House
Karachi

THEN AND NOW

1799–1974

Commemorating 175 years of

Law Bookselling and Publishing

London

Sweet & Maxwell

1974

Published in 1974 by
Sweet and Maxwell Limited of
11 New Fetter Lane, London
and printed in Great Britain
by The Eastern Press Limited
of London and Reading

S.B.N 421 20490 7

Preface

It is natural for companies to celebrate important anniversaries and for a publisher, whatever other means of celebration may be adopted, the publishing of a commemorative volume is an obvious one.

It may be asked why celebrate 175 years, particularly when the year 1799 saw only the foundation of one of the businesses which subsequently became what is now Sweet & Maxwell. Of course, 150 years could have been made the occasion for some special work—and, indeed, I believe there was a private celebration—but a glance at the Statute Book for 1949 will show that the very small editorial staff (three people) had more than enough to do publishing material for the legal profession and would spare little time for assembling such a work as this.

What is worth commemorating is the fact that, after 175 years, out of many who have started selling law books, only two families have continued to provide members of succeeding generations to carry on the business, and it is with regret that one notes that the current members of the two families are nearing retirement age.

The theme of a collection of essays inevitably bears some relation to the event or period commemorated, and for law publishers in 1974 the simple theme of "Then and Now" is appropriate. From the end of the eighteenth century and the middle of the Napoleonic Wars to a new era of social revolution and Britain's entry into Europe is a period spanning tremendous changes in law and its administration. Under broad headings wellknown legal authors have been kind enough to contribute to this volume. Other than the theme and a suggested length, no advice or restriction has been placed and each author has treated his subject in his own way, which makes this a varied and attractive collection of essays. The directors of Sweet & Maxwell express their gratitude to our authors, who have found time to contribute to a volume created for sentimental rather than commercial reasons.

PETER ALLSOP.

All Fool's Day, 1974.

Contents

II COMMERCIAL LAW

CLIVE M. SCHMITTHOFF, LL.M. (Lond.), LL.D. (Lond.),
DR. JUR. (Berl.), Barrister of Gray's Inn, Visiting Professor
of International Business Law at the City University and the
University of Kent, Hon. Professor of Law at the Ruhr-Univer-
itat Bochum

III COMMON LAW

A. W. B. SIMPSON, M.A., J.P.
Professor of Law at the University of Kent

IV CONSTITUTIONAL LAW

J. D. B. MITCHELL, C.B.E., PH.D. (Lond.), LL.D. (Edin.),
DR. (h.c.) Lille
Solicitor; Salvesen Professor of European Institutions, Uni-
versity of Edinburgh

VIII *PROCEDURE*—continued

Civil Procedure since 1800—continued

IX *PROFESSIONS*

TOM HARPER
Editor of *The Law Society's Gazette* 1950–1965; Editor of
The New Law Journal 1965–1972

X *PROPERTY AND EQUITY*

EDWARD F. GEORGE, LL.B., A.T.I.I.
Solicitor of the Supreme Court; Joint Editor of the
Conveyancer and Property Lawyer

X PROPERTY AND EQUITY—continued

I
Authors

Legal Authors since 1800

O. HOOD PHILLIPS

JURISTS: BENTHAM AND AUSTIN

WHEN we look back from our present vantage point to the literature of
the law in this country at the beginning of the nineteenth century, one
figure of international significance appears to loom over all other legal
writers—that of Jeremy Bentham, already over fifty years old at the turn
of the century. Of Bentham's work published in his lifetime, some was
published in the eighteenth century, but much of what he wrote did not
appear at all in his lifetime. The first collected edition was the eleven
volumes edited by John Bowring in 1843. All his manuscripts, legal and
non-legal, are now in the process of being re-edited or prepared for first
publication. Bentham was called to the Bar by Lincoln's Inn in 1769,
but never practised and could well afford not to do so. His study was not
the law as it was, but the science of legislation or " censorial jurisprudence." Yet he was not censorious: his criticisms of the law were always
positive and constructive. He adopted the doctrine of sovereignty, for
legislation by an unlimited legislature was to be the mechanism for his
ambitious schemes of law reform. He also accepted from James Mill the
principle of utility which, although it lies open to philosophical criticism,
served the purpose of providing a criterion both of existing law and possible reforms during an age of rationalism. On the other hand, Bentham
ignored the lessons of history and made little attempt to understand
human nature. Many of his proposals were taken up later, in a modified
and more practical form, by such influential followers as Brougham and
Romilly. From his vast output we may select for mention here: *A Fragment on Government* (1776; ed. 1948), a reaction against Blackstone's complacency: *A Comment on the Commentaries* (ed. E. W. Everett, 1928), the
context of the *Fragment; The Principles of Morals and Legislation* (1789; ed.
1970); *Principles of Penal Law; Rationale of Judicial Evidence* (ed. J. S. Mill,
1827); *The Theory of Legislation* (ed. C. K. Ogden, 1931); and *Of Laws in
General* (ed. H. L. A. Hart, 1970), replacing *The Limits of Jurisprudence
Defined* (ed. Everett, 1945). Bentham's style is prolix and difficult, and
contains many neologisms some of which, like " codify " and " international law," are undoubtedly useful. To render Bentham's general
theory of law readable by undergraduates, we need someone to do for him
what Jethro Brown did for Austin. Bentham wrote incessantly but left
most of his works uncompleted, some being put into publishable form

3

by Dumont in France and J. S. Mill and others in this country. He died
at a ripe age on the eve of the passing of the Reform Act 1832, and his
fame was largely—though by no means entirely—posthumous. Dicey,
writing of the relation between law and public opinion, called the period
1825–70 the age of Benthamism. Macaulay's verdict was that Bentham
found jurisprudence a gibberish and left it a science.

John Austin was a follower of Bentham in his view of sovereignty and
political society, in his use of the analytical method, in embracing the
principle of utility (which he identified with the law of God), and in
accepting with modifications the imperative definition of a law. It is
therefore convenient to mention Austin here, although his influence was
felt—and that mainly in this country—in the second half of the nineteenth
century. At the end of that period an Oxford undergraduate could
satisfy the examiners in the jurisprudence paper after merely reading
through the two volumes of Austin's *Lectures*. Austin was born in 1790.
After five years in the army he was called to the Bar by the Inner Temple
in 1818. He carried on some practice until 1825, being a good draftsman.
Having been appointed Professor of Jurisprudence at the new University
of London (now University College), he began to deliver his carefully
prepared lectures on jurisprudence in 1828, but resigned in 1832 because
of inadequate attendance. So he became the patron saint and martyr
of lecturers who have seen their audiences dwindle. The first fruits of this
course were *The Province of Jurisprudence Determined* (1832; ed. H. L. A.
Hart, 1954). Austin then served on a Criminal Law Commission, which
he upset by agitating for a criminal code, and more successfully on a
commission on the government of Malta. After residing for a few years
in Germany and Paris, he lived in retirement on slender means and with
a delicate constitution at Weybridge. He died in 1859, and his *Lectures
on Jurisprudence, or The Philosophy of Law* were published in 1863. The
analytical method had soon to contend with the new school of historical
jurists, but Austin's work was of permanent value in the attempt to
clarify legal concepts and to distinguish legal from non-legal rules;
further, the doctrine of sovereignty came to be applied rigorously by
Dicey and others to the British Parliament. Austin's style has been con-
demned for being unreadable as an Act of Parliament. He himself said
that his vocation was the untying of intellectual knots, and that he ought
to have been a twelfth-century schoolman or else a German professor.
The present tendency is to think that Austin as a jurist is a pale reflection
of Bentham, and that if all Bentham's juristic writings had been published in his lifetime Bentham would have held the predominant position
in English legal theory that has been held by Austin. But do we know
how much of Bentham's thinking was familiar to his friend Austin, either
through reading Bentham's manuscripts or through conversation with
him? It may be, for example, that Austin's definition of a command is an

intentional simplification of Bentham's excessively complex analysis. For student purposes Austin's work, apart from *The Province of Jurisprudence Determined*, was displaced in the first thirty years of this century by Sir Thomas Erskine Holland's *Elements of Jurisprudence* (1880; 13th ed. 1924), with growing competition from Salmond's book.

SURVIVORS FROM THE EIGHTEENTH CENTURY

Among practitioners' law books surviving from the eighteenth century and still in common use in the early nineteenth were Burn's *Justice of the Peace* and Tidd's *Practice*. Richard Burn, who was Vicar of Orton in Westmorland for fifty years, first published his *Justice of the Peace and Parish Officer* in 1755 and his *Ecclesiastical Law* in 1760, after which he took a well-earned D.C.L. at Oxford. The former work continued to be the most authoritative and complete book on local government during the first half of the last century, the thirtieth edition being published in 1869. William Tidd, the most famous of special pleaders—whose function it was to draw all the written proceedings in a suit at law in the various kinds of actions—published his *Practice of the Courts of King's Bench and Common Pleas* in 1790. He practised as a special pleader under the Bar for more than thirty years before being called by the Inner Temple. His pupils included the future Lord Chancellors Lyndhurst, Cottenham and Campbell, and Denman, a future Chief Justice of the Queen's Bench. The last (ninth) edition of Tidd's *Practice* appeared in 1828, followed by Supplements in 1837. It was unequalled as a statement of procedure, but it contained no criticism or suggestions for reform. Its style has been described as harsh and unattractive, which points the humour of Uriah Heep's remark to David Copperfield: " Oh, what a writer Mr. Tidd is, Master Copperfield." A companion volume, *Forms of Practical Proceedings in the Courts of King's Bench and Common Pleas* was published in 1799, the last edition being the eighth in 1840.

AUTHORS WHO BECAME JUDGES

The fact that a legal author was, or became, a judge is not supposed to add authority in court to his writings. Of those authors in our period who became judges the first to demand notice is Edward Burtenshaw Sugden, Lord St. Leonards. A conveyancer called to the Bar by Lincoln's Inn, Sugden was for some years a Tory Member of Parliament, becoming Solicitor-General. In that capacity he introduced a number of Bills to reform the law of wills and trusts. He was Lord Chancellor of Ireland from 1834–35 and from 1841–46. In 1852 he was appointed Lord Chancellor of Great Britain, but held this post for less than a year owing to the fall of the government. A man of great learning in the law of real property and equity, he gained the reputation of being almost infallible. At the Bar his practice was enormous. On the Bench he was described as

flippant, conceited and overbearing. Sugden's best-known work—
although not the one he rated the most logical—was his *Practical Treatise
on the Law of Vendors and Purchasers of Estates*, first published in 1805. He
says in the Preface that when he had finished writing the work his courage
failed him and he nearly committed the manuscript to the flames, but he
was eventually persuaded to share the risk of publication equally with a
bookseller. As soon as the book was printed another bookseller bought
out his interest, so that he received very little for this edition. However,
he saw the book, which reached its fourteenth edition in 1862, as the
foundation of his early success in life, and earned altogether more than
£40,000 from his writings. The *Treatise on Powers* followed in 1808, an
original and exhaustive book which has always been accepted as of the
highest authority on the history and exposition of this branch of the law,
and it remained the standard work until superseded in 1874 by one with
the same title by Sir George Farwell, a Lord Justice of Appeal. Peel said
that, if *Sugden on Powers* was a legal Euclid, the section on the *Scintilla Juris*
was the *pons asinorum*. Sugden's books were closely reasoned and packed
with detail; according to Bryce their authority was unsurpassed by any
other legal writings of the nineteenth century. In 1858 Lord St. Leonards,
as he had become, published *A Handy Book on Property Law* for students
which was so popular that it went through six editions in its first year, and
Chief Justice Campbell said he would be willing to support a Bill declaring that everything in the *Handy Book* was law. Even in his nineties he
retained the habit of vaulting over gates. After his death no will could be
found, although half-a-dozen codicils came to light, and the court
allowed his daughter (who had acted as his amanuensis) to prove the
contents of the missing will by oral evidence.[1]

Sir John Barnard Byles, of the Inner Temple, was created one of the
last Queen's Serjeants in 1867, preparatory to his appointment to be a
judge of the Common Pleas. For fifteen years he greatly strengthened the
commercial side of that court. His *Treatise on the Law of Bills of Exchange*,
generally known as *Byles on Bills*, was published in 1829, and was
authoritative both as a historical explanation and a practical exposition.
Byles used to ride to the courts on a white horse, which inevitably became
known to the legal public as " Bills." The book reached its twenty-third
edition in 1972. Here we may notice the custom in the world of legal
publishing of continuing to bring out new editions of standard treatises
under the name of the original author but posthumously by other hands.
Colin Blackburn was born in Scotland, but according to one biographer
he was refined and civilised by Eton and Cambridge. A barrister of the
Inner Temple and law reporter, he became a judge of the Queen's Bench
and a Lord of Appeal. He was one of the greatest masters of the common

1. *Sugden* v. *St. Leonards (Lord)* (1876) 1 P.D. 154.

law, a jurist as well as a judge. It was said that Chief Justice Cockburn learnt his law from sitting with him. Blackburn's *Contract of Sale* (1845), written in his early days at the Bar, set out to show the effect of a contract of sale on the legal rights of property and possession in goods. The sources included Roman Law and Pothier as well as the Year Books. A third edition was published in 1910. Lord Campbell was responsible for the appointment of Blackburn from the junior Bar to be a judge at the early age of forty-five, which came as such a surprise to the public that *The Times* issued a leader headed " Who is Mr. Blackburn? " After twenty-seven years on the bench Blackburn retired and is said to have read nothing thereafter except French novels. Nathaniel Lindley, who lived from 1828 to 1921, was equally learned in both common law and equity. The last serjeant-at-law, he was appointed a judge of the Common Pleas Division in 1875, when the Judicature Acts came into force, although he had carried on a large practice on the Chancery side. Later he became successively a Lord Justice of Appeal, Master of the Rolls and a Lord of Appeal in Ordinary. He had translated Thibaut's *System des Pandekten Rechts* five years before publishing his classic *Law of Partnership* in 1860, of which the thirteenth edition appeared as recently as 1971. The first edition included the Law of Companies, later hived-off into a separate book that did not enjoy the sustained celebrity of his *Partnership*.

Sir James Fitzjames Stephen, a brother of Leslie Stephen, came of a gifted family with wide intellectual connections and acquaintance, including the Austins. Maine was a friend of his from Cambridge days. Stephen, who was a member of the Inner Temple, practised at the Bar for fifteen years as well as writing innumerable articles in literary periodicals, and then followed Maine as legal member of the Council of the Governor-General of India. During his three years there he was able to indulge to the full his appetite for codification. Stephen said that an ideal code ought to be drawn by a Bacon and settled by a Coke. He also uttered the well-known dictum that in drafting it is not enough to gain a degree of precision which a person reading in good faith can understand, but it is necessary to attain if possible to a degree of precision which a person reading in bad faith cannot misunderstand. We should not be surprised to learn from Bryce that Stephen's capacity for drafting was not equal to his fondness for it. He tried without success to bring about the codification of English criminal law. For a short time he was Professor of Common Law at the Inns of Court, and then from 1879 to 1891 a judge of the High Court. He will be remembered, however, rather as author and codifier than as judge. Stephen's *General View of the Criminal Law* (1863), criticising the form which English criminal law derived from the three elements of the old common law, heterogeneous statutes and case law, was something of a pioneering work with its use of the comparative method. It was the germ from which grew his most celebrated works—

Digest of the Criminal Law (1877; 9th ed., 1950), *Digest of the Law of Evidence* (1876; 12th ed. revised, 1946), and *History of the Criminal Law* (3 vols., 1883). Stephen inaugurated the scientific study of criminal law in this country, although the historical side of his work has merited criticism.

Sir Edward Vaughan Williams, of Lincoln's Inn, was a pupil of Patteson and Campbell and a son of "the renowned Serjeant" Williams, editor of Saunders' *Reports* ("the Pleader's Bible"), which he himself helped to re-edit. He was appointed a judge of the Common Pleas in 1846. After twenty-two years he retired but continued to sit in the Privy Council. He was an insatiable reader, modest and reserved. *The Law of Executors and Administrators* (1832; 15th ed., 1970) was always regarded as of great authority, with its comprehensive analysis of common law, Chancery and ecclesiastical cases. Several editions were edited by his son, Sir Roland Vaughan Williams, a Lord Justice of Appeal, himself the author of a well-known book on *Law and Practice of Bankruptcy* (1870; 18th ed. revised, 1968). Sir Edward Fry, of University College, London, and Lincoln's Inn, was one of the greatest technical masters of equity and enjoyed a successful practice at both the Chancery and parliamentary Bars. After five years as a puisne judge in the Chancery Division he was appointed in 1883 a Lord Justice of Appeal. As a member of the Rule Committee of the Supreme Court he is said to have invented the originating summons. Surviving his retirement from the Bench by a quarter of a century, he remained in demand as chairman of government commissions and as an international arbitrator. His *Specific Performance of Contracts* (1858), the first and highest authority on the equitable remedy of specific performance as opposed to the contract of sale, reached a sixth edition in 1921. Another member of a well-known legal family educated at Westminster school was Sir Robert Phillimore, civilian and jurist, learned in ancient and modern languages, barrister of the Middle Temple and D.C.L. of Oxford. He became judge of the Cinque Ports and in 1867 succeeded Dr. Lushington as the last judge of the High Court of Admiralty. His *Commentaries on International Law* (1854–57) formed the most important book on international law to appear in this country since Zouche produced his *Jus inter Gentes* 200 years earlier. Volume 4 (1861) covered private international law, incorporating the author's *Law of Domicil* (1847). This part was somewhat overweighted with foreign authorities, and did not compete with Westlake's work on *Private International Law*. Phillimore also wrote a treatise on *Ecclesiastical Law of the Church of England* (1873; 2nd ed., 1895).

Henry Burton Buckley, a Cambridge wrangler called to the Bar by Lincoln's Inn, became a judge of the Chancery Division in 1900 and was a Lord Justice of Appeal from 1906 to 1915. He published in 1873 his widely used *Law and Practice under the Companies Acts*, which in 1957 reached its thirteenth edition. In 1915 Buckley was created Lord Wrenbury, and for some years he continued to take an active part in the judicial and legislative business of the House of Lords.

Thomas Edward Scrutton enjoyed brilliant success at Cambridge, where he was President of the Union, and in the Bar examinations. He was called to the Bar by the Middle Temple and while still a pupil in chambers he was appointed Professor of Constitutional Law and Legal History at University College, London. His practice lay mainly in commercial law and copyright. As a judge of the Queen's (King's) Bench Division from 1895 to 1910 he was unpopular with counsel on account of his rudeness, but as a Lord Justice of Appeal (by which time he looked like an old sea captain) he mellowed with age. He died in 1934 aged nearly eighty, after almost forty years on the Supreme Court bench. Scrutton's *Charterparties and Bills of Lading* (1886; 18th ed., 1974) was immediately recognised as the standard treatise on this subject. *The Influence of Roman Law on the Law of England* (1885) is the most celebrated of the four successful Yorke Prize essays Scrutton wrote on different topics. He also published books on mercantile law, commons and copyright.

County court judges are represented in this survey by Charles James Gale, who began his career as a special pleader and law reporter. He was called to the Bar by the Middle Temple in 1832, and doubtless inspired by the Prescription Act of that year, he published *The Law of Easements* seven years later (14th ed., 1972). Prominence was given in the early editions to rights in respect of water, which were then of current interest.

PROLIFIC AUTHORS

The most prolific writers of English law books must include among their number Joseph Chitty, with his family, and J. F. Archbold. Joseph Chitty Senior was an eminent pleader, first special and then at the Bar, and besides writing more than twenty practitioners' books he founded a well-known family of lawyers. His most successful works were *Law of Bills of Exchange* (1799; 11th ed., 1878), *Pleading and Parties, with precedents* (1809, 7th ed., 1844) and *Collection of Statutes of Practical Utility* (1829; 6th ed., 1911). His *Criminal Law, comprising Practice, Pleadings and Evidence* (1816) was soon rendered obsolete by reforms in the law and was superseded by Russell and Archbold. Other subjects on which Chitty published books were apprentices and journeymen (of topical interest following the Industrial Revolution), game laws and fisheries, the legal effect of war on commerce (1812), stamp laws (actions often failed because documents were not sufficiently stamped), and medical jurisprudence, of which only the part on medical information appeared in print. His eldest son, Joseph Chitty Junior, a special pleader, enjoyed most success with his *Law of Contracts* (1826), of which the twenty-third edition was published as recently as 1968. Its purpose was to cover the substantive

law of contracts not under seal in such a way as would be of use to the
practitioner. It became a standard work, and the twentieth edition of
1947 was modernised and made academically respectable under the
general editorship of Harold Potter. Joseph Junior also wrote books on
bills of exchange, the office and duties of constables, precedents of
pleading, and *Law and Prerogatives of the Crown* (1820) which is still
referred to by constitutional lawyers. Thomas Chitty, Joseph Senior's
second son, was as distinguished a pleader as his father, and counted
among his pupils the future Lord Chancellors Cairns and Herschell, a
future Master of the Rolls, A. L. Smith, and a future judge of the
Common Pleas, Willes. His *Forms of Civil Proceedings in the Queen's Bench
Division* (1833) reached its twentieth edition in 1969. Edward Chitty,
the third son of Joseph Senior, an equity draftsman, not only published
a popular *Commercial and General Lawyer* (1823–36; 14th ed., 1865), but
compiled an *Index to Equity, Privy Council and House of Lords Cases* (1831)
which was eventually incorporated in Mews' *Digest*. Grandsons of
Joseph Chitty Senior were Sir Joseph William Chitty, of Lincoln's Inn,
who was appointed a judge of the Chancery Division in 1881 and a Lord
Justice of Appeal in 1897, and Thomas Willes Chitty who edited a
number of the family books and also collaborated with Mews in com-
piling his *Digest of English and Irish Cases*.

John Frederick Archbold, a member of Lincoln's Inn, was sufficiently
industrious to produce some forty books, clear, concise, comprehensive
and usually well arranged. The publishers owned the copyright of
Practice of the Court of King's Bench in Personal Actions (1819) and to Archbold's annoyance they commissioned Thomas Chitty to prepare the
later editions, which competently included the practice of the Common
Pleas and Exchequer (14th ed., 1885). *Pleading and Evidence in Criminal
Cases*, first published in 1822, was of course Archbold's most important
and successful book. He had intended to write a digest of criminal law
based on all the authorities from Bracton onwards, but in view of the
competition from other authors he substituted for this a book concentrat-
ing on pleading and evidence. The aim was intensely practical, the plan
being to treat first of pleading and evidence in criminal cases generally
and then pleading and evidence in particular cases. The edition current
in 1877 was criticised by J. F. Stephen for bad arrangement. " It is an
invaluable work of reference," wrote Stephen, " but to try to read it is
like trying to read a directory arranged partly on geographical and
partly on biographical principles." Nevertheless a series of able editors
have kept the book very much alive, and 1973 saw the thirty-eighth
edition. Of Archbold's other books his *Poor Law* (1840) reached a sixteenth edition by the time the Poor Law was abolished in 1930; the
volumes of *Justice of the Peace and Parish Officer* on summary convictions
(1840) reached a seventh edition in 1859, and a work on the duties of

Justices out of Sessions (Jervis's Act) met the needs of the profession for rather more than twenty years; *Law and Practice in Bankruptcy* (1825) called for eleven editions down to 1856; *Practice of the County Courts*, which appeared in 1847 soon after those courts were established, reached a tenth edition in 1889; *Parish Officer* (1852) survived until the eighth edition of 1895; and *Practice of the Court of Quarter Sessions* (1836) saw a sixth edition in 1908. Archbold's other books on such subjects as arbitration, landlord and tenant, lunacy, partnership, pleading and evidence in civil actions, and Crown Office practice enjoyed a shorter life.

OTHER EARLY NINETEENTH-CENTURY AUTHORS

Other law books of the early nineteenth century included William Woodfall's *Law of Landlord and Tenant*, first published in 1802, which was remodelled and enlarged by other hands from 1831 onwards. Woodfall was a barrister of the Middle Temple. The twenty-seventh edition of 1968 remains a standard work on this branch of the law. Edward Christian, brother of Fletcher Christian who led the mutiny in the *Bounty*, was a Fellow of St. John's College, Cambridge, and a barrister of Gray's Inn. He did not succeed at the Bar but appropriately wrote two short-lived books on bankruptcy and in later life one on the game laws. It was said that he died in " the full vigour of his incapacity." Nevertheless he became Treasurer of his Inn, and was appointed in 1788 to be the first Downing Professor of the Laws of England. Christian is mentioned here because he produced a good edition of Blackstone's *Commentaries*. William Oldnall, barrister of Lincoln's Inn, adopted the name Russell. He was created a serjeant-at-law in 1827 and was knighted in 1832 on appointment as Chief Justice of Bengal. Russell's *Treatise on Felonies and Misdemeanours* (1819) was the best and (except that it excluded treason) the fullest work on the criminal law at that time. Evidence was added in the second edition. The arrangement, however, was strongly criticised in 1877 by J. F. Stephen, who likened the cases on homicide to the British army stores at Balaclava during the Crimean War. " Everything is there, nothing in its place," Stephen wrote, " and the few feeble attempts at arrangement which have been made serve only to bring the mass of confusion to light." The continued usefulness of the book to the profession is shown by the fact that a twelfth edition was brought out in 1964. Thomas Lewin, an Oxford graduate, member of Lincoln's Inn and for twenty-five years conveyancing counsel to the Court of Chancery, wrote on a variety of archaeological and other topics, including the life and epistles of St. Paul. His *Law of Trusts*, first published in 1837 and dedicated to Lord St. Leonards, has always been regarded as the standard textbook on this subject. The sixteenth edition was published in 1964.

LEGAL HISTORY IN THE EARLY NINETEENTH CENTURY

Here we may take a look at the literature on legal history in the first half of the nineteenth century. John Reeves, a graduate of Merton College and Fellow of Queen's College, Oxford, and a member of the Inner Temple, was an expert on shipping and navigation laws. After acting as Chief Justice of Newfoundland for a year or two he wrote a history of the government of that colony, giving the proceeds for the relief of refugee French clergy in the British dominions. Later he was appointed King's Printer. Reeves, a high Tory, was prosecuted for seditious libel—somewhat paradoxically, because it was in respect of a pamphlet exaggerating the royal prerogative in relation to Parliament.[2] He was acquitted. Reeves's *History of English Law*, issued in several editions between 1783 and his death in 1829, was the first general history of English law to be written, the only general history of English law until Pollock and Maitland, and the only history of English law after Edward I to be written before Holdsworth's. Holdsworth agreed with the common view that Reeves's book was indescribably dull, but he denied that it was unreadable. George Spence, a graduate of Glasgow, studied Roman law and the Code Napoléon as well as Anglo-Saxon and medieval English law. A member of the Inner Temple, of which he became Treasurer, he practised in the Court of Chancery. In 1826 Spence published a learned inquiry into the origin of the laws and political institutions of modern Europe, particularly those of England, and in the following year translated the Code Napoléon. As a Member of Parliament and in his *Evils and Abuses of the Court of Chancery* (1831) he continued to advocate reforms in the Court of Chancery. After taking silk Spence found time to write his *Equitable Jurisdiction of the Court of Chancery*, the aim of which was to explain how the laws relating to property came to be administered by separate courts of common law and Chancery, and to point out the boundaries between their jurisdictions. Part I, published in 1846, was an interesting and useful history of equity, beginning with the Roman occupation of Britain and continuing down to the middle of the nineteenth century, so as to bring out the reason why common law and equity came to be administered in separate courts. It was the best account of this topic at that time, and Holdsworth regarded it nearly a hundred years later as an important authority on the history of equity. Part II, published in 1849, gave a full and systematic account of the equitable jurisdiction of the Court of Chancery. This incorporated Henry Maddock's treatise on the *Principles and Practice of the High Court of Chancery* (1815; 3rd ed., 1837), the first general treatise on modern equity and dedicated to Lord Eldon. Spence's book covers trusts of various kinds, the rules against perpetuities

2. (1796) 29 St.Tr. 530.

and accumulations, and such doctrines as conversion and election, as well as the defence of fraud and equitable remedies.

LAW STUDENTS' READING IN THE EARLY NINETEENTH CENTURY

There was no systematic legal education at the beginning of the nineteenth century. Textbooks were comparatively few, and a knowledge of the principles of the legal system had to be extracted largely from Littleton, Coke and Blackstone. A syllabus prepared in 1817 for the instruction of a student intending to become an attorney is described in Lord Hanworth's memoir of his grandfather, Chief Baron Pollock. The course was to take four years, beginning with such general reading as Hume and Paley. The legal programme began with the text of Volumes 1, 3 and 4 of Blackstone's *Commentaries* (persons, private wrongs and public wrongs), after which the student was to read these Volumes again, referring to every case quoted by Blackstone. There followed Selwyn's *Nisi Prius Cases* (first published in 1806 and already in the fourth edition) and Peake's *Law of Evidence* (published in 1802 and then in its fourth edition) in the same manner, " never to pass over a single case or position of the text without proving it." The student was to go on to read Tidd's *Practice*, followed by Littleton's *Tenures*, Butler and Hargreave's edition of *Coke upon Littleton* (all cases to be looked up), Volume 2 of Blackstone (rights of things), the seven volumes of Cruise's *Digest of the Laws of England respecting Real Property* (1804–07) and Fonblanque's *Treatise of Equity* (1793–94; 4th ed., 1812).

MID-NINETEENTH-CENTURY AUTHORS

Legal literature towards the middle of the nineteenth century was generally of a higher quality than in the previous period. We find clear statements of legal principles based on a co-ordination of statutes and judicial precedents, some showing an interest in the history of English law and a comparison with Roman law, occasional reference being made to Justinian and Pothier. Bulky tomes compiled from accumulations of judicial decisions also abounded, but these did not always receive a demand for successive editions. The revival of legal education in the middle decades of the century influenced the production of books intended primarily for students. Where these formulated general principles concisely, as in the works of Joshua Williams, they were found useful by practitioners as well. From the last quarter of the century we have a growing number of scientific treatises written by distinguished academic lawyers.

One of the best-known titles from the mid-nineteenth century is Stone's *Justices' Manual*. Samuel Stone, solicitor, was Clerk to the Leicester Justices and originally prepared the manual for his own use.

It was first published in 1842 at 5s. 2d. Stone himself brought out the first seventeen editions down to 1874. Editions were roughly biennial in its first fifty years, then annual since 1897 and are still current. The hundredth edition appeared in 1968 with a photograph of Samuel for a frontispiece. Stone's *Justices* may be called the magistrates' clerk's bible, except that both Volumes contain the New Testament. The Court of Appeal have recently said that magistrates ought to look at reports of cases referred to in passages of Stone cited in court, but one may doubt whether they (as distinct from their clerks) often go as far as to look at Stone itself. Samuel Stone also wrote a *Town Councillor's Manual* (1869), but it never got beyond a second edition.

The idea of making a collection of leading cases was suggested by Samuel Warren in his *Popular and Practical Introduction to Law Studies* (1835). Warren, a Q.C. of the Inner Temple, D.C.L. of Oxford and Fellow of the Royal Society, Recorder of Hull and Master in Lunacy, was the author of a novel well known in legal circles, *Ten Thousand a Year* (1841). The idea of such a collection was acted on by John William Smith, a Dublin graduate and member of the Inner Temple. *Leading Cases in various branches of the Law*, whose two volumes first appeared in 1837–40, is Smith's best-known work. It is a selection of common law cases with history and commentary, a work of high quality used by practitioners as well as students for more than a century. Later editors have included Sir James Shaw Willes and T. W. Chitty, and the thirteenth edition appeared in 1929. Smith's *Compendium of Mercantile Law* (1834; 13th ed., 1931) and *Law of Contracts* (1847; 8th ed., 1885) were also well received and helped his practice at the Bar. Smith also lectured for the Incorporated Law Society. He was a man of wide learning but delicate health, and died young. Smith's collection prompted Frederick Thomas White, equity draftsman and conveyancer of the Middle Temple, and Owen Davies Tudor to prepare a similar collection of *Leading Cases in Equity*, which first appeared in 1849–50 and reached its ninth edition in 1928. Tudor, also a barrister of the Middle Temple, a year after the passing of the Charitable Trusts Act 1853 published *Charitable Trusts*, which had become *Charities* by the sixth edition of 1967.

The roll-call of standard practitioners' books dating from the mid-nineteenth century must include such old warriors as Fisher, Prideaux, Copinger, Addison, Taylor, Best, Jarman, Mayne, Bullen and Leake, and Benjamin. *Law of Mortgages* by William Richard Fisher, equity draftsman and conveyancer of Lincoln's Inn, was first published in 1856. It became in later editions a treatise on securities of various kinds, and rejuvenated by the learned J. M. Lightwood as *Fisher and Lightwood* it merited a revised seventh edition in 1947. Frederick Prideaux, conveyancer of Lincoln's Inn, enjoyed his best publishing success with *Forms and Precedents in Conveyancing*, with a commentary giving an account of the law and practice of conveyancing. The first publication in 1853 was in one volume, but recent editions including the twenty-fifth in 1958 have occupied three fat volumes. Charles Greenstreet Addison, of the Inner Temple, special pleader, formed the meritorious purpose of producing the first scientific studies of the law of contracts and torts, but he had not quite the equipment needed for the task. His *Law of Contracts* (1845–47) was a well-intentioned and laborious attempt, partially successful, to elucidate the whole English law of contract in an intelligible form, as based on some principles and not merely an assortment of arbitrary rules. It was inspired by the works of Pothier. Later editors greatly improved the book, and an eleventh edition was called for in 1971. Addison's *Law of Torts* (1860) was an exhaustive treatise of the law of civil wrongs and their remedies, in which the trees of judicial decisions obscured the wood of principles. This book also was improved by later editors, though still without much discussion of general principle, and an eighth edition was brought out in 1906.

Thomas Jarman's *Treatise on Wills*, published in two volumes in 1841–44, became the standard monograph on the subject, treating exhaustively of the making, revocation, construction and effect of wills, and with the administration of assets. The eighth edition of 1951 was in three volumes. Jarman, a member of the Middle Temple and conveyancing counsel to the Court of Chancery, suffered from poor health. Consequently he did much of his work in the open, and was found on one occasion standing at a desk in the middle of a field with lawbooks strewn around him. He had previously written the volume on devises in W. M. Blythewood & Jarman's *Precedents in Conveyancing* (10 vols. 1821–34; 4th ed. 1884–90) based on manuscript drafts by counsel, with dissertations on the law and practical notes. J. D. Mayne's *Law of Damages* when published in 1856 was the first book on the subject of damages in this country for nearly a century. It examined the measure of damages, the mode in which they were assessed, judicial review of the jury's assessment and the law of set-off. The twelfth edition appeared in 1961 under the names of Mayne and MacGregor, becoming MacGregor in 1972. Two books on evidence were published in the middle of the century within a year of each other. First came J. Pitt Taylor's *Law of Evidence* in 1848, founded on a book by the American, Greenleaf. This standard treatise reached a twelfth edition in 1931. Then followed W. M. Best's *Principles of the Law of Evidence* in 1849. Best made use of the comparative method, and was also familiar with Bentham's criticism. The last (12th) edition was in 1922. Best had previously written books on jury trial and on evidentiary presumptions especially in criminal cases, and later he collaborated with G. J. P. Smith in issuing ten volumes of Queen's Bench Reports for the years 1861–69. One of the few works on the esoteric subject of copyright was published by Walter Arthur

Copinger in 1870, a year after being called to the Bar by the Middle Temple. His *Law of Copyright*, which covers the history and statute law of copyright in literature, music and art, received its eleventh edition in 1971. Copinger practised for some years in Manchester as an equity draftsman and conveyancer, and in 1892 was appointed Professor of Law at Owen's College. He was also an antiquary, bibliographer and composer, publishing books on such subjects as predestination and the history of the Copingers.

The *Precedents of Pleadings* (1860) by two barristers of the Middle Temple, Edward Bullen and Simon Martin Leake, was called for by the passing of the Common Law Procedure Acts. These precedents of pleadings in actions at common law have always been relied on for their accuracy, and the notes earned a high reputation for learning. The third edition of 1868 by Leake, containing more notes than precedents, provides the best explanation we have of the working of the forms of action at common law just before they were abolished by the Judicature Acts. After those Acts came into force *Bullen and Leake* continued to be brought up to date as providing precedents of pleading in the Queen's (King's) Bench Division down to the eleventh edition of 1959. Leake, after retiring from practice at the Bar on account of deafness, wrote a useful book on the *Law of Contracts* (1867; 8th ed., 1931) in an attempt to treat this branch of law in its general and abstract form, apart from its specific practical applications.

BENJAMIN, THE COLOURFUL OUTSIDER

No more colourful figure adorned the English Bar at this period than Judah Philip Benjamin. He was born of Jewish parents in St. Croix in the West Indies and so was a British subject by birth, but he spent most of his early years in New Orleans, taking American citizenship. After graduating at Yale he practised at the New Orleans Bar, thereby acquiring an extensive knowledge of Roman, French and Spanish law. Later he practised before the Supreme Court at Washington, and is said to have declined appointment to the Supreme Court Bench. For a few years he served as a Senator for Louisiana. On the outbreak of the Civil War he attached himself to the Southern Confederacy, for whom he became Attorney-General and Secretary of State. On the defeat of the Confederacy, Benjamin just succeeded in escaping to England. Six months after joining Lincoln's Inn as a student, having been excused his terms, he was called in 1866 to the English Bar at the age of fifty-five. Two years later he published his *Law of the Sale of Personal Property*, which at once established his reputation in this country. *Benjamin on Sale* is regarded as a classic. It formed the most complete treatise on the contract of sale of personal property, thereby supplementing Blackburn. A ninth edition appeared in 1974. Benjamin made use of Roman law, the

Code Napoléon and American cases, and his presence at the English Bar did much to influence the practice of our courts in referring to American decisions. He became the leading counsel in commercial cases and was appointed a Palatine silk, his practice consisting largely of Privy Council appeals from the colonies. Benjamin was single-minded in his devotion to the legal profession. His professional skill was said by Serjeant Ballantine to have been characterised by unimpassioned reasoning and immovable persistence in enforcing his argument. He retired on the ground of ill-health at the age of seventy-two, and died a year later.

BOOKS ON THE CONSTITUTION

We may now turn to some leading works on constitutional law. Sir Thomas Erskine May spent his career in the service of the House of Commons, rising from Assistant Librarian to Clerk to the House. He first published his *Law, Privileges, Proceedings and Usage of Parliament* in 1844. This work, generally known as " May's Parliamentary Practice " or " Erskine May," has been revised and re-edited by successive Clerks to the Commons and is regarded as of great authority not only at Westminster but also in all Commonwealth legislatures that operate on the Westminster model, and it has been translated into a number of foreign languages. The latest edition is the eighteenth (1971). In 1861 Erskine May published a *Constitutional History of England from 1760–1860*, beginning where Hallam left off. In this work he was so modern as to discuss such topics as ministerial responsibility to Parliament and the Sovereign's obligation to act on the advice of Ministers, but he drew no formal distinction between laws and constitutional conventions. A new (twelfth) edition appeared in 1912. On his retirement May was created Lord Farnborough, but died soon afterwards. The pioneering textbook *Institutions of the English Government*, published in 1863 by Homersham Cox, a barrister, has not enjoyed the celebrity it deserves, probably because it was so soon followed by the works of Hearn and Todd. Cox anticipated Bagehot by discussing the Cabinet, and he influenced Hearn who influenced Dicey in their treatment of the themes of constitutional conventions and the rule of law. William Edward Hearn, LL.D., Q.C., was an *alumnus* of Trinity College, Dublin, who became successively Professor of Greek at Queen's College, Galway, Professor of Modern History and Literature and the first Dean of the Faculty of Law at Melbourne University, a member of the Legislative Council of Victoria and Chancellor of Melbourne. Besides books of analytical jurisprudence, *The Theory of Legal Duties and Rights*, and comparative jurisprudence or anthropology, *The Aryan Household*, Hearn wrote sociological works. The second edition (1886) of his *Government of England*, first published in 1867, was used by Dicey. Working independently of Bagehot, Hearn emphasised the importance of the Cabinet and the doctrine of responsible government. Alpheus Todd, LL.D., C.M.G., was an Englishman whose family emigrated to Canada when he was eight years old. In the year that saw the passing of the British North America Act 1867, having become Librarian of the Legislative Assembly of Canada he published the first volume of his *Parliamentary Government in England*, the second volume following two years later. It gave the fullest account of the working of the English Constitution, and contained discussions not only of the " Cabinet Council " but also of the Prime Minister and constitutional " usage " or " custom." This book was found useful by Anson in writing his standard work on the law and custom of the Constitution. Todd later published *Parliamentary Government in the British Colonies* (1880; 2nd ed., 1894), a pioneer authority on responsible government in the colonies, only superseded by Berriedale Keith's work on responsible government in the dominions.

LATE NINETEENTH-CENTURY AUTHORS

Coming to practitioners' books of the later nineteenth century we notice first Maxwell's *Interpretation of Statutes*. Sir Peter Benson Maxwell, a graduate of Trinity College, Dublin, and barrister of the Middle Temple, became successively Recorder of Penang and of Singapore and Chief Justice of the Straits Settlements. This book, published in 1875 after his retirement, was the fruit of much experience in litigation involving the construction of statutes. Some later editions were by Sir Gilbert Jackson, puisne judge of the High Court of Madras. It has often been cited in the courts, although recent editions would have been improved by closer contact with the movement (at first academic only) for reform in the methods of statutory interpretation. The *Precedents in Conveyancing* of T. Key and Sir Howard Elphinstone have long provided a rival to Prideaux. Elphinstone, a third baronet, Cambridge wrangler and member of Lincoln's Inn, was appointed Reader in Real Property to the Inns of Court, and from 1895 to 1914 was conveyancing counsel to the court. He also wrote valuable books on conveyancing and property law. *The Law of Torts* (1895; 13th ed., 1969) by John Frederic Clerk, of the Inner Temple, and William Henry Barber Lindsell, of Lincoln's Inn, was a comprehensive survey of the cases. Since the tenth edition of 1947 issued under the general editorship of Harold Potter it has become more than a work of reference. Hood and Challis, *Property Statutes* was a collaboration between Henry William Challis and Henry J. Hood to bring out an annotated edition of the Acts relating to landed property, settled land, trustees and administrators. First published in 1882 it was frequently revised, and an eighth edition appeared in 1938. The learned Challis, a barrister of the Inner Temple, besides publishing a monograph on the Settled Land Act 1882, wrote the authoritative *Real Property Law* (1885; 3rd ed., 1911). Wolstenholme and Cherry's *Conveyancing Statutes*, which went through two editions on its publication in 1882, was a collaboration between two eminent conveyancing counsel of Lincoln's Inn, E. P. Wolstenholme and Sir Benjamin Cherry, the latter a former Cambridge rowing blue. Each of them by himself or in collaboration with others also produced works of practical use to conveyancers, including Cherry's *Lectures on the New Property Acts* (1926), of which Acts he was one of the chief draftsmen. Lewis E. Emmet, whose *Notes on Perusing Titles* have been found invaluable by conveyancers since they were first published in 1895 (15th ed., 1967), was a Sheffield solicitor. The growth of limited liability companies created a ready market for *Company Law* by Sir Francis Beaufort Palmer, Oxford graduate and bencher of the Inner Temple (two editions in 1898; 21st ed., 1968), *Company Precedents* (1877; 16th ed., 1951–52), *Private Companies* (1877; 41st ed., 1950) and *Company Guide* (36th ed., 1950). In 1907 Palmer published *Peerage Law in England*, the first treatise on this topic since Cruise *On Dignities* and a prophetic transfer of interest in view of the fact that peers now form companies to manage their stately homes.

STUDENTS' BOOKS IN THE MID-NINETEENTH CENTURY

The most important general students' lawbook in the middle of the nineteenth century was the four volumes of Stephen's *Commentaries*. Henry John Stephen (uncle of Sir J. F. Stephen) brought Blackstone's *Commentaries* up to date in 1841–45. He was a serjeant-at-law and commissioner in bankruptcy, and is said to have declined a judgeship because he was unwilling to impose the death sentence. He also wrote a classical treatise *On Pleading* (1824; 7th ed., 1866). Stephen's *Commentaries* remained a set book for the first part of the Law Society's examinations until recent years, the twenty-first edition appearing in 1950. Joshua Williams's *Law of Real Property* (1845) was an excellent textbook, with the right blend of history and modern law, by a complete master of his subject. Joshua Williams, special pleader and then barrister of Lincoln's Inn, was not only steeped in both history and current practice, but he took a critical view of this branch of law, and was a pioneer in advocating such reforms as the repeal of the Statute of Uses and the establishment of a registry of deeds. He became conveyancing counsel to the court, a Q.C. and bencher of his Inn, and from 1875–80 Reader in the Law of Real Property and Personal Property to the Council of Legal Education. He wrote at least ten other books, some of them series of lectures delivered at the Inns of Court, on such subjects as seisin and rights of common, the best known of which was the pioneer *Law of Personal Property* (1848) which was hived off his *Real Property* and reached an eighteenth edition in 1926. Some editions of *Real Property* after Joshua's death in 1881 were prepared by his almost equally learned and well-known son, T. Cyprian

Williams, himself the author of the successful *Law Relating to Vendors and Purchasers of Real Estate and Chattels Real* (1904–06; 4th ed., 1936). R. A. Eastwood's twenty-fourth edition of Williams's *Real Property* (1926), incorporating the effect of the new property statutes, is the most valuable edition of any textbook for a student who wants to understand the pre-1925 land law. The student's main standby in equity for many years was Snell's *Principles of Equity*, first published in 1868 and achieving a twenty-seventh edition in 1973. Edmund H. T. Snell was a graduate of Edinburgh and Oxford, and a barrister of the Middle Temple. A generation or two ago the book was dull but essential; more recently it has been revivified although now it meets with more competition.

A TWENTIETH-CENTURY ENCYCLOPEDIA

Halsbury's *Laws of England* is a product of the early years of the present century. It has long been recognised that the uncodified English legal system in its entirety does not lend itself to any scientific order of exposition, other than the alphabetical. This comprehensive work of reference appeared between the years 1907 and 1917. It is not a mere collection of cases and statutory provisions, but a series of concise though detailed treatises written by experts in their field. H. S. Giffard made such varied use of his time at Merton College, Oxford, that the examiners in classics placed him in the fourth class. His career in law and politics began when he was called to the Bar by the Inner Temple in 1850, and culminated in holding the office of Lord Chancellor for periods totalling more than seventeen years. Many law students have wondered whether Lord Halsbury, who relinquished the office of Lord Chancellor in 1905 in his eighty-third year, really wrote the *Laws of England* himself. More sceptical elders have assumed that the aged Earl merely lent it the prestige of his name, being content with the position of a figurehead. In fact Halsbury carried out the task of Editor-in-Chief (for which he was paid 10,000 guineas) with zeal, and infected the various contributors with his enthusiasm. Not only did he plan or approve the general scheme of the work, but he selected or approved the names of all the contributors. His personal contribution was made to the title " Parliament," in which he rewrote the paragraph on the powers of the House of Lords relating to finance after the Parliament Act 1911. Later editions have appeared or are appearing under the auspices of his successors Viscount Hailsham, Viscount Simonds and Lord Hailsham of St. Marylebone, but in the legal profession the work is always referred to as " Halsbury."

THE REVIVAL OF LEGAL EDUCATION

A revival of legal education, both in the profession and at the universities, took place during the middle decades of the nineteenth century. The Incorporated Law Society established lectures for articled clerks in

1833, and some provincial law societies soon followed. The new University College and King's College in London provided courses in law from the first. Other reforms were introduced during the next forty years. Examinations for intending solicitors became compulsory, individual Inns of Court began to establish readerships or lectureships and lecture courses, and made some provision for examinations; and then in the 1860s and 1870s the Council of Legal Education was set up and the passing of examinations became a compulsory qualification for the Bar. During the third quarter of the century Oxford and Cambridge at last began to make provision for teaching, examinations and degrees in English law.

MAINE: HISTORICAL AND COMPARATIVE JURISPRUDENCE

An illustrious product of this development was Sir Henry Sumner Maine, Scottish on his father's side. A classical scholar at Cambridge he was elected Regius Professor of Civil Law there at the age of twenty-five. He was called to the Bar by Lincoln's Inn in 1850 and two years later became the first Reader in Roman Law and Jurisprudence at the Inns of Court. He spent the years 1862–69 in India as a legal member of the Governor-General's Council, and like his predecessor, Sir James F. Stephen, was an advocate of codification, one of his measures being an Indian Succession Act. He declined the office of Chief Justice of Bengal. Meanwhile Maine had published his most famous book, *Ancient Law* (1861), in which by the use of the historical and comparative methods he traced the development of progressive legal systems. In this approach he was influenced not only by Savigny and Ihering but also by Darwin, as well probably as Herbert Spencer's pre-Darwinian evolutionism. His style was excellent, both as writer and lecturer. In 1862 Maine was admitted to the Middle Temple, of which he became a bencher. In 1869 Maine was appointed the first Corpus Professor of Jurisprudence at Oxford; eight years later he was elected Master of Trinity College, Cambridge, for the last year of his life being also Whewell Professor of International Law. His *Village Communities in the East and West* (1871) compared Indian and Teutonic village communities, *Early History of Institutions* (1875) dealt with the ancient Brehon laws of Ireland as well as the doctrine of sovereignty, and *Early Law and Custom* (1883) discussed Hindu, Mohammedan and Slavonic laws and customs. As Pollock said, the common law within living memory had been treated merely as a dogmatic and technical system; at one stroke Maine forged a new and lasting bond between law, history and anthropology, and jurisprudence became a study of the living growth of human society through all its stages. Maine's work is of lasting value for his aims and methods, even though later research may cause us to modify many of his general conclusions.

POLLOCK: TEXTBOOKS, REPORTS AND PERIODICALS

The revival of legal education exercised a double effect on the writing of lawbooks. First, it stimulated the explanation of fundamental legal principles in textbooks intended primarily for students; secondly, it fostered a demand by university-trained practitioners and judges for the scientific and systematic exposition of the various branches of English law. In this context pride of place must be given to Sir Frederick Pollock, another third baronet. He was born in 1845 into a legal family: Chief Baron Pollock was his grandfather, his father was Queen's Remembrancer and Lord Hanworth M.R. was a cousin. Educated at Eton and Trinity, he was called to the Bar by Lincoln's Inn in 1871, and was a pupil of Lindley and Willes. Six years after call Pollock published *Principles of Contract*, dedicated to Lindley, and in 1887 *The Law of Torts*, dedicated to Willes. These were attempts to restate the law of contract and torts, formulating substantive principles rather than describing procedure, and they were the first books in which these branches of English law were treated in both a scientific and literary manner. His *Principles of Contract* showed, like Anson's which soon followed and supplemented it, the influence of Savigny, generalisation being facilitated by the predominance of the action of assumpsit. The thirteenth edition was edited by Winfield in 1950. The *Law of Torts* (of which a fifteenth edition was edited by Landon in 1951) aimed at showing that there really is a Law of Tort and not merely a number of rules about various kinds of torts, an exercise that was impossible before the abolition of the forms of action and is difficult even now. Pollock held the Corpus Professorship of Jurisprudence at Oxford from 1883 to 1903. On the Chancery side he wrote an excellent little book on the *Land Laws* (1883; 3rd ed., 1896) and a *Digest of the Law of Partnership* (1877; 15th ed., 1952), and he drafted the Partnership Act 1890. His collaboration with Maitland in their *History of English Law* extended to a general responsibility for the whole, although he himself wrote only the introductory parts and most of the early history of contract. In addition to publishing several collections of essays and lectures, Pollock was the first Editor-in-Chief of the *Law Reports* for forty years and the founder-editor of the *Law Quarterly Review* (to which he contributed innumerable notes) for thirty-five years. He was elected a bencher of his Inn, was given silk in 1920, was appointed Judge of the Admiralty Court of the Cinque Ports in which capacity he never had to decide a case, and became a Privy Councillor who was consulted on the drafting of Edward VIII's Abdication Bill. Pollock was a polymath, at home in a number of ancient and modern languages, philosophy and mathematics as well as history and law. Although he was a poor public speaker, his literary style was clear, polished, critical and witty. His writings were cited in court probably more than any other writings in their authors' lifetime. They could claim, in Lord Wright's words, a place in the category of our unwritten law. He died at the age of ninety-two, after being at the centre of the law—practical as well as academic—for sixty years.

MAITLAND: MEDIEVAL LEGAL HISTORY

A few years after Pollock at Eton and Trinity followed the brilliant Frederic William Maitland, running blue, President of the Cambridge Union and fellow-member of " The Apostles " and " Sunday Tramps," a slight, ascetic figure with expressive eyes. Called to the Bar also by Lincoln's Inn in 1876, Maitland practised in Chancery chambers for seven years before being enticed to the scholar's life by the offer of a Readership in English Law at Cambridge. In deciding to devote most of his working life to the study of the history of English law in its social context, Maitland acknowledged the inspiration of Savigny and Stubbs. Five years later he became Downing Professor, and Lincoln's Inn subsequently elected him an honorary bencher. Vinogradoff encouraged him to edit *Bracton's Notebook* (1887). Among Maitland's other scholarly works published in 1897 and 1898 were *Domesday Book and Beyond, Township and Borough* and *Roman Canon Law in the Church of England*. The monumental *History of English Law before the time of Edward I* (1895), written in collaboration with Pollock, stands mainly to Maitland's credit. Founder and first literary editor of the Selden Society he edited a number of volumes for that Society, especially editions of the Year Books. The originality and depth of his learning were matched by a scintillating style, vivid and epigrammatic. Chronic ill-health dogged him in his last years, so that he used to winter abroad taking with him photo-copies of the manuscripts on which he was invariably working, and at the age of fifty-six he died in the Canary Islands. After his death his lectures on the *Constitutional History of England* were published in 1908, and form what is still the most useful book of English constitutional history for law students. His lectures on *Equity* were similarly published in 1909, in which Maitland illuminated the relation between common law and equity and emphasised the importance of the trust in English society. In 1911 appeared three volumes of his *Collected Papers*. Balfour's offer of the Regius Professorship of Modern History was declined, partly on the ground of health. Lawyers place him in the front rank of lawyers, historians place him in the front rank of historians, and Holdsworth wrote that " as a legal historian English law from before the time of legal memory has never known his like."

ANSON: CONTRACT AND THE CONSTITUTION

Sir William Reynell Anson, yet another third baronet, got a first in classics and was elected Fellow of All Souls in 1867. A pupil of Thomas Chitty and the future Lord Justice Thesiger he was called to the Bar by the Inner Temple. He practised at the Bar for a time—earning, it is said, two guineas at Quarter Sessions—but was appointed Vinerian Reader in English law in 1874. Dicey considered him the best teacher of English law in Oxford during the next twenty-five years. Elected Warden of All Souls in 1881 he remained for the rest of his life " the ideal Warden." He received the Prince of Wales in 1912 as his last undergraduate pupil. From 1899 until his death Anson was also Unionist Member of Parliament for Oxford University, serving as Parliamentary Secretary to the Board of Education for three years and being created a Privy Councillor in 1911, so that he gained considerable knowledge of public affairs. Anson published *Principles of the Law of Contract* in 1879, three years after Pollock's book on this branch of the common law, and showing even more strongly the influence of Savigny. This book, together with Pollock's, inaugurated the scientific study of the law of contract in England. It was the first textbook to explain to the student the nature of a contract. Later editions catered also for practitioners, a twenty-third edition being called for in 1969. Volume 1 of *Law and Custom of the Constitution* came out in 1886 (5th ed., Gwyer, 1922) and Volume II in 1892 (4th ed., Keith, 1935). Here Anson's aim was not (like Blackstone's) to eulogise the British Constitution or to criticise its working, nor was it (like Dicey's) to select for emphasis a few leading ideas, but to state the existing mechanism of the Constitution, checked by information supplied by government departments. The volume on Parliament, although now out of date, is still a reliable treatise and work of reference.

DICEY: A GREAT VINERIAN PROFESSOR

A cousin of Sir J. F. Stephen and pupil of Jowett at Balliol, Albert Venn Dicey was elected President of the Oxford Union and gained first class honours in *literae humaniores*. He was called to the Bar by the Inner Temple in 1863, read in the chambers of the future Chief Justice Coleridge and entered practice, becoming Treasury counsel and last appearing in court (in spite of lifelong delicate health) at the age of eighty. As Vinerian Professor of English Law from 1882 until he resigned on account of deafness in 1909, Dicey fully restored the faded prestige of that chair and inspired the revival of the Oxford Law School. After his resignation he continued as All Souls Lecturer in Private International Law. Dicey's only textbook was his monumental treatise on *Conflict of Laws* (1896). This incorporated his *Law of Domicil* (1879), and covered comprehensively and in detail a field at that time largely untilled except by Westlake. The ninth edition, under the names of Dicey and Morris, appeared in 1973. John Westlake's book on *Private International Law* was published as early as 1858, four years after his call to the Bar by Lincoln's Inn. Westlake was a scholar of civil as well as English law. His book had a considerable influence on the development of private international law, which in England was still inchoate, for example in respect of the doctrine of the proper law of a contract. Westlake followed Maine as Whewell Professor of International Law, and was a member of the Court of Arbitration at The Hague. Dicey's *Law of the Constitution* (1885; 10th ed., E. C. S. Wade, 1959) consisted of lectures given as Vinerian Professor. They immediately gained him an international reputation, and their powerful influence has continued almost undiminished down to our own day. The book is not a textbook but emphasises certain selected principles or ideas, namely, the " sovereignty " of Parliament, the importance of constitutional conventions and the " rule of law." Its treatment of administrative law has long been controversial. A work of more interest to the general reader is *The Relation between Law and Public Opinion in England during the Nineteenth Century* (1905; 2nd ed., 1914), consisting of lectures delivered at Harvard Law School. Dicey wrote in an easy and attractive style. He did not eschew polemics, as in his opposition to home rule for Ireland.

HOLDSWORTH: HISTORY OF THE ENGLISH LEGAL SYSTEM

Serried volumes of the *History of English Law* stand as a massive monument to the most eminent historian of the English legal system. After gaining first class honours in both history and jurisprudence at Oxford, William Searle Holdsworth was called to the Bar by Lincoln's Inn in 1896, spent a year in Chancery chambers without holding a brief and was then elected a Fellow of St. John's College. From 1922 to 1944 he occupied the Vinerian Chair of English Law as a worthy successor to Blackstone and Dicey. For many years he was also Reader in Equity and later Constitutional Law to the Inns of Court. For his work on the Committee on Indian States in 1928 he was knighted, and much of the report of the Committee on Ministers' Powers, 1932–34, reflected his historical knowledge and somewhat conservative thinking. Early in his career Holdsworth was commissioned to write a history of English law in one volume. The first volume when completed covered only the history of the courts, and this has become the leading textbook on that topic. Holdsworth's plan was to deal with the sources and substantive and adjective law down to the Judicature Acts, and he intimated that it would take two more volumes to reach the end of the period to 1485. The publishers in their wisdom gave Holdsworth his head, and commissioned Dr. Edward Jenks to write the one-volume history, which he did (*A Short History of English Law*, dedicated to Maitland, 1912). Holdsworth published twelve large volumes of his *History* before the war, all written in longhand from cryptic notes. Early in the war he sent a mass of typescript and manuscript to America for safe-keeping, but he died in 1944. His two literary executors (A. L. Goodhart and H. G. Hanbury) accomplished the difficult task of completing and editing Volumes XIII to XVI, which were published between 1952 and 1966. These have been followed by a general index to the whole series prepared by the publishers (Vol. XVII, 1972). It is surely unlikely that any one scholar will ever again attempt such a colossal undertaking on his own as this *History of English Law*. Such tremendous energy, tenacity of purpose and capacity for sustained work, combined with profound learning, are rare indeed. A number of other books based on special lectures came from his pen on such topics as the sources and literature of English law, some lessons from our legal history and some makers of English law, most of which material became incorporated into the *History*, as well as a delightful book on *Charles Dickens as a Legal Historian*. The style in which the *History* is written is workmanlike rather than elegant, and not so readable as that of his shorter books. Holdsworth's appearance was impressive, with the famous moustache, the well-rounded cranium, and the pince-nez secured by black ribbon, but the manner in which he lectured to note-taking students was not stimulating. Holdsworth became a K.C. and an honorary bencher of his Inn, dying a year before he would have been Treasurer, and it is fitting that the life-work of the greatest British academic lawyer of the twentieth century was crowned by the award of the Order of Merit.

ROMAN LAWYERS

English Scholars of Roman law are rare, and William Warwick Buckland was probably the most erudite of these in modern times. A native of Devon, Buckland was educated at Caius College, Cambridge, and was called to the Bar by the Inner Temple. He soon became a law don at Cambridge, and was Regius Professor of Civil Law from 1914 to 1945. His mature researches were published in *The Roman Law of Slavery* (1908) and *Equity in Roman Law* (1911), while his best-known work was his *Textbook of Roman Law* (1921; 3rd ed., 1963). Buckland also wrote three smaller—though not easy—students' manuals. Another Cambridge man who became a very distinguished Roman lawyer was Herbert Felix Jolowicz, of Trinity College. He possessed a wide knowledge of languages, studied in Germany under Mitteis and Lenel, and became a brother-in-law of Martin Wolff. He was a pupil in the chambers of the future Lord Justice Slesser, and was called to the Bar by the Inner Temple in 1919. In 1931 he was appointed Professor of Roman Law at University College, London. He also lectured there on Jurisprudence for twenty-five years, and these lectures were published posthumously. The post of Regius Professor of Civil Law at Oxford became his in 1948, and he occupied it for the remaining six years of his life. Jolowicz's main work, used with profit and enjoyment by teachers and students, was *Historical Introduction to Roman Law* (1932; 3rd ed., 1972). He also edited the title of the *Digest* on theft. *Roman Foundations of Modern Law* was published posthumously. Not the least of the activities by which Jolowicz will be remembered is that of founder-editor of the *Journal of the Society of Public Teachers of Law* for thirty years. About ten years of academic life were lost by service volunteered in two world wars, in which his knowledge of languages was found valuable by the authorities.

TORT AND ITS BOUNDARIES

Cambridge also produced in much the same period Sir Percy Henry Winfield, of St. John's College, the most successful law student of his time. Called to the Bar by the Inner Temple, Winfield began to practise but shortly returned to Cambridge as a law teacher, renowned for his problem classes. He was Rouse Ball Professor of English Law from 1928 for fifteen years. *Chief Sources of English Legal History* (1925) most usefully filled a gap in bibliography, but his main work was done in the field of tort, the *Textbook of the Law of Tort* (1937; 9th ed., 1971) being intended primarily for students though found useful also by practitioners and cited by the courts, and also the " shadowy boundaries " between tort and its neighbours: *Province of the Law of Tort* (1931) and *Law of Quasi-Contract* (1952). He edited the *Cambridge Law Journal* for its first twenty years, and served on committees on law revision and law reporting. Winfield completed the first edition of Salmond's unfinished *Law of Contracts* (1927). Although Sir John Salmond[3] was a New Zealander, successively government draftsman, Solicitor-General and judge of the Supreme Court of New Zealand, his *Law of Torts* (1907; 15th ed., 1969) and *Jurisprudence, or the Theory of Law* (1902; 12th ed., 1966) have always been accepted as part of the legal literature of this country.

RECENT CONSTITUTIONAL LAWYERS

Of two distinguished British constitutional lawyers of recent times one was a Scotsman and the other of Welsh origin. Arthur Berriedale Keith graduated at Edinburgh with a first class in classics before taking high honours in oriental languages and *Literae humaniores* at Oxford. From 1901 to 1914 he served in the Colonial Office, being called to the Bar by the Inner Temple in 1904. From 1914 for the remaining thirty years of his life Berriedale Keith occupied the post of Regius Professor of Sanskrit and Comparative Philology at Edinburgh, in which he made important contributions to Vedic and Sanskrit studies. What is more relevant for

---

3. The name has to do with psalms, not fish, and should be pronounced to rhyme with *almond.*

our present purposes, Keith was also for much of this time an honorary
Lecturer in Constitutional Law. It is said that he could write a book on
constitutional law while his secretary was reading detective stories to
him, and that—although a Scotsman—he could memorise the bowling
analyses of the first-class English cricketers. Keith's most important book
was *Responsible Government in the Dominions* (2 vols. 1912; 2nd ed., 1928).
Among a number of other works—he preferred to write new books with
different titles rather than to bring out new editions—were *The Governments of the British Empire* (1935) and *The Dominions as Sovereign States*
(1938). With his notes on current developments in the *Journal of Comparative Legislation* Keith was an indispensable, if sometimes polemical,
writer on constitutional law in the inter-war period. Overlapping Keith's
career came Sir William Ivor Jennings. After a first-class student record
in mathematics and law at Cambridge, Jennings was called to the Bar
by Gray's Inn, of which he later became a bencher and Q.C. His early
academic life was spent as Lecturer and then Reader in English Law
at the London School of Economics. From 1940 to 1955 he was the
first Vice-Chancellor of the University of Ceylon, during which period
he acted as constitutional adviser to the government of Ceylon in its
negotiations for independence. He then returned to England as Master
of Trinity Hall and Downing Professor of the Laws of England. The
most important of Jennings's numerous publications were *Cabinet Government* (1936; 3rd ed., 1959), *Parliament* (1939; 2nd ed., 1957), *Law and the
Constitution*, a provocative introduction for students (1933; 5th ed., 1959),
Principles of Local Government Law (1931; 4th ed., 1960), and *Party Politics*
(1960–62). He also wrote a number of works on local government for
practitioners, mostly before the war, and on Commonwealth constitutional problems after the War. Various Commonwealth countries
including Ceylon, Pakistan and Malaya, sought his advice on the
drafting of their independence constitutions. The leading British constitutional lawyer of his time, he was interested in the practical working
of institutions rather than their theory, for example, the importance of
political parties behind the constitutional structure. Jennings was an
exceedingly hard worker, seldom allowing himself leisure even at week-
ends. Not long before his death the liner in which he was taking a con-
valescent cruise caught fire in the eastern Atlantic, and after the crew
of the lifeboat stopped rowing Jennings navigated the boat to safety
with the help of two amateur rowers.

MODERN INTERNATIONAL LAWYERS

The study of international law following the Napoleonic wars was
much occupied with war and neutrality, notably prize law. More recently
it has been concerned rather with international institutions, and has
taken on a new importance with the European Convention of Human

Rights and the Common Market. Hersch Lauterpacht was born in Eastern Galicia and studied under Kelsen in Vienna. He came to England in 1922, obtained his Doctorate of Laws at London, took British nationality and accepted a teaching post at the London School of Economics. As a barrister of Gray's Inn he carried on a consulting practice in international law, becoming a bencher and taking silk. In 1938 Lauterpacht became Whewell Professor of International Law. He was appointed a judge of the International Court of Justice in 1954 and was knighted in 1956, but he died in office before he had much opportunity to deliver important opinions in the International Court. Our survey of legal authors no longer living must end with an enumeration of Lauterpacht's most original publications. These include *Private Law Sources and Analogies of International Law* (1927), *The Function of Law in the International Community* (1933), *The Development of International Law by the Permanent Court of International Justice* (1934), *Recognition in International Law* (1947) and *International Law and Human Rights* (1950), this last being a subject close to his heart on account of the persecution of Jews in Europe. In addition to all this Lauterpacht revised the two volumes of *International Law*, a standard work first published in 1905 by L. Oppenheim, the German-born successor to Westlake in the Whewell Chair, and he also edited the *Annual Digest of International Law Cases* (now *International Law Reports*) for twenty-eight years and the *British Year Book of International Law* for ten years.

CONCLUSION

This selection of legal authors writing in the last 175 years must omit some with strong claims to be included. Further, it excludes living writers and therefore does not do justice to learned editors who have not only preserved but rejuvenated works still bearing the names of their original authors, who would be proud of their long-lived progeny even if they would hardly recognise it. Our period begins by being strong in works on civil procedure, land law, conveyancing and magisterial law. Attention is transferred to trusts, other branches of equity and equitable remedies, mercantile law and the higher levels of criminal law, followed by more sophisticated studies of the British Constitution. Then comes the systematic treatment of other branches of the common law, contract in general and tort, and the conflict of laws. A gathering interest is shown by legal authors in Roman law, the work of continental jurists like Pothier and Savigny, and the history of our own legal system. Treatises of the greatest use to practitioners, and retaining a place on publishers' lists for the longest time, have not surprisingly been written by leaders of the profession, some of whom became eminent judges. The most significant new feature in the latter part of the period has been the appearance of textbooks of high creative and critical quality written by academic lawyers, ostensibly for students and fellow law teachers but sometimes providing a valuable synthesis for practitioners and judges and even legislators.

II

Commercial Law

Commercial Law in the 19th and 20th Centuries

CLIVE M. SCHMITTHOFF

Mr. MAXWELL'S CATALOGUE

In 1825, some years after he commenced business as law bookseller and publisher, Mr. Alexander Maxwell published a *Catalogue of Law Books, Ancient and Modern*. The catalogue was arranged " to enable the student to select, at one view, such works as may treat on the subject of his particular study." In a Chapter entitled " On Personal Property, Commercial Law, Shipping Insurance, Contracts, Bills of Exchange, Partnership, Bankruptcy, etc." we find not less than 112 titles on commercial law. This wealth of literature should be compared with the feudal attitude which still dominated Blackstone's *Commentaries*.

" Blackstone's mind," writes Mr. Fifoot,[1] "was still dominated by the legacies of feudalism, and he was content, in discussing mercantile usage and negotiable instruments, to assert that ' knowledge of these things would be much easier learnt on the Royal Exchange than in the courts of Westminster Hall.' "

The change in the legal mind between the publication of the first edition of the *Commentaries* in 1765 and Mr. Maxwell's Catalogue in 1825 is significant. It reflects the economic and political changes brought about in Great Britain by the consolidation of her mercantile empire and the progress of the industrial revolution.

While at the beginning of the eighteenth century books on the *lex mercatoria* were almost entirely written by merchants and civilians,[2] the scene changed at the end of the century and the beginning of the nineteenth century. Mainly as the result of Lord Mansfield's great contribution to commercial law, English lawyers began to take notice of the legal complexities of that branch of law and to publish learned treatises on individual topics of commercial law.[3]

This tendency is perhaps best exemplified by James Allen Park's *A System of the Law of Marine Insurance*, first published in 1787. It should be viewed in the light of the general development of English legal literature.

---

1. C. H. S. Fifoot, *Lord Mansfield* (Oxford, 1936), p. 26.
2. See *e.g.* Wyndham Beawes' *Lex Mercatoria or a Complete Code of Commercial Law*. The sixth edition of this work (1813) was edited, " considerably enlarged and improved," by Joseph Chitty, Senior.
3. W. S. Holdsworth, *A History of English Law*, Vol. XII, p. 383.

The common law, as is well known, is developed from cases decided by the courts in matters which arise in them rather haphazardly. If a particular area is covered by numerous cases and thus shown to be a focal topic of interest, a practitioner will attempt to systematise the cases in a law book, mainly for the use of other practitioners or for the students. Only later is it realised that the area in question forms part of a wider subject which is then treated in a general compendium. In modern days such a general treatise is usually written by an academic teacher who wants to make the subject " teachable." Thus, the treatment of the law of husband and wife and of infants existed long before the first book on family law was published. The law of master and servant and of the cases under the Factories Acts preceded the treatment of industrial law. Dicey's great *Conflict of Laws* originated in his book on the *Law of Domicile*. In commercial law, at the end of the eighteenth and the beginning of the nineteenth centuries, numerous books on individual topics were published. In Mr. Maxwell's catalogue we find references to titles on shipping,[4] marine insurance,[5] life annuities,[6] bills of exchange,[7] bankruptcy,[8] arbitration,[9] patents,[10] mercantile guarantees,[11] usury,[12] and other topics. Several works on partnerships are noted,[13] but in the Chapter on Corporations, Charters, Public Records, etc.,[14] there are listed only a few works which appear to bear on commercial corporations,[15] except that several books deal with the stannaries; that is not surprising since the Bubble Act was only repealed in 1825 and the first Joint Stock Companies Act was passed in 1844. Several works on foreign law are listed, such as G. T. Standfast's " Laws of Hamburgh concerning bills of exchange, copied from the original MS. in the archives of the senate of Hamburgh, now first translated " (1805), and, most important of all, Pothier's " Treatise on the Law of Obligations or Contracts, with notes illustrative of the English cases on the subject," translated into English by Sir William D. Evans, a disciple of Lord Mansfield (1806).[16] The great influence which Pothier's work exercised on the common law of that period, may be gathered from the statement of Brett J. in a case decided

4. Lawe, 1814.

5. Annesley, 1808; Park (6th ed.), 1807.

6. Blaney, 1817.

7. Bayley (3rd ed.), 1813; Chitty (6th ed.), 1822; Cunningham (6th ed.), 1778.

8. Christian (2nd ed.), 1820; Cullen, 1800; Green (4th ed.), 1780; Montagu (2nd ed.), 1819, Scott, 1786.

9. Bacon (3rd ed.), 1770; Kyd (2nd ed.), 1799.

10. Collier, 1803; Davies, 1816.

11. Fell (2nd ed.), 1820.

12. Bentham (3rd ed.), 1818; Plowden, 1797.

13. Montagu, 1815; Watson (2nd ed.), 1807.

14. Chapter X of the Catalogue.

15. E. G. Kyd, 1794 and 1796; Sheppard, 1659.

16. Pothier, who lived from 1699 to 1772, was a native of Orleans where he became a judge in 1720; see Schmitthoff's *Sale of Goods* (2nd ed., 1966), pp. 9–11.

in 1822[17] that " the authority of Pothier is... as high as can be had, next to a decision of a court of justice in this country." An American author, L. S. Cushing,[18] referred to Pothier's Law of Contracts as " the standard work without which even a moderately sized law library would scarcely be complete."

In spite of this wealth of literature on individual subjects and on the *lex mercatoria*, written by and for merchants, Mr. Maxwell's catalogue does not advertise a modern general treatise on commercial law as such. The recognition that the various mercantile topics were intrinsically connected and worthy of treatment by a modern English lawyer in one volume was reserved to a man who was perhaps the greatest commercial lawyer of the nineteenth century, John William Smith, whose *Compendium of Mercantile Law* was first published in 1834.

JOHN WILLIAM SMITH

John William Smith (1809–1845) was a remarkable man. He was not endowed with the graces which make an immediate impression on a person's acquaintances, and he was embarrassingly shy. We are told by Sir Samuel Warren, one of his contemporaries and friends, that his personal appearance was " insignificant and unprepossessing."[19] His was not the advocate's mellifluous voice, but when he addressed the court in his harsh tones and dry manner, he commanded attention at once by the clarity of his exposition and the precision of his statements. He was an accomplished scholar, having won the gold medal in classics at Trinity College, Dublin, where he was educated. He was also well read in English, Italian and Spanish literature, a devout Christian well versed in theological writings.

When he was a young, practically unknown barrister, hardly twenty-five years old, he published his *Mercantile Law* (1834).[20] He writes in the Preface that he attempted to present his subject-matter with " clearness, brevity, and accuracy." Warren sums up his achievement as follows[21]:

" The calm, practised skill with which this young unknown jurist moved about in these regions of subtle intricacy—*inter apices juris*—excited the cordial admiration and respect of all competent judges. He was manifestly a master of his subject; and having quietly detected important but unoccupied ground, had possessed himself of it with skill and resolution."

Although Smith was primarily a practitioner, he held an academic appointment. In 1837 he was appointed common law lecturer to the

17. *Cox* v. *Troy*, a case dealing with bills of exchange (1822) 5 B. & Ald. 474, 480.
18. L. S. Cushing, in the Preface to his translation of Pothier's *Treatise of the Contract of Sale* (Boston, U.S.A., 1839).
19. Samuel Warren, " Memoir of John William Smith," in *Miscellanies*, Vol. 1 at pp. 116, 130 (1855).
20. The complete title is *Compendium of Mercantile Law*.
21. Warren, *loc. cit.*, p. 138.

Incorporated Law Society and lectured on contract. His *Leading Cases* were praised by Judge Joseph Story as being " among the most valuable contributions to judicial literature which have appeared for many years." [22]

Smith died of consumption at the early age of thirty-six years. Touching is the story of his last legal assignment. On the morning of his death, when he lay exhausted on his death bed, he slightly elevated himself and suddenly demanded to get pen, ink and paper. To the amazement of his friend who had come to visit him, " in a perfectly calm and collected manner, but with great difficulty of utterance [he] dictated not only an appropriate, but a correct and able opinion on a case of considerable difficulty." [23]

The elegant structure of the *Mercantile Law* can be gathered from its arrangement. It is divided into four books: " Of Mercantile Persons," " Of Mercantile Property," " Of Mercantile Contracts," and " Of Mercantile Remedies." In the first book Smith treats partners, corporations, and principal and agent. In the second book he considers, *inter alia*, the goodwill and negotiable instruments, but bills of exchange and promissory notes are treated in the third book, together with most other commercial contracts. The last book deals with stoppage *in transitu*, lien and bankruptcy, and an appendix is added on insolvency. This is indeed a comprehensive coverage of the various topics of mercantile law, facilitated by the fact that the work was written before Gladstone introduced the first Companies Act. Smith devotes only about three pages to corporations; he treats mainly the principle that a corporation shall contract under its common seal and considers in detail the exceptions from that rule.

The author of this contribution confesses that he has always felt a bias in favour of first editions of law books. Often they reveal the original plan of the author more clearly than subsequent editions in which that plan is liable to be obscured by the understandable desire of the editor to keep the work up to date. To no work does this comment apply with greater force than to Smith's *Mercantile Law*.

It is rewarding to browse over the first edition. The chapter on contracts of sale opens with a long discourse on market overt of which only the following may be quoted here [24]:

" This market overt, in the country, is only held on special days provided for particular places by charter or prescriptions; but in the City of London, every day, except Sunday, is market day; the market place or spot of ground, set apart by custom for the sale of particular goods, is also, in the country, the only market overt; but in London every shop, in which goods are exposed publicly

22. *Law Magazine*, Vol. XXXV (1846), pp. 177, 179.
23. Warren, *loc. cit.*, p. 180.
24. Smith's *Mercantile Law* (1st ed.), 290.

to sale is market overt, but for such things only as the owner professes to trade in."

Almost one quarter of the *Mercantile Law* is taken up by the treatment of bankruptcy and insolvency, an indication of the difficult times in which the book was written. Characteristic of Smith's style, an amalgam of dry legal precision and the traditionally florid prose of his period, is the following passage which occurs in the introduction to his treatment of bankruptcy[25]:

"And thus we see that, as upon the one hand, the bankrupt law is a law of severity, inasmuch as it compels a total cession of the bankrupt's property, whether he will or no, and subjects him, as we shall hereafter observe, to very heavy punishment, in case of misconduct; so, upon the other hand, it is a law of mercy, rescuing him from the pressure of embarrassment, which might otherwise have damped his spirits, and crippled his future exertions, and providing him with the means of re-commencing his trade, and again claiming the support of former connexions; who, if during the legal scrutiny to which he is subjected, his conduct prove to have been blameless, are, we find from experience, often very forward to assist him."

Smith's *Mercantile Law* provided a firm framework for English commercial law for almost a century.[26] The *Compendium* was the foundation on which the commercial lawyers of the nineteenth century could carry out the consolidation and reform of commercial law which culminated in its codification in the Bills of Lading Act 1855, the Mercantile Law Amendment Act 1856, the Factors Act 1889, the Bills of Exchange Act 1882, the Partnership Act 1890, the Sale of Goods Act 1893 and eventually the Marine Insurance Act 1906. The great commercial judges of that time, Blackburn, Esher, Theo. Mathew and MacKinnon, the gifted draftsmen, MacKenzie Chalmers and Pollock, the authoritative writers, such as Benjamin, Byles, Carver and Arnould, completed the work initiated by John William Smith.

FRANCIS BEAUFORT PALMER

In 1855 the Limited Liability Act was passed which was consolidated with the Joint Companies Act 1844 in the Joint Companies Act 1856, the first great Companies Act in this country. A new topic was added to the commercial law of the United Kingdom. The new legislation had a bad press. Legal periodicals and the daily press saw in the device of limited liability a possibility of defrauding one's creditors and a legal journal commented that the legislator had now legalised fraud. William S. Gilbert, himself a barrister by training, made fun of the new form of business organisation in Utopia Limited,[27] which Hesketh Pearson[28]

25. *Ibid.*, 344.
26. The last—thirteenth—edition, prepared by H. C. Gutteridge, was published in 1931.   27. First performed October 7, 1893.
28. Hesketh Pearson, *Gilbert and Sullivan*, 1935 (Penguin ed., 1954), p. 174.

rightly describes as " one of the best efforts of the famous pair " but which was a partial failure, due to Gilbert's savage attack on the English establishment. In this opera the famous promoter's song occurs:

" Some seven men form an Association
(If possible, all Peers and Baronets),
They start off with a public declaration
To what extent they mean to pay their debts.
. . .
They then proceed to trade with all who'll trust 'em,
Quite irrespective of their capital
(It's shady, but it's sanctified by custom) ;
Bank, Railway, Loan, or Panama Canal.
. . .
If you come to grief, and creditors are craving
(For nothing that is planned by mortal head
Is certain in this Vale of Sorrow—saving
That one's Liability is Limited)—
Do you suppose that signifies perdition ?
If so you're but a monetary dunce—
You merely file a Winding-up Petition,
And start another Company at once! "
. . .

How wrong were the prophets of gloom! In retrospect, the form of the limited company has contributed to a tremendous expansion of British business. Today, in 1974, after successive Companies Acts have attempted to eradicate the unacceptable face of capitalism, some 530,000 businesses use that form.[29] Company law has become a cult, and its high priest was Sir Francis Palmer, the most important company lawyer produced by this country.

Francis Beaufort Palmer (1845–1917) began his career at the Chancery Bar without any special advantages, such as connection with leading solicitors or big commercial firms. He was a man of great quickness of perception and exceptional power of work, coupled with a remarkably placid temper and courteous manner. With his increasing work in chambers he found it impossible to attend court regularly, and in the early nineties he devoted himself wholly to chambers work. No doubt his deafness and his shy and sensitive nature had something to do with that decision. He was so familiar with company law that he was frequently called upon by the judges to act as amicus curiae. He assisted in the drafting of several Companies Acts, notably the Companies (Consolidation) Act 1908. Apart from his books on company law, of which his great reference book and *Company Precedents* were the most important, he published a book on *Peerage Law* which was much quoted.

Palmer was a man of refined taste; he collected works of art, including old tapestry and Tanagra ware. In his house in Bryanston Square, he and

29. *Companies in 1972* (Department of Trade and Industry, H.M.S.O., 1973), p. 12.

Lady Palmer entertained their friends with thoughtfulness and care. *The Times* wrote in his obituary [30]: " There was not a set of barristers' chambers or of solicitors' offices in England in which his famous books were not to be found," and the *Law Times* wrote [31] that " his *Company Precedents* and his *Company Law* have a world-wide reputation."

Palmer's most important work is undoubtedly his *Company Law*, published in 1898.[32] It originated in six lectures which he gave in January and February 1897 in the Inner Temple Hall upon the request of the Council of Legal Education. Palmer indicated the object of his work in the Preface:

" The object of the author in putting the work together has been to set forth the leading provisions of the Companies Act 1862 to 1893, and at the same time to show, by reference to the principal decisions, how the Acts have been interpreted by the Courts, and how the provisions thereof have been supplemented by the application of the general rules of law and equity.

The Acts alone afford a very inadequate view of the law regulating companies incorporated thereunder; but the Acts *plus the decisions* constitute a great and, for the most part, admirable system of Company Law built up with the assistance (at the Bar and on the Bench), and illuminated by the genius of a host of great lawyers, including such names as Cairns, Chitty, Cockburn, Cranworth, Chelmsford, Davey, Giffard, Halsbury, Herschell, James, Jessel, Lindley, Macnaghten, Rigby, Selborne, Selwyn and Watson, and this great system prevails not only in the United Kingdom, where the paid-up capital of such companies exceeds £1,200,000,000, but, with slight variations, in most of our colonies and dependencies.

The author trusts that the work may be found practically useful not only to lawyers and to students of law, but generally to businessmen; for nowadays, looking to the vast number of persons interested as directors, shareholders, officials, customers, creditors and otherwise in companies, there are but few businessmen who can escape the task of acquiring some knowledge of Company Law."

The fact that the *Company Law* is written for lawyers and laymen alike and that it originated in a set of lectures, accounts for some of its unique features. Although the list of cases quoted in the first edition covers not less than twenty-nine pages, the presentation of the text is lively and easy to understand. The original arrangement of the work was rather casual and a more systematic order had to be adopted in later editions. Palmer usually sets out the facts of the cases which he considers, explains the reasoning of the court and adds his own observations which are always original and often critical. The last chapter of the first edition consists of a summary of leading cases, with references to the pages on which they are treated fully in the text; that chapter must have been heaven sent to the students preparing for an examination.

Interesting is the comment of Palmer on aspects of company law

30. *The Times*, June 16, 1917. The sketch of his life is taken from that obituary.
31. *The Law Times*, Vol. 143, p. 139 (June 23, 1917).
32. The twenty-first edition was published in 1968.

which are still relevant. In his discussion of *Salomon* v. *Salomon & Co.*[33]
he considers at length the judgment of the Court of Appeal which, lifting
the veil of corporateness, held that it was a fraud on the policy of the Act
to devise a scheme under which a company should consist of one sub-
tantial person and six dummies. Heaving a sigh of relief, Palmer continues[34]: " This decision caused great anxiety, as well it might, but it
was unanimously reversed by the House of Lords."

His critical approach may best be seen from the following passage
which occurs in his treatment of the *ultra vires* doctrine[35]:

"An ingenious perversion of the doctrine of ultra vires has sometimes led to its
being contended that, inasmuch as the funds of a company can be applied only to
the promotion of its objects, they cannot be applied in making good damage
caused by the fraud, or negligence, or misconduct of its agents or servants.

This is a fallacy. There is nothing in the rule of ultra vires which in any way
protects a company acting within its legitimate sphere from liability, to the extent
of its assets, for the consequence of the acts of its agents, done by them on behalf of
the company and in the course of the company's business. This liability is derived
from the ordinary law of principal and agent, and it makes no difference whether
the agent's wrongful act or default takes the form of malice, negligence, nuisance,
or fraud."

Palmer adopted a slightly reactionary attitude to the Directors' Liability Act 1890, which overruled the unfortunate decision of *Derry* v.
Peek[36]; he said[37]:

" Whether this exceptional legislation is fair to directors or not, it is certainly a
significant commentary on the supposed necessity of the Act, that—so far from
the crop of litigation anticipated—there is scarcely a reported case to be found on
the Act. . . . This may perhaps be attributable to the Act having rendered directors more careful as to the contents of the prospectuses to which they are parties.
It undoubtedly, at first, frightened away some good directors."

Soon, however, the fears of promoters proved to be unfounded. Today
these necessary provisions are enacted in sections 43 and 44 of the Companies Act 1948 and nobody criticises them. Indeed, how far we have
travelled since Palmer expressed his strictures on the Directors' Liability
Act in 1898, may be seen from the suggestions of the Companies Bill of
1973 that the directors shall observe the utmost good faith towards the
company[38] and that insider trading shall become a criminal offence.[39]

JOHN CHARLESWORTH

Charlesworth was a very learned lawyer, of that there can be no
doubt. He was not only a Doctor of Laws of the University of London, but

33. [1897] A.C. 22.
34. Palmer's *Company Law* (1st ed., 1898), p. 39.
35. *Ibid.* p. 47.
36. (1889) 14 App.Cas. 337.
37. Palmer's *Company Law* (1st ed. 1898), p. 239.
38. Companies Bill, cl. 52.   39. *Ibid.*, cls. 12–16.

his *magnum opus*, *The Law of Negligence*, bears witness to his erudition. What is surprising is that that learned man should be the author of two of the most popular textbooks for students, one on mercantile law and the other on company law.

The most valuable feature of a students' textbook is its selectivity. There are some who believe that the best students' books are written by authors whose learning does not represent the acme of perfection. This view is wrong. These authors often fail in their selection. Only an author who is a complete master of his subject has the discernment of knowing what to treat and what to omit in a students' book. Charlesworth's absolute mastery of the wide range of subjects covered by his books is one of the secrets of their success.

John Charlesworth (1893–1957) was a busy practitioner in the North of England. Before being called to the Bar, he had seen distinguished service in the First World War; he had served in France, Italy and Gallipoli and was mentioned in despatches. The general esteem which he enjoyed may be seen from the fact that he was recorder of Pontefract, Scarborough and Middlesbrough before he was elevated to the Bench as a county court judge in 1953. His circuit included Durham, Northumberland and Newcastle-on-Tyne. From 1950 he was Chancellor of the county palatine of Durham.

The author of this contribution met Charlesworth in court after the Second World War and before he went to the Bench. He was a quiet man who wore his great learning with modesty.

This modesty expressed itself in the titles of his two famous students' books. He called them *Principles of Mercantile Law* [40] and *Principles of Company Law*.[41] He indicated thereby that the books were selective and did not aspire to treat every detail of the law. In the Preface to the first edition of *Mercantile Law*, published in 1929, Charlesworth states that that book was founded on six years' experience in lecturing on the subject. The method which he employs is to use illustrative cases to explain how the principles of law are applied to the problems which arise in the conduct of business. This method conveys a sense of reality to the reader and is particularly attractive to the novice. In this treatment the hand of the practitioner is discernible. It is not surprising that many thousands of students of the legal and business professions have been introduced to the study of mercantile law by these books.

However, it is not only the novice who profits from a perusal of *Mercantile Law*. A reviewer of a later edition wrote [42]:

"A lawyer sometimes realises at the end of his career that in matters of legal knowledge he can hardly see the trees for the wood. Reading a student book re-

40. First published in 1929. The twelfth edition was published in 1972.
41. First published in 1932. The tenth edition was published in 1972.
42. G. E. Garrett, in *Law Society Gazette*, Vol. 69 (1972), p. 356.

veals once again the original planting and true qualities of the individual trees which have become obscured by an undergrowth of special applications and compromises. This book—whose impeccable parentage and elegant upbringing render criticism almost an impertinence—performs this revealing function extremely well and is a first-class introduction to its subject."

In his *Mercantile Law* Charlesworth takes account of the fact that, strictly speaking, in England that branch of law does not exist. It is not a special body of legal rules, comparable with the *droit commercial* of France or the *Handelsrecht* of Germany which is the law of the *commerçants* and *Kaufleute*. In English law mercantile law forms part of the general law of contract. That explains why Charlesworth treats the law of contract extensively in his *Mercantile Law*. In the eighth edition, the last prepared by him, about one third of the book deals with the law of contract in general.

1974

In 1974 English commercial law presents the picture of a mature, well-developed branch of law. It is one of the leading systems of commercial law in the world and its literature reflects that fact. There exists a plethora of excellent reference and students' books. Only the history of commercial law is relatively unexplored.

Today a clear distinction is drawn between practitioners' reference books and students' books and there are only a few books which serve the need of both types of readers. That distinction, however, is not typical of commercial law. It exists also in other branches of law. Moreover, it is of considerable antiquity. Littleton's *Tenures*, we learn from Holdsworth,[43] " was designed to assist the author's son Richard to a knowledge of the law, and it soon obtained and long retained its position as a first book for the student."

What is, however, new in our time is that the general one-volume reference book for the practitioner has disappeared. Smith's *Mercantile Law* was last published in 1931 and is not likely to be republished. We have returned to the time when Mr. Maxwell published his catalogue. The various branches of commercial law have grown so far apart and have become so detailed that they have destroyed the unity of the subject, as far as the practitioner is concerned. Thus, Halsbury's *Laws of England* do not contain a section on commercial law and its entry under commerce [44] refers to agency, banking, bills of exchange, carriers, contract, insurance, sale of goods, shipping, trade and labour.

The place of the practitioner's single-volume compendium has been taken by monumental series devoted wholly or in part to commercial

43. William Holdsworth, *Some Makers of English Law* (Cambridge University Press, 1966) (paperback), p. 57.
44. Halsbury's *Laws of England*, (3rd ed. (Lord Simonds), 1955), Vol. 5, p. 293.

law or by loose-leaf encyclopedias. Reference may be made to the following collections:

> *British Shipping Laws,* including
>> *Admiralty Practice* (McGuffie, Fugeman and Gray);
>> Carver's *Carriage by Sea* (Colinvaux);
>> Marsden's *Collisions at Sea* (McGuffie);
>> *C.I.F. and F.O.B. Contracts* (Sassoon);
>> *Forms and Precedents* (Colinvaux and Steel);
>> Lowndes and Rudolf's *General Average and York-Antwerp Rules* (Donaldson, Ellis and Staughton);
>> *International Conventions* (Singh);
>> Arnould's *Marine Insurance* (Chorley and Badblacke);
>> Temperley's *Merchant Shipping Acts* (Porges);
>> *Ship-Owners* (Singh and Colinvaux).

> *The Common Law Library,* including
>> *Chitty on Contracts;*
>> *Clerk and Lindsell on Torts;*
>> *Chitty and Jacob's Queen's Bench Forms;*
>> Bullen and Leake's *Precedents of Pleading;*
>> Charlesworth's *Law of Negligence;*
>> *Bowstead on Agency;*
>> *Gatley on Libel and Slander;*
>> *McGregor on Damages;*
>> *Phipson on Evidence.*

> *British Tax Encyclopedia.*
> *Encyclopedia of Labour Relations Law.*
> *Encyclopedia of European Community Law.*[45]

Only a few great works on commercial law have escaped the trend towards serialisation, notably *Russell on Arbitration, Scrutton on Bills of Lading and Charterparties,* and *Lindley on Partnership.*

Whilst in the field of practitioners' books this diffusion of legal literature has obtained, the position is different in the area of students' books. Here a number of one-volume works exist which treat commercial law as a whole. Many of them are excellent, and amongst them Charlesworth's *Mercantile Law* has maintained its leading place.

In 1974, three trends are discernible in English commercial law.

First, it is felt that commercial law can no longer be regarded in isolation as a collection of abstract legal rules but that it must be related to the realities of modern business. It is now recognised that commercial law has relevance to the modern man only if it is seen in its interaction

---

45. There exist other encyclopedias which do not affect commercial law directly or indirectly.

with related disciplines, such as economics, finance, taxation and accounting because it is in that setting that legal questions arise. Commercial law has thus developed into business law which is eminently
practically orientated. Since 1957 a periodical has been published which
treats in its columns these aspects of commercial law. Its title is *The
Journal of Business Law* and it describes business law thus [46]:

> " Business law is a modern concept which has developed from conventional
> mercantile law. Whilst the latter contents itself with the description of the posi-
> tive rules of law regulating the organisation and transaction of business, business
> law includes within its ambit the practical application of legal principles which
> have to be related to their economic and social environment.
>
> In short, business law is the living law which is applied by the business execu-
> tive and his legal and other professional advisers in the day-to-day conduct of
> business affairs. As such it includes of necessity the law-creating practice of pro-
> fessional accountants, company secretaries, bankers, insurers, exporters and
> other sections of the business community."

David A. G. Sarre, the Legal Adviser of British PetroleumCompany Ltd.,
one of our most experienced business lawyers, writes [47]:

> " Practice in international business law requires a knowledge and under-
> standing of practice in international business transactions. For it is as new devel-
> opments arise in the conduct of business internationally that the lawyer is called
> upon to help devise the framework within which the parties may enter into
> mutual commitments, without ambiguity in their terms and with some measure
> of predictability as to their interpretation and enforcement in the event of
> differences in the future."

Secondly, while at the time when Mr. Maxwell published his catalogue
and Smith wrote his *Mercantile Law* the prevailing philosophy of commercial law was that of economic liberalism, modern commercial law,
in keeping with its time, reflects the philosophy of social justice. The
underlying idea of commercial law at the beginning of the nineteenth
century was that of equality of the contracting parties, whether they
were factory owner or labourer, merchant or consumer, rich man or
poor, and only occasionally did the law take notice of the inequality of
bargaining power, as *e.g.* in the rules relating to restraint of trade. At
the end of the twentieth century, the position is different. We recognise
that unequal bargaining power is relevant and that the economically
weak require protection against powerful interests which make unin-
hibited use of their financial weight or threaten to dominate the market
by establishing a monopoly position. The new society in which we live
has been described as the protective society [48] and it is now thought that it
is the function of the legislator to provide protection for the consumer, the
investor and the employee.

46. [1957] J.B.L. 1.
47. D. A. G. Sarre, " The Lawyer in International Business " in [1973] J.B.L. 104,
116.   48. [1973] J.B.L. 4.

In the law of consumer protection, the first measure of importance was Helen Wilkinson's Hire-Purchase Act 1938. Today we have a series of enactments which pursue that aim: the Restrictive Trade Practices Acts 1956 and 1968, the Resale Prices Act 1964, the Hire-Purchase Act 1965, the Trade Description Acts 1968 and 1972, the Unsolicited Goods and Services Act 1971, the Supply of Goods (Implied Terms) Act 1973, the Fair Trading Act 1973, and a Consumer Credit Bill is before Parliament.

The increasing pace of consumer protection legislation should be noted. It is characteristic of this development that the Supply of Goods (Implied Conditions) Act 1973 provides that in consumer sales the implied conditions of the Sale of Goods Act 1893 cannot be contracted out—what a difference in the philosophy of these two Acts which are separated by eighty years! The Fair Trading Act 1973, which has created the office of Director-General of Fair Trading, provides for the constitution of a Consumer Protection Advisory Committee, for references to the Committee and additional functions of the Director-General for the protection of consumers; this Act is firmly founded on the idea that consumers as a class deserve the special attention and protection of the legislator.

In the law of investor protection, apart from the many important provisions which are now contained in the Companies Acts 1948 and 1967, the first special enactment pursuing this aim was the Prevention of Fraud (Investments) Act 1939. The Act was directed against share-hawking and other practices harmful to the investing public. Today the relevant legislation is contained in the Prevention of Fraud (Investments) Act 1958 and the statutory instruments made thereunder, and the Protection of Depositors Act 1963.

Today this regulation of investor protection is antiquated. The emphasis is no longer on the prevention of fraud but on the need to prevent discrimination in favour of the larger shareholders and to the detriment of the small investors. The present statutory regulation would be unworkable were it not supplemented by the voluntary self-regulation of the City. Here the regulations for Admission of Securities to Listing at the Stock Exchange [49] and the City Code on Take-overs and Mergers [50] issued by the Panel on Take-overs and Mergers should be mentioned. The proposed regulation in the Companies Bill of 1973 to make insider trading a criminal offence [51] serves likewise the protection of the investor. Like the City Code, it is founded on the idea of equal availability of price-sensitive information and non-discrimination of shareholders in that respect. Sir Francis Palmer, who criticised the obviously necessary intro-

49. In the version of March 1973.
50. In the version of February 1972.
51. Cls. 12–16 of the Companies Bill (1973).

duction of the Directors Liability Act 1890, would raise his eyebrows if he could read the new proposals against insider trading.

In the law of the protection of employees, we have gone a long way since the Tolpuddle Martyrs (1834) and the repeal of the Combination Laws (1824–25). Today the protection of the contract of employment and of the employee against unfair industrial practices is a recognised policy of the law, as the following enactments show: the Redundancy Payments Act 1965, the Employers' Liability (Defective Equipment) Act 1969, the Industrial Relations Act 1971, the Contracts of Employment Act 1972.

How deeply the philosophy of social responsibility has penetrated commercial law can be seen from the proposal in the Companies Bill of 1973[52] that " the matters to which the directors of a company are entitled to have regard in exercising their powers shall include the interests of the company's employees generally as well as the interests of its members." Thus even the erstwhile citadel of capitalism, the limited company, could not withstand the onslaught of the idea of social responsibility.

Thirdly, in a world of growing international integration on the global and regional plane, commercial law has proved itself to be the most susceptible branch of law. The reason is not far to seek. Commercial law has always had an international flavour, even after it ceased to be the cosmopolitan custom of the merchants and was incorporated into the national systems of law. It was only natural that it should be the first branch of law to react when the rigid predominance of the national state was mitigated by the rise of global and regional political organisations and the growing influence of transnational economic empires, founded on the concept of the multinational enterprise. That even at the high tide of nationalism commercial law retained its international flavour was recognised by judges and writers. Lord Mansfield, who completed the incorporation of the law merchant into English common law, said in *Pelly* v. *Royal Exchange* [53]: " The mercantile law, in this respect, is the same all over the world. For from the same premises, the same conclusions of reason and justice must universally be the same." And Sir Frederick Pollock wrote[54]:

"Yet the law merchant has not wholly lost its old character. It has not forgotten its descent from the medieval law of nature which claimed to be a rule of universal reason embodied in the various forms of cosmopolitan usage. Conforming to English procedure and legal method, it can still be reinforced by additions from established general custom."

On the global level the internationalisation of commercial law finds expression in the growing number of enactments giving effect to inter-

52. Cl. 53.   53. (1757) Burr. 341, 347.
54. Sir Frederick Pollock in his Introduction to the *Commercial Law of Great Britain and Ireland*, in Vol. I (Vol. XIII of the *Commercial Laws of the World*), p. 11.

national conventions. Only the following may be mentioned here: the Carriage of Goods by Sea Act 1924,[55] the Arbitration Act 1950, the Carriage by Air Act 1961, the Carriage of Goods by Road Act 1965, the Uniform Laws on International Sales Act 1967. The clearest evidence of this tendency, however, is the formation of a special agency of the United Nations for the coordination and promotion of the law of international trade. The United Nations Commission on International Trade Law (UNCITRAL) was established by unanimous resolution of the General Assembly on December 17, 1966. It became operative on January 1, 1968. UNCITRAL consists of the representatives of twenty-nine states, namely, seven African states, five Asian states, four East European states, five Latin American states, and eight Western European and other states. The United States of America, the Soviet Union, the United Kingdom, France and Hungary are amongst the countries elected to sit on the Commission. The *Yearbook*[56] of UNCITRAL indicates the immensity of the task with which the Commission is confronted; it has chosen four priority subjects, namely, the international sale of goods, international payments, international commercial arbitration and shipping law. The *Register of Texts*,[57] published by UNCITRAL, is the most valuable collection of international conventions and other instruments relating to international trade. The work of UNCITRAL is ably supported by the efforts of the International Institute for the Unification of Private Law (Unidroit) in Rome, the International Chamber of Commerce in Paris, and the Comité International Maritime in Antwerp and other organisations.

On the regional level the harmonisation of basic concepts in the commercial laws of the member states is necessary for the implementation of the aims of the European Community. This is not a novel experience. The technique of harmonising some aspects of commercial law was used as an instrument for the economic and political unification of Germany. In 1834 the Zollverein sponsored a Uniform German Bills of Exchange Act which was promulgated in 1848, and in 1861 the German Confederation adopted a Uniform Commercial Code which was the forerunner of the German Code of 1897. In the European Community company law is the spearhead of the movement for the harmonisation of basic principles of commercial law. Already the first Council Directive on harmonisation of company law, dated March 9, 1968, has been given effect in the United Kingdom by section 9 of the European Communities Act 1972, and various other Directives and measures relating to that

55. The Carriage of Goods by Sea Act 1971 has not been activated yet.

56. So far three volumes have been published, Vol. I (1968–70), Vol. II (1971), Vol. III (1972).

57. The full title is *Register of Texts of Conventions and other Instruments concerning International Trade Law*. So far two volumes have been published, Vol. I (1971) and Vol. II (1973).

subject are in preparation. The drafts of ambitious projects, such as the European Company and a European Co-operative Grouping (ECG), are discussed. There can be no doubt that the European development will influence the shape of British company law considerably. English judges and writers have proved themselves equal to the challenge of European law. In their decisions the judges deal with European Community law in the same manner as they are wont to deal with English law,[58] and a flood of books on that branch of law or certain aspects of it has been poured out by British lawyers. The monumental *Encyclopedia of European Community Law*, under the general editorship of Professor K. R. Simmonds, the director of the British Institute of International and Comparative Law, seeks to inform the English practitioner of this new branch of law.

CONCLUSION

It would be trite to state that in 1974 commercial law is entering into a new phase of its development because it is suspected that that can be said of commercial law at any point of its development. It can, however, be asserted with confidence and without complacency that, on the whole, English commercial law today shows an awareness of the practical, social and international problems of our time.

---

58. See the judgments of Bridge J. in *Esso Petroleum Co. Ltd.* v. *Kingswood Motors (Addlestone) Ltd.* [1973] 3 W.L.R. 780 and Graham J. in *Lowenbrau Munchen* v. *Grunhalle Lager International Ltd.*, [1974] C.M.L.R. 1.

III

Common Law

The Survival of the Common Law System

A. W. B. SIMPSON

By 1800 the English common law system was already very ancient. It had developed without any major discontinuity for some 700 years or more, and if its antiquity did not rival that of Civilian systems it was, nevertheless, sufficiently venerable to be mistaken for senile. A century and a half after the beginning of the assault of reformers upon the system we find, very curiously, that it has survived all that they have done to it, and continues to flourish. Nor has it simply survived in a form which would be unrecognisable to an eighteenth-century lawyer; far from it. Whatever set of characteristics one selects as typical of the common law system, it is difficult to locate fundamentally significant changes in the past century and a half. The unsystematic character of the substantive law, the conceptual distinction between law and equity, the centrally dominant position of the judiciary, the superiority and pre-eminent influence of the Bar, the importance of case law—plainly nothing has really changed. This seems very remarkable. For since the early nineteenth century virtually every branch and every aspect of English law has been to some degree in the melting pot, to be transformed or at least modified either by legislation of one kind or another, or by judicial decision, or by some shift in the manner in which discretionary powers have come to be exercised. Yet the system itself has assimilated these changes.

The period following the first Reform Act of 1832 is commonly described as an age of legal reform, but this means little more than that since then a continuous state of legal change has persisted; this fluid condition has come to be regarded as normal, and at the moment there is no sign of any slackening in the process. Existing legal institutions have indeed been reformed, but there has also been much legal innovation, that is to say, the establishment of wholly new institutions. Schemes of legal innovation have not been characteristic of any particular political party, and today it has come to be accepted that a primary function of any government is the alteration of existing laws and the making of new ones. Indeed many citizens of twentieth-century Britain would find it difficult to conceive of a society in which the spirit of the Medes and Persians was more in evidence, and unchangeability conceived to be the

51

chief merit of law. Law has come to be regarded as an instrument of social improvement and not simply the expression of a just regulation of life within a society whose leading characteristics are given; hence a conception of law according to which its function was thought to be the achievement of individual justice—giving to each man his due—has come to seem quite inadequate in a society which employs law to pursue a more extended list of social and individual values. Today we value rule through law rather than the essentially static conception of the rule of law.

We can study a period of such change and innovation from various points of view; in this essay I wish to concentrate upon one only. What effects have been produced upon the common law system in this country *generally*? Why (to anticipate a conclusion) have these effects been relatively slight? Will the common law system continue to digest the incessant modification of the laws?

This approach needs some explanation. There are a variety of ways in which a period of legal evolution may be studied, and these correspond with distinguishable ways of conceiving of law, laws and legal systems. I shall contrast three such approaches. The first involves conceiving of a national legal system (if that is the object of study) as a *corpus* of rules, principles, doctrines, *et cetera* which are in operation at a particular time. Legal history then concerns itself with the identification, analysis and explanation of the changes which have taken place in the law, so conceived, over a given period. And since the past is even more obscure than the present, a great deal of effort will be devoted to the task of establishing just what rules were " in force " (not *enforced*) at a given time, a somewhat artificial inquiry in a system which solves problems as they arise rather than in advance. This is doctrinal legal history, and it is important to see that it leads to a certain view of the relative significance of particular historical events. For example, consider the history of the law relating to stealing. A doctrinal historian will be concerned in our period with certain judical decisions such as *Riley's Case* (1853),[1] *Ashwell's Case* (1885)[2] and indeed with some more venerable still, such as *The Carrier's Case* (1473)[3] which constitute the formal " authorities " for certain legal rules, and he will be concerned too with certain statutes, in particular the Larceny Acts of 1861 and 1916, and the Theft Act of 1968. The Theft Act will appear, reasonably enough, as something of a landmark in the doctrinal history of the subject, and future doctrinal historians may well regard it as involving an important discontinuity in the history of the subject. The Criminal Law Revision Committee, whose eighth report generated the Act,[4] certainly supposed that this was so, for after consideration of the

1. (1853) Dears. 149.
2. (1885) 16 Q.B.D. 190.
3. Y.B. 13 Edw. IV P. f. 9, pl. 5. 4. Cmnd. 2977 (1966).

merits of gradual evolution they decided that what was needed was " a new law of theft, based upon a fundamental reconsideration of the principles underlying this branch of the law." [5] Some caution is perhaps needed here, for perhaps it will turn out that the new Act, together with the encrustation of decisions which is already forming (there being in the common law system no equivalent to the seaman's anti-fouling paint), was not so very innovatory after all. Be that as it may, the Theft Act will certainly retain a considerable doctrinal significance in that it employs a different range of concepts and categories from earlier law, and it is with these—with the history of legal thought—that the doctrinal historian is concerned.

Now contrast a second approach—that of the historian whose concern is with the social effects generated by legal rules and doctrines. It is, *a priori*, likely that each year some people will be convicted, and others not, because of the changes in the law made in 1968 by the Act; the members of the Committee were indeed in favour of change because one of the two chief defects in existing law was " its failure to deal with certain kinds of dishonesty which ought certainly to be punishable." [6] It may indeed be possible to produce specific examples, and supply a sort of anecdotal proof of success in this aim, particularly by taking examples from appeals by way of case stated. But quantification will be impossible, and strict proof very difficult, for we can only guess at the reasoning which led particular juries or benches of magistrates to reach decisions for conviction or acquittal. Those who have experience, whether as jurymen or magistrates, may feel more cynical here than do professional judges; my own experience as a magistrate makes me doubt whether any of my colleagues (apart from one who was legally trained) had ever read the Theft Act or could give any acceptable account of its provisions; magistrates convict for " stealing," not for breaches of the Theft Act. But whatever view one accepts of the reality of legal decision, it seems wholly implausible to suppose that the *social* effect of the changes made in the Theft Act could be more than piffling. I suppose that the employment by one large department store of an extra and enthusiastic store detective would cause more of a bump in the statistics, and prevent more thieves from " getting away with it," than all the labour of the Law Revision Committee. The same point can be made in relation to much lawyers' law reform. The abolition of trial by battle in 1819,[7] or the modification of the rule against perpetuities in the Perpetuities and Accumulations Act of 1964 are both events of little social significance, the first because trial by battle had for all practical purposes been laid to rest by 1300, and

5. Para. 7.
6. Para. 15.
7. Appeals of Murder Act 1819 arising out of *Ashford* v. *Thornton* (1817) 1 B. & A. 405 The last actual battle was fought in Henry VII's reign but this was an isolated revival

the second because the number of persons annually affected by the changes made (granted the existence in the world of the draftsman of more than one way of killing a cat) must be tiny. Of course for some few individuals the changes are very significant indeed, but one reason why " lawyers' law reform " is left to lawyers is that in many instances it affects very few people, or at least is thought to do so. The same point may be made in relation to certain changes in the law produced by judicial decisions which seem doctrinally of first importance. It is not likely that human happiness has been affected very much by such a celebrated decision as *Rylands* v. *Fletcher*,[8] and I should myself doubt whether even *Donoghue* v. *Stevenson*[9] ranks as socially very significant, if one bears in mind the realities of the consumer world and the mechanisms for the evasion of legal liability.

A third approach, and the one I wish to follow, starts from an appreciation that a national legal system such as our own is either (and very rarely) unique or, what is much more common, constitutes an example of a particular type of legal culture or tradition. It is in this sense that we speak of the common law system as existing, in one form or another, in very many different countries, including large parts of the Commonwealth and the United States of America. From this point of view concern ceases to be centred upon the particular rules and their evolution; instead it is focused upon an attempt to identify the salient features, whether ideas or institutions, which locate a given system within a legal culture. This generates different historical questions and different views as to the relative significance of particular events. In England in our period the common law system certainly survived, and did so with no obvious lack of continuity, just as it survived earlier periods of rapid legal change. We may ask however if there were modifications in the essential features, the identifying features, of the system, and if so what relationship there is between such change and particular modifications of the law and of legal institutions during the same period. And if change was minimal how is this to be explained?

From this viewpoint the Theft Act of 1968 by itself is hardly significant, but its context may be, for it forms an example of something very typical of the English system during our period—the lawyers' Law Reform Committee. In this instance it was the Criminal Law Revision Committee, set up in 1959 by the then Home Secretary; in the last century and a half an enormous amount of legal revision has originated in similarly constituted bodies, for example: the Real Property Commissioners first set up in 1829, the Common Law Procedure Commission of 1850, the Judicature Commission whose work led to the Judicature Acts 1873–75, The Law Commission of our own time. The list of such bodies is long and such

8. (1868) L.R. 3 H.L. 330.
9. [1932] A.C. 562.

committees, heavily dominated by eminent members of the Bar and Bench, must now be regarded as a typical institution of the common law system in England. Of such bodies the Criminal Law Revision Committee is a prime example, and a consideration of the membership of the Committee which generated the Theft Act is not without significance. No less than six were currently judges of the High Court or Court of Appeal, and one was a retired judge. Other members included the Common Serjeant and the Director of Public Prosecutions. Plainly what is involved here is internal law reform—in effect little more than the Bar washing its own dirty linen through a different institution, different that is from the courts in which the high priests of the legal profession normally operate. For complex reasons the opportunities for modifying the common law to suit ideas of convenience current in the profession has come to be limited, limited that is if the modification is to take place through judicial decisions. Hence the work, if it is to be done, must be done through different mechanisms. The law revision committee keeps the matter as it were, within the family. The recent Beeching Commission whose work has led to the Courts Act of 1971 is a remarkable example of a rather different approach to law reform, where an attempt is made to inject layman's values into the operation by the choice of a lay chairman with a reputation for iconoclasm.

One way of conducting the inquiry with which I am concerned is to select certain changes in the law and in our legal institutions which would seem on the basis of historical and comparative study likely to cause radical modifications in the common law system in its homeland, and to see how if at all these changes have in reality operated. Plainly any list one compiles will be open to argument, but my list would contain five factors. They are: first, the change in the scale of the system, secondly, the rise in the importance of legislation as a source of law, thirdly, the development of an academic legal tradition, fourthly, the modification of the structure of the courts and fifthly, the decline in the jury as the characteristic method of trial. (One might add entry into the European community, but here the event is too recent and the relationship perhaps ephemeral, so judgment must be deferred.) All these changes *ought* to have had repercussions; if they have not then this is something which calls for special explanation.

THE CHANGE IN THE SCALE OF THE SYSTEM

The common law system developed around the activities of a very small highly centralised judiciary and Bar; the law just was what went on in Westminster Hall and certain adjacent premises. In 1800 the central profession was hardly larger than it had been in the fifteenth century. In that year the central courts of common law [10] were entirely

10. *i.e.* the King's Bench, Common Pleas and Exchequer.

run by two chief justices, one chief baron and nine puisne judges and barons. The Court of Chancery possessed two professional judges—the Lord Chancellor and the Master of the Rolls. There regularly appeared before the central courts a very small number of counsel, probably under a hundred. Here figures are misleading, but there were seventeen serjeants (who alone could appear before the Common Pleas *in banc*) and twenty-five King's Counsel. The total number of barristers called was 597, but of these the majority would have no London practice; there were also some six draftsmen in equity, sixty-eight special pleaders and ninety-seven conveyancers.[11] Of course there existed other courts of civil, ecclesiastical and criminal jurisdiction, and a very considerable number of attorneys and solicitors. But in the main these other legal functionaries and institutions had little significance on the legal system in the sense under discussion—one must exclude courts administering other types of law, but I am concerned only with common law. And not only was the size of the judiciary tiny; it was also the case that remarkably little time was devoted to the consideration of matters of law. The common law judges spent most of their time either on circuit or in London conducting trials, and there were no appellate courts in the full sense understood today at all. Though figures are not available for 1800, they are for 1827, and it is plain that the time spent by the judges sitting as a full court *in banc* was very scanty—thus the King's Bench sat for only forty-five days a year as a full court, a figure to be put against the 66,459 actions commenced in the court in that year.[12]

If we contrast the situation with that prevailing today the difference is very remarkable. Professional judges of High Court status and above total ninety-nine in the *Law List* for 1973. There are some 243 circuit judges—full-time professionals—and 294 Recorders. The number of Queen's Counsel listed as in practice is just under 300, and the practising Bar has risen to well over 2,000, the number called being over 6,000.[13] The increase in the size of the professional judiciary and Bar has been steady throughout the period, and the increase has not been proportional to the growth of population. In comparison with other countries the number of professional judges in England and Wales remains extraordinarily low; thus the Justice Report on the Judiciary in 1972 noted that the figure was eight per million as compared for example with France's eighty-two: the explanation for this is principally the fact that around 98 per cent. of all criminal cases are tried by lay magistrates. But the fact remains that the professional judiciary has been increased abso-

11. These figures are based on the *Law List* for 1800.

12. See the evidence submitted to the Commission appointed to inquire into the Practice and Proceedings of the Superior Courts of Common Law.

13. All figures based upon the *Law List*, 1973, which only includes the names of those non-practising barristers who have applied to be included.

lutely, and one would expect that this increase would have produced first by dilution a sharp reduction in the status and authority of professional judges within the system, and thereby a weakening of the judge-centred character of the system, and secondly a decline in the cohesion and internal consistency with which the system operates.

So far as the first point is concerned the threat has, to a considerable degree, been countered by a sort of redefinition of the requirements for counting as a high priest of the system. There have always been judges—typically justices of the peace—who were not the sort of people one had in mind in saying that the common law system was judge-made, or that law was what the courts said it was, *et cetera*. The views of Justice Shallow on the doctrine of *mens rea* are thought to possess no general interest or importance in the traditional common law conception of the system. One way to cope with an increase in the number of judges is to degrade a higher proportion of the judiciary to something like the status of Justice Shallow, and this is precisely what has happened. This has in reality been the fate of the county court judges since 1846,[14] and will obviously be the fate too of the barristers and solicitors who have joined them as circuit judges as a result of the Courts Act of 1971. The vast majority of English judges are out in the cold—they are in reality mere functionaries. The modern High Court judge is in a slightly better case—his decisions are very occasionally reported, and he has at least a chance of promotion to a higher and more significant status. But it is idle to suppose that a modern High Court judge is as important a person as was one of the twelve men in scarlet in 1800, for the role they once performed has been largely taken over by the Lords Justices of the Court of Appeal and the Law Lords, who have become the high priests of the contemporary system. The existence of regular appellate courts, staffed by special judges, has meant that these judges of raised status have a very considerable amount of time to devote to the elaboration of abstract law, far more than their predecessors. This has not of course been planned by anyone—it has simply happened, and thereby made possible the continuance of the dominance of a small group of judges within the common law system. The incidental consequence of confining the conception of law to the law of a smaller proportion of the judiciary—indeed a tiny minority—has been to introduce a very considerable element of myth into that conception.

So far as lack of cohesion and consistency is concerned it is obvious that an increase in scale is likely to create difficulty. Where there are effectively few judges and counsel, and they live and work together, as they did in the conditions obtaining in 1800, an unsystematic body of law such as English law can be made to work acceptably. Those conditions no

14. County Courts Act 1846, first establishing the modern system.

longer obtain. Various expedients have been used to attempt to produce a greater degree of cohesion—the evolution of rules of precedent, the increased use of appeals, the production of semi-official restatements like Halsbury's *Laws of England*, sentencing conferences, to mention some which will come readily to mind. The degree of success achieved in these and other ways is impossible to quantify, but that in one way and another there is today much inconsistency few would deny. Thus on some issues there can be differences between the House of Lords and Court of Appeal, or between different divisions within the Court of Appeal, or trial judges in criminal cases can *de facto* decline to follow the House of Lords. Lower down the system studies have revealed very considerable differences between different magistrates' courts. None of this need surprise anyone; no large legal system is ever monolithic, though the degree to which this is recognised and regarded as a matter for complaint may differ. If however the idea becomes current, as it has to some degree in the United States of America, that the ideal of " the law " as an objective body of rule to be administered to all by an impartial judiciary is chimerical, and instead judges and lawyers come to be viewed as very wise " problem solvers " situated under palm trees doing what seems sensible, it is plain that a somewhat different system of law has emerged. This may be happening in England, but it has not yet come about.

THE RISE IN THE IMPORTANCE OF LEGISLATION AS A SOURCE OF LAW

The common law system has always known legislation, and indeed the further one goes back into legal history, the more shadowy becomes the distinction between legislation and adjudication, both conceptually and institutionally. But once the distinction becomes clearer we can say that the common law has developed mainly in the central courts, and the evolution of the law has at most periods been little affected by legislation. The use of legislation in Edward I's reign, under the Tudors and under the Commonwealth has appeared exceptional; more important, it has been thought of as ancillary, being used to remedy what were conceived to be defects in the customary common law—to put things right when they had gone wrong. Much nineteenth and twentieth-century legislation has been of this character—typically the legislation reforming the law of real property, if one excludes the legislation establishing the modern system of registration of title. Although the sheer bulk of remedial legislation has increased enormously, its character remains similar to earlier legislation integral to the customary common law. But in addition to this type of legislation there has been and continues to be much legislative innovation—for example the factory statutes of the nineteenth century and the road traffic and planning legislation of our own time. Here again the sheer quantity of legislative material produced by Parliament or by delegated legislation under powers conferred by Parliament has been enormous, and the flow continues unabated. The history of the rise of legislation has been traced by a master, and it would be purposeless to repeat Dicey's analysis of the reasons for it or his explanation of the forms which it took.[15] Plainly the consequence has been first that in sheer quantum the major part of English law is now statutory, and, secondly, that legislation has come to be far and away the major instrument of legal change. This is not to say that pure common law development has ceased, or that it is always of trivial importance; one has only to think of the development of vicarious tortious liability. But the social importance of such developments as have occurred has been *relatively* small. It is idle to claim that, for example, the evolution of tortious liability of hospitals has altered our lives to the same extent as the establishment of the health service or the enforcement of statutory controls over public health. Indeed it has commonly been the case that case law development has done little more than echo legislative change, or changes in the current of legislative opinion. To date the technique employed in the United States of using litigation as an instrument of social change has been little developed.

By the light of nature one might expect that the rise of legislation would bring about the extinction or at least radical modification of the common law system. This indeed was precisely what Bentham hoped and expected. Plainly it would be possible, as Bentham saw, to use the instrument of legislation to reap advantages which are just not possible in a system based predominantly upon the use of case law as authority. In principle it would seem practicable to reduce the whole of the law to a systematic form embodied in a code or codes, with resulting gains in consistency of application, simplicity, accessibility and intelligibility. Such a scheme would ideally suit the majority of English courts whose judges are mere functionaries; its direct advantages to ordinary citizens are probably secondary in importance, though considerable. To this aim of codification Bentham worked. And in addition to the huge gains in convenience which he envisaged there was also a political aim—the reduction of the power of undemocratic " Judge and Co." Bentham's ultimate objectives are as far off now as they ever were, for not only is the common law going strong in all its chaotic glory, but the mass of spasmodic and utterly unsystematic legislation which pours from the legislature has, as it were, magnified the demerits of the common law. There is indeed something quite paradoxical in the almost complete lack of any legislative impact upon the vitality of the common law system.

In part the explanation for this must be seen in terms of our political history and political system, and I do not propose to do more than

15. A. V. Dicey, *Lectures on the Relation between Law and Public Opinion in England during the Nineteenth Century.*

mention more than a few points in this connection. The form in which a political party offers a programme to the electorate produces a list, not a principle or set of principles designed to attract support, and the ensuing legislation is predestined in consequence to have an unsystematic character. Shortage of parliamentary time, changes of government, the diverse sources of legislation in different departments, commissions, *et cetera*, all tend to the same result. More significant, however, though less easy to explain, has been the lack of any serious pressure throughout most of the period even for the introduction of a criminal code. Since the failure of Fitzjames Stephen's attempt in the later nineteenth century, no further attempt of any significance has been made, and this remains true even since the establishment of the Law Commission. It is of the first importance to appreciate however that there is a special connection between the lack of legislative impact upon the common law system and the status of the higher judiciary in that system, and one which seems to me of particular relevance to any scheme of codification which the Law Commission or its successors may envisage.

In a professionalised system of law the high priests of the system are its authoritative expositors, and vice versa, and in the case of legislation the dominant status can, if it is to belong to anyone outside the legislature, only be enjoyed by authoritative expositors and glossators. Now the ideal of the codifier in its purest form is that the law should be identical with the text of the legislated code or codes, and nothing else but the text. This ideal, if fully realised, leaves no place for high priests, be they professional jurists, university professors or judges; no dominant role remains to them. Now it is commonly said and believed that the codifier's ideal is futile, since a text is bound, through the nature of language and the imperfect nature of man (for men draft codes), to require interpretation. This is an error, and it is important to understand why. Suppose for example a simple code of criminal law which contained the following provision: " Anyone who steals shall be punished by a fine of £10." Obviously someone will have to decide what counts as stealing, and whether a particular person has stolen; let us give this task to the local bench of magistrates. In most cases there will be little doubt as to whether what the accused is said to have done counts as stealing; in some cases there will be legitimate grounds for doubt or disagreement, and the bench will need to make up its mind. There is in principle however no reason why the system should provide for any investigation into their view of what counts as stealing; for legal purposes we can simply establish a cut-off point at the word " steal ". Our conception of law can by definition extend so the words of the code, and no further. What is important to notice is that we are bound at any given moment to establish a cut-off point tomewhere, even though it may be a movable cut-off point which can be altered whenever a decision is given on the interpretation of the code by a court which has a creative role in the system. If we allow expounded interpretation and count it as a source of law, we may say that " steal " means " dishonestly misappropriate," and thus gloss the text, but we then merely shift the problem of decision from the text to the gloss. What is to count as " dishonest "? If we are not careful the gloss will need glossing. This process can reach utterly ludicrous proportions; thus Professor J. C. Smith's gloss of the Theft Act 1968, published in that year, ran to 178 pages of text as contrasted with 23 pages of the text of the statute itself, a proportion of nearly eight to one; he referred to approximately three hundred decided cases in addition, the text of which must run to thousands of pages. At the date of publication not a single problem of interpretation had or could have arisen, nor is there any reason to suppose that the availability of the gloss has prevented disputes as to the proper interpretation of the Act.

Plainly it is *in principle* possible to achieve the codifier's pure ideal—to embody the whole corpus of the law in a code or set of codes, and reduce the function of the judiciary to mere application. Indeed, very considerable bodies of statute law are in fact treated in just this way, or in something very closely approximating to it. For example, most English criminal law is administered by magistrates; large parts of the law so administered are statutory, and much of that innocent of case law. Statute apart, Stone's *Justices' Manual* is treated as the equivalent of a code. Every day of the week countless decisions are taken by magistrates as to what counts as this or that, but the system is such that this activity generates no law whatsoever. Law is only produced when a case goes on appeal to the Divisional Court and beyond. It is important to see that the production of law through the interpretation of a text is not some sort of logical necessity, arising out of the nature of things; it is the result of the existence of certain types of legal institution, and if such institutions do not exist, the text can operate without giving rise to a mass of interpretative gloss.

Once it is seen how the interpretation of texts generates law, it is plain that to achieve the codifier's ideal one must attempt to prevent the evolution of any form of authoritative gloss; in the context of the common law this would mean in the first instance the deliberate reduction in the status of the higher judiciary. All judges must be reduced to the status of mere functionaries, as was attempted in France after the Revolution. Since the early nineteenth century nothing of the kind has been attempted in England. The institutional changes which would be needed to achieve such a reduction are an essential prerequisite to any radical alteration in the common law system through the rise in legislation as a predominant source of law. What has happened is that as the mass of legislative material has increased in a gradual and fragmentary way, the common law courts have simply behaved as before, applying to it their traditional methods—the hotchpotch of so-called principles of statutory interpretation, the rambling judicial opinion, the citation of precedents and the use of analogies drawn from earlier material. Legislation has been absorbed into the system, and this development has gone hand in hand with the preservation of dominance by the upper echelons of the judiciary.

THE DEVELOPMENT OF ACADEMIC LAW IN THE UNIVERSITIES

At the beginning of our period academic common lawyers, and the teaching and study of English law in the universities, hardly existed. Something had been achieved in Oxford by the establishment in 1758 of the Vinerian Chair, and in Cambridge in 1788 by the establishment of the Downing Chair, but the real pioneer was University College London, closely followed by King's College: nothing much was achieved in the establishment of English legal studies in Oxford and Cambridge until the middle of the nineteenth century.[16] Of course law had been taught and studied in the old universities from a very early period, but what was involved was civil and, until the reformation, canon law. Indirectly this influenced the common law system, particularly through the medium of what we now call equity, for the fifteenth-century Chancellors who initiated that system were almost all practising lawyers who had graduated in the Oxford law school. But after the reformation equity became naturalised and cut off from this influence. University law, with this exception, never had any profound influence upon the common law system, and to say this is the same as to say that there was never a reception. Continental legal history followed an utterly different course. University law, based upon the creative exposition of the *Corpus Juris Civilis* which began in the University of Bologna in the late eleventh century, came in the end to become the common law of all Europe except England, and remains the basis of those many systems in the civilian tradition. University law triumphed, it must be noticed, not because the universities taught and studied the existing law in force around them, but because they obstinately taught and studied what they thought to be better law, and in the end their obstinacy prevailed. There must be a moral in this somewhere.

We now have a large academic legal profession and many thriving law schools in English universities; the question naturally arises whether the development of academic law has up to date constituted an important modifying force on the common law system in England. No such development as took place on the Continent can now be expected. It is true

16. See H. G. Hanbury, *The Vinerian Chair and Legal Education*; F. H. Lawson, *The Oxford Law School 1850–1965*; G. W. Keeton, " University College, London, and the Law, " 51 *Juridical Review*, 118.

that there existed in nineteenth-century university legal education a movement towards civilianising the common law, and this has to some degree survived into the twentieth. Much of what was taught as jurisprudence fell into this category, aided and abetted by the emphasis placed upon the teaching of Roman law; the idea, still commonly held, that it is the function of a university course in law to provide a " theoretical " basis for further legal education tended towards the inculcation of a civilian basis, since the common law system lacks much in the way of an explicit theory: hence Austin's *General Jurisprudence*. But although there was this tendency, too much water had flowed under the bridges for there to be much prospect of a reception of civilian ideas today, and general jurisprudence has had its day, though some civilian influence lurks in modern analytical jurisprudence, where dogmas of continental law reappear masquerading as general characteristics of law. But the influence of taught jurisprudence has been slight.

If university law in England could hardly at so late a stage romanise the common law, what was left? Plainly young law students could be more congenially and efficiently taught English law if there were law schools, and the lot of the law student has been enormously improved in consequence. The teaching of law is intimately connected with the production of systematic expository literature, and the development of law in universities has produced a very considerable improvement in legal literature. Expository, systematising legal literature produced in universities can of course be to some degree innovatory and creative, and whether overtly through citation in legal argument or judgment, or indirectly through professional use in the preparation of arguments or other ways—particularly through the early indoctrination of students—legal literature can exercise a very considerable though rather intangible effect. But in so far as the university law schools have confined themselves simply to an expository role, they become simply one of the mechanisms whereby continuity in orthodoxy is maintained within the legal system; as Maitland long ago observed, taught law is tough law. More particularly will this be so if their exposition is confined to a narrow and well-worn group of legal subjects, the list being largely dictated by the practitioners.[17] It is true that the law can be transmitted in a critical spirit, but what passes as this in much academic teaching and writing is no more than the advancing of arguments of a type which *could* in principle currently sway a court; such criticism keeps, as it were, within the system, and hence its innovatory force is necessarily slight. Any attempt by the academics to displace the higher judiciary from their central place as expounders and modifiers of the law seems to me to have always been foredoomed to failure. In the absence of some quite radical scheme of

17. This is now more true than in the past.

modification the judges, and in particular the members of the Court of Appeal and House of Lords, are hardly likely to abdicate their status in favour of the professors. Why should they? All that can be observed at present is a slight tendency to imitation in the judicial opinion, which appears to be rivalling the learned article in its self-conscious erudition.

It seems to me therefore that the rise of the academics has so far exercised little effect upon the common law system as such; whether this is a good or a bad thing is not a matter with which I am concerned. Radical change in the system, or even extensive revisionist reform within it has not originated in the schools of law, nor to date have the law schools been much concerned with such things. If one confines attention to the world of learning I suppose the penologists and the doctors have had far more profound effects upon the practical working of the legal system than have the academic lawyers. Whilst the academics have tended to behave as if their chief aim was to be really accepted as part of the system—that is as barristers without portfolio—those who have had most influence upon the law have kept a safe distance between themselves and the Inns of Court. Things may be changing, and one speculation is that the different way they do things across the Atlantic may be more influential in the long run than the home-grown tradition of the law schools. The reception, if it comes, may be from the North American law-schools.

THE MODIFICATION IN THE STRUCTURE OF THE COURTS

There have been four major schemes of alteration in the structure of the courts during our period. The first involved the establishment and progressive extension in the functions and powers of the new county courts, the second was the reorganisation of the higher civil courts through the Judicature Acts of 1873–74, the third was the establishment of the Court of Criminal Appeal in 1907 and the fourth was the reorganisation of the criminal courts in the Courts Act of 1971, which is too recent for evaluation here. The organisation of the courts before 1846 was such as to provide no mechanism for the enforcement of small claims; legal rights which cannot be reasonably cheaply enforced are worthless, and there is no doubt that the establishment of the county courts was a reform of great social significance. The Act of 1846 forms one of the long series of procedural measures which continue in our own day and which are designed to make justice available to the people; arrangements for the provision of legal aid fall into the same category. But the new institution of the county court and the judges and officials who staff these courts have, as I have said, no significance for the evolution of the common law system; when one conceives of that system as centred upon the activities of the judges and the courts, one no more has in mind the world of the county court, which contains most civil judges, than one has in mind the magistrates' courts where sit the vast majority of the criminal judges.

The effect of the Judicature Acts must also be sought largely in social advantages secured through procedural simplification, and it is easy to read into some provisions an institutional importance which they do not possess. For example, consider the relationship between law and equity. The so-called " fusion " of law and equity has never occurred, and was never intended; the catch phrase is most misleading. The principle that equity trumped law had been established at least since the early seventeenth century, and in the only two senses in which fusion could occur it had occurred. These senses are first the development of settled, customary or precedent-based principles; rules and concepts of equity came to differ only in substance (if at all) from common law. Secondly, long before the Judicature Acts there had been worked out a scheme of harmonious relationship between the two systems, one in which equity presupposed the law to which it was merely supplementary. The chief effect of the Judicature Acts upon the common law system derived from its establishing a three-tiered structure of civil courts, manned by three different (though to an unimportant extent overlapping) categories of judge. Leaving on one side the Chancery Division which is of course in all ways peculiar, the High Court judge spends his time in the main sitting alone trying cases. He does not, as his predecessor did in the early nineteenth century, sit *in banc* with his fellow justices in what resembled an appellate capacity, nor does he have anything whatever to do with the activities of either the Court of Appeal or the House of Lords. His institutional status has been very considerably reduced, as has the status and significance of the Chief Justice in the world of civil law. The centre of gravity of the system has moved to the Court of Appeal, whose Lords Justices are split into courts rather like the three traditional courts of common law. Though these divisions of the court possess a certain collegiate character, the court as a whole does not. Its justices have largely inherited the legal status of the twelve men in scarlet at the expense of the High Court judges, though through the system of promotion and the system of law reporting they have not yet been put out in the cold to join the county court judges. The Lord Justices and Master of the Rolls, who now exercise quantitatively the greatest formative influence upon the law, are isolated from the trial system, and that as we shall see is in civil matters isolated from lay participation. Once upon a time the more bizarre flights of legal fancy were to be found in the world of pleading and procedure (a preserve of the lawyers alone) and in those areas of the law which were not, as it were, kept with their feet on the ground by close involvement with trial by jury. The increased abstraction and unreality which seems to me at least to be a character of Court of Appeal law may be a consequence of this isolation. That court, in its turn, is subsidiary in status to the House of Lords though in a somewhat spasmodic way, so that the centre of gravity of the system wobbles. There the degree of isolation is very great, and the application of House of Lords' law to trials is extremely difficult. The Lords had for a long part of our period a special function—that of imposing finality on legal argument.[18] This they have now abandoned, without acquiring any other special function in the system, and the organisation and practice of the court exclude such a development at present. One could perhaps develop, though it is not easy to see the form it could take.

There remains the establishment in 1907 of the Court of Criminal Appeal, and its subsequent development into the criminal division of the Court of Appeal. There was previously no regular system of appeal in criminal cases tried by juries, though some of the functions of an appellate court were in fact exercised by proceedings in error, the reservation of points of law for consideration in the Court for Crown Cases Reserved and the exercise of the Royal prerogative of pardon by the Home Secretary. The general effect of the establishment of this court is generally acknowledged—a general improvement in the quality of administration of English criminal law, a branch of the law whose history has been neatly summed up by Professor Milsom: " The miserable history of crime in England can be shortly told. Nothing worthwhile was created. There is no achievement to trace."[19]

The direct effect of the court on jury decisions as such has been limited, and it must remain a matter of speculation to what extent its control over trial judges has reduced the number of wrong convictions. Of course it remains true that the administration of the criminal law in England remains an unattractive business, and nobody would, I suppose, wish to claim of English criminal law any notable intellectual content or sophistication. But matters have certainly improved, and it may be that it is intrinsic to the nature of the activity that the administration of criminal law, like the running of an abattoir, just *is* an unpleasant business however hard everyone tries to make it better.

THE DECLINE IN THE JURY AS A METHOD OF TRIAL

Jury trial, like parliaments, universities and cathedrals, is a legacy of the Middle Ages; originally conceived as a system under which members of the local community answered of their own knowledge matters of fact arising in legal proceedings, jury trial came, in the course of time, to involve the employment of a college of laymen to determine on evidence issues of fact presented to them by the court. Long before 1800 jury trial had at common law superseded less rational methods such as wager of

18. This was the case at least from 1898 to 1966, and the principle was more or less settled by the mid-nineteenth century.

19. *Historical Foundations of the Common Law*, p. 353.

law and the even more archaic battle,[20] and a position had been reached in which the primary function of a trial at common law was to formulate some precise issue to be submitted for trial to a jury. The primary occupation of common law judges was to preside over the proceedings where this task was performed, and the elaborate system of pleading at common law was of course designed to provide a system whereby the parties could be brought to agree upon the issue which divided them, and whose determination one way or the other would determine which party was in law entitled to win. All law was essentially subsidiary to this basic aim of the system; though it is true that the issue could be an issue of law which was determinable by the court and not by the jury, the function of the court as the instrument for determining such issues arose secondarily out of its control over the procedures leading to trial by jury, or in earlier times trial by some other method such as wager or battle. The obvious alternative to jury trial at common law was trial by the court, typically the system of civil and canon law, and this at the beginning of our period was the mode of proceeding in Chancery, whose procedure had been in all essential respects settled in the fifteenth century by the civilians and canonists who were concerned in the early evolution of the Chancery as a regular court. The predominance of jury trial at common law is one of the more striking consequences of there having been no reception in England, or to put the matter somewhat differently, there having been only a partial reception institutionalised in the form of the distinction between law and equity. Within the common law world the only alternative system of trial of issues of fact of any importance was trial by justices of the peace out of sessions of minor offences—the petty sessional jurisdiction which had evolved piecemeal over the centuries.

Since 1800 jury trial has progressively declined in importance.[21] In civil cases the first step was taken in 1846 with the establishment of the new county courts, in which originally the judge determined issues of fact as well as issues of law; in 1888 provision was made for jury trial if one party wished it. Since 1846 the jurisdiction of the county courts has been progressively increased and in practice juries are virtually never employed. Consequently a very large body of civil litigation has come to be determined without the intervention of a jury. So far as the High Court is concerned the first step was taken in 1854 by the Common Law Procedure Act, which made possible for the first time the trial of issues of fact by the judge alone, though only with the parties' consent. Since then the jury in civil cases has come to the verge of extinction, though the story of the legislation which has brought this about has its ups and downs. Up

20. Wager of law had been virtually abolished by the early seventeenth century: its formal abolition was in 1833 by the Civil Procedure Act. For battle, see above, note 7.

21. What follows is largely based on R. M. Jackson," The Incidence of Jury Trial During the Past Century," 1 M.L.R. 132.

to 1918 parties in common law actions had a right to jury trial, subject
to one exception given by the Rules of the Supreme Court. These in 1883
gave the court power to dispense with a jury in any matter " requiring
any prolonged examination of documents or accounts, or any scientific
or local investigation " which could not be conveniently conducted by
jury. 1883 also saw the introduction of the rule that if a party wanted a
jury he must ask for it. In the late nineteenth century the use of juries
declined very significantly, but no radical change was made until 1918,
when, apart from cases involving reputation (defamation, false imprisonment, malicious prosecution, seduction, breach of promise, and allegations of fraud), jury trial ceased to be a right, but rested with the discretion
of the court. In 1925 the right to jury trial was again restored, but by the
Administration of Justice Act of 1933 it was taken away once again by
putting the clock back to 1918. Between 1939 and 1947 no *right* to jury
trial in civil cases existed at all, and a jury could not be awarded unless
the court was of opinion " that the case ought to be tried by jury." Since
then the earlier position has been restored in that a party is entitled to a
jury in a case involving reputation unless the court is of opinion that the
case cannot be conveniently tried by jury (in accordance with the exception introduced in 1883); otherwise the matter rests at the court's discretion. The restoration of a qualified right to jury trial, and the existence of
a discretionary power to award a jury, have had little effect on the
statistics, and the jury in civil cases is now virtually extinct. Thus the
Annual Civil Judicial Statistics for 1972 note only twenty-three jury
trials in the Queen's Bench Division out of some 1,129 actions tried. In
criminal cases matters have not progressed so far, but the tendency,
though concealed, has been the same. Serious criminal charges, at least
in the case of adults, are still determinable by jury trial, but the vast
majority of criminal charges are dealt with by lay or stipendiary magistrates sitting without juries. Jury trial in criminal law is now the exception
rather than the rule. Over a considerable area of the criminal law there
is a choice of method of trial, which rests in part with the prosecutor
(either formally or through the choice of charge) and in part with the
accused and the court. And where jury trial does exist it is not quite what
it used to be—there is now the possibility of the majority verdict, and
jury decisions to convict are at risk of review more than in the past. Jury
trial is currently under attack from some quarters, principally upon the
ground that juries acquit too readily, and the future may well see further
restrictions in its use within the system, the alternatives being an extension of the powers of magistrates or, more radically, the extension of the
powers exercised in the Crown Court by professional judges.

The effect of the decline in jury trial in civil law has been very considerable. When the institution was flourishing its existence restricted the
areas in which the professional lawyers could develop their natural love

of intricacy, which is itself merely a consequence of a laudable desire to get matters exactly right. There grew up a complex body of law governing the isolation of the issue to be submitted to the jury, which culminated in the extreme rationality of the Hilary Rules of 1834. There also developed to a lesser extent complex law governing the admissibility of evidence and the general conduct of trials, and of course much law governing process. But jury trial imposes, as it were, an end to the generation of law; there comes a point when the jury just has to decide the matter, however it is formulated, and their reasons, being suppressed, do not generate law. Furthermore, the last stage in the process—the direction to the jury—is of necessity compelled in general to be fairly simple and uncomplicated, and this remains so whatever the appellate court says. Similarly, law applied by magistrates is by the nature of the institution pretty straightforward stuff. Magistrates, however conscientious, cannot in any real sense apply the elaborate dogma to be found in a set of speeches by the Law Lords, any more than a devout but unlettered Irish peasant can accept the doctrines of the faith in the same sense in which this is possible for a Jesuit. Law courts never operate out of their own depth, and for many courts the safe depth is very limited. When the use of the jury declines, this leads to some modifications in the previous law—thus the law governing pleading has been extensively modified—but it does not naturally produce any overall simplification, nor has it done so. What is bound to happen if professional judges of the English tradition are put in its place is that an irresistible opportunity is provided for the replacement of the terse and oracular verdict of the jury by an extravagant body of doctrine. This has happened, the best illustration being provided by the baroque movement in the modern law of torts, in which one scarcely intelligible doctrine succeeds another without anyone at the end of the day being any the wiser. In criminal law the existence of appellate courts, especially if they are not staffed by judges contemporaneously engaged upon the management of trials, leads to the same type of result—a luxuriant mass of increasingly abstract law. Matters are aggravated in the common law system by the continuance of the tradition of the individual " judgment " or judicial opinion, whose rambling and undisciplined style derives from its origin in an argument intended to persuade the other judges, such arguments having by a curious evolution got into the wrong place. They are now delivered too late to serve the function for which alone their style suits them.

My thesis has been that the common law system in England at least has, up to date, been relatively little affected by the multifarious changes in detail during the past century and a half; it operates in much the same way as it did in the eighteenth century. How long this state of affairs will continue is a matter of speculation, though at the moment there is nothing obviously threatening on the horizon. But as the survival of the system was unplanned, so may its radical modification be too, and amongst the factors I have discussed there may exist pointers to the way in which future developments may move.

IV

Constitutional Law

Constitutional Law

J. D. B. MITCHELL

INTRODUCTION: THE MYTH OF ETERNAL VIRTUE

Just why it was that in 1799, or more probably in 1798 or earlier, Mr.
Sweet should have said to Mr. Maxwell, " Come, let us publish " and
the idea met with Mr. Maxwell's favour, I do not know. No doubt Mr.
Maurice Maxwell will correct my ignorance,[*] as the products of the firm
which those two started have done from time to time. What is at least
clear is that constitutional law would not, as will appear, have been high
in their list of priorities, if it even appeared at all. By " constitutional
law " in that sentence I mean that law written in critical, and not in
adulatory, terms. Possibly the successors in title may, for different
reasons, hold to the same view. It may be that serious books on the subject
are frequently a drug on the market, and that there are more fashionable
subjects. That however is a commercial judgment. In 1798–99 it would
have been a political judgment. Such a work could have meant certain
death to a new-born publishing firm. Some things have changed meanwhile. It is indeed a pity, save for one reason, that the ghosts or the
corporate successors have chosen to celebrate 175 years. The one hundred
and fiftieth anniversary would have been much better. In 1949 we were
at the flood of the revolution which we call the arrival of the Welfare
State. There was, even in the midst of upheaval, some certainty. Now we
are in uncertainty, uncertainty even about how to deal with that state.
There is perhaps the justification that 1799 was a dull year (except notably for the miserable Wolfe Tone) but constitutionally there was a flat
tide, if one sticks to strict chronology. Writing in 1973, the chances are
that again constitutionally 1974 will also be dull, except for passing
eddies. Elections or other uncertain events may falsify that view, but, at
the moment of writing, a year of dull and niggling uncertainty seems the
most probable forecast. (The Election has happened. The forecast
remains.) Hence, in this series on " then and now " there must be a give
and take at the margins.

To look at the two situations in such a way is unhelpful. Uncertainty
in politics is an enduring feature, and constitutional law is, at least, a
half-brother to politics. Of course there have been changes. Indeed it is
tempting to take as a title, or at any rate sub-title, the " Appleby to

---

[*]As he has done; see his article at p. 121, *post.*

Bexley line." As a railway journey it sounds uncomfortable, even if it be
not impossible, but in any event it is one which publishers would reject.
Booked equally for rejection would be " Canute—the patron of constitutional law." Each rejected title would highlight one major theme. To
move from a Tory Prime Minister sitting for a pocket borough (before
moving to a university seat), presiding over a ministry in a clear minority
in the Commons, heavily defeated there as soon as it faced Parliament
and yet one which survived, with the help of the King and the Lords, to
a Tory Prime Minister, the first to be elected as leader of his party, sitting
for a seat which must in 1973 be called marginal, with no hope if things
went wrong that the Lords or the Queen could do anything to help, is to
jump at one stride over fundamental political and constitutional changes.
The second rejected title would suggest a great deal of passivity in constitutional change. Events like the waves took control in betweenwhiles,
and little was done to think coherently about the whole nature of constitutional law. It may even be that failure is even more important than
those changes, for the link between " then and now " could well be the
fact that each year was in its way a prelude to a revolution (used in a
sense closer to that of Kelsen than that of Madame Guillotine). Ahead of
Pitt lay the Reform Acts and their consequences, together with those of
the Industrial Revolution. In 1973 there lies ahead, at any rate, talk of
devolution of government internally, and all the constitutional consequences which flow from British membership of the European Communities. Thus behaviour in the years between has also its importance.

What is at least clear is the underlying falsity of such propositions as
one finds in the Kilbrandon Report: " The United Kingdom already
possesses a constitution which in its essentials has served well for some
hundreds of years."[1] Such statements come far too glibly to pen or tongue
and in themselves, and combined with the complacent sentiments which
normally follow, have, to our loss, become part of popular mythology.
How was 1799 constitutionally situated? It followed 1794, with the
Suspension of Habeas Corpus Act 1795, with the Treasonable Practices
Act, the Seditious Meetings Act 1795 and the Unlawful Combinations
Act 1799. In modern terminology the spirit of seeking a Jacobin under
every bed was abroad. On the judicial side, in Scotland, the trial in 1793
of Muir cannot be said to stand as one of the triumphs of the defence of
liberty. For Lord Cockburn it was a trial which evoked memories of
Lauderdale and of Judge Jeffreys at the full flood of popular belief about
their behaviour. More generally, it was a constitution which called forth
Cobbett's description of a " great jaggle of monopolies, churchcraft and
sinecures " for, after all, " the Closet " had to do its best for Pitt. In this
age in which Pitt ruled England, and Henry Dundas ruled Scotland for

1. Royal Commission on the Constitution (Cmnd. 5460), para. 395.

him, Cockburn would write of the conditions in Scotland: " In other words, we had no free political institutions whatever."[2] It was the age in which John Galt described, at a lower level of government, in the *Provost*, a world in which " the cloven foot of self interest was now and then to be seen aneath the robe of public principle," and in which the provost's greater objections were perhaps to the sight, rather than to the existence, of that cloven foot. Certainly neither of the Royal Commissions did anything to suggest that John Galt's perception was wrong. In England the Report spoke of " revenues . . . diverted from their legitimate use and are sometimes wastefully bestowed for the benefit of individuals, sometimes squandered for purposes injurious to the character and morals of the people."[3] In Scotland it was reported " it is almost superfluous to state the general conclusion, that the dilapidation of the common good of burghs royal, the misapplication of their revenues, . . . have been carried, in the greater number of cases, to their utmost extent."[4] At the higher level it has been said: " We no longer believe that George III's system of personal government came to an end in 1784 and that power was then transferred from the King to the Prime Minister. The power of the Crown, though tending to decline, remained substantially unchanged until the Reform Act of 1832 gradually transformed the situation."[5] One might, to take Popper's analogy, say that to move back from " now " to " then " is equivalent to a change of physical environment from Crete to Greenland.[6] Unless the " essentials " of which the Kilbrandon Report speaks are reduced to the meaninglessness of institutions described by names such as King, Lords, Commons, boroughs and deprived of any content, it is impossible to say that these essentials have continued over even this short span.

THE CONSTITUTION AT THE END OF THE EIGHTEENTH CENTURY

If one looks at the setting of those institutions, the same contrast is apparent. Of all the supposed essential doctrines of the Constitution of today few existed with certainty in any identifiable form. In the conditions which have been indicated it is really too obvious to require stating that none of the essential doctrines relating to the Cabinet (which must be regarded as one of the central institutions of the present Constitution) could or did exist. There could be no idea of collective responsibility, when questions of the significance of Catholic emancipation were left as open questions, when a Prime Minister was not himself free in the choice

2. *Memorials*, p. 87.
3. " Report of Royal Commission on Municipal Corporations," p. 49.
4. " Report of Royal Commission on Municipal Corporations," p. 30.
5. Aspinall, *The Cabinet Council 1783–1835*, p. 225.
6. *The Poverty of Historicism*, p. 100.

of his Cabinet, but largely dependent on the King, when it was not even clear that the resignation of a Prime Minister involved a fall of the Government, and when the incapacity of a former Minister to take his seat in the new Cabinet was not evident to all. On the parliamentary side, what now some would call the sovereignty of Parliament was not a clearly established doctrine. The concepts of Locke implying limitation of parliamentary power had taken root on the far side of the Atlantic, and still had their adherents on this side,[7] and the whole doctrine was certainly not accepted in the extended meaning which later was attributed to it.[8] Our ideas of the separation of powers were not so clear as to prevent Lord Ellenborough maintaining that he could have a seat in the Cabinet and be Chief Justice at the same time (or else again ideas of the Cabinet were so unclear). One main pillar of the modern constitution existed neither in theory nor in practice—the civil service; and its origins lay, in the minds of politicians, as much with a desire to limit the patronage of the Crown, as in any practical necessity. Indeed it emerged as a consequence of a later Constitution. It has been remarked: " As the monarchy rose above party, so the civil service settled below party. Constitutional bureaucracy was the counterpart of constitutional monarchy." [9] It must though be noted that if it did so emerge as a consequence, it was not a necessary consequence. Other choices, other solutions, were open, including a spoils system. There was no inevitability in this evolution.

Between the two ages there are, of course, continuities. Externally, there were troubles with France, though ones of a different order from those now current, and the mode of reaching a solution has changed. Questions of Ireland were there too, but with the marked difference that the Union of the two Kingdoms lay just ahead. Domestically fears have arisen that the situation elegantly hinted at by John Galt, and brutally described by the two Royal Commissions on Municipal Corporations, has not entirely changed, and the Committee on Local Government Rules of Conduct has been established. That should cause no surprise, for while constitutions can do something to make men free, they can do remarkably little to make men good, though measures below that level of constitutional law can help and have done so. In these matters, there is simply a continuity of problems. The statement that organised labour produces problems is simply a neutral assertion of fact, as is the statement that organised capital produces problems. The way in which problems are met, through Combination Acts or through an Industrial Relations Act, through a fumbling and obscure law on monopolies, forestalling and regrating or through various forms of Monopolies and Restrictive Prac-

7. Gough, *Fundamental Law in English Constitutional History*, Chap. XII.

8. *Donald* v. *Magistrates of Anderston* (1832) 11 S. 119; apart from *Mackenzie* v. *Stewart* (1754) 1 Pat.App. 578, only recently rediscovered by the generality.

9. Parris, *Constitutional Bureaucracy*, p. 49.

tice Acts or through Fair Trade Acts can have more interest, but as such they are not in the forefront of this essay which remains concerned with constitutional law in the traditional sense of law related to the organisation of government, and its powers.

Taken in that sense, 1799 has a greater interest. It was in the midst of the period when, partly stimulated by outside events, a traditional Constitution was under heavy attack and was also heavily defended. At the time defence was most obvious. Blackstone's ideas were pre-eminent. For him, Great Britain was singularly blessed as against the unhappy situation which theories had created in other countries. " Happily for us of this island the British constitution has long remained, and I trust will long continue a standing exception "—specifically an exception to Tacitus' proposition that a mixed government was an unattainable ideal, but implicitly an exception also to the disastrous course upon which other nations had set themselves. The idea was, though, a combination of a mixed system—which was to be found in Parliament, and of a single person having the executive power.[10] These two were for him, in many places in the *Commentaries*, the whole of government,[11] and magistrates were an admixture of judges and administrators.[12] Indeed higher courts were left out of the discussion of general structure in his Introduction, and relegated to Part III and for technical discussion. Much of this is also to be found in De Lolme, in a work largely remembered for one misleading sentence.[13] The key to understanding the virtue of the Constitution was the acceptance of the fact that " This authority has been made in England one single indivisible prerogative; it has been made for ever the unalienable attribute of one person . . . and all the active forces of the state have been left at his disposal " [14]; in marked contrast to Scotland " that seat of anarchy and aristocratical feuds."[15] Again there is the " mixed system " as the essential element of the legislature, with an ultimate dominance of the Crown through the veto.[16] There are more fundamental resemblances between the two. There was an acceptance of the eternal perfection of the Constitution as it existed. For De Lolme it satisfied " all the political passions of mankind."[17] For Blackstone[18] the bounds of prerogative were " so certain and notorious that it is impossible he [the King] should ever exceed them." One other facet is notable. For De Lolme the constitution should be studied in abstraction, detached

10. *Commentaries*, Introduction, para. 2.
11. *Cf.* Book 1, Chap. 2.
12. Book 1, Chap. 9 and Pt. III.
13. *The Constitution of England*—all references are to the fourth edition, 1784.
14. pp. 281–282.
15. p. 402.
16. p. 487.
17. p. 489.
18. Book 1, Chap. 7.

from all consideration of its content, " disengaged from the apparatus of fleets, armies, foreign trade, distant and extensive dominions." [19] Both attitudes persist. There is a clear element of unreality in proposing, as does the Kilbrandon Report, an Exchequer Board " concerned with two main functions: the first would be to decide the total amount of money and resources to be devoted to regional services and the second would be to decide how that amount should be distributed among the regions," [20] and at the same time to suggest that in some way that Board can be detached from politics. This is to attempt to return to habits of putting government out to arbitration which were demonstrated to be unworkable in the nineteenth century, and rightly the idea is criticised in the Minority Report. Serious problems are still approached on the basis that the past has achieved all that is required. " We do not want to create any new institution which would erode the function of Members of Parliament in this respect [*i.e.* of taking up the grievances of constituents] nor to replace remedies which the British Constitution already provides " [21] was the proclaimed hypothesis on which reform was to be built, when both that function and those remedies were in question because of either inappropriateness or inadequacy. At an intermediate stage Maitland had complained: " They [our institutional writers] go on writing as if England were governed by the Royal prerogatives." [22] At the end of the eighteenth century the combination of these attitudes meant that there was a failure to perceive that the mixed system of government worked, not because of its perfection but, because of its corruption. It was the management of the House and of elections which was the essential hinge upon which the system depended. [23] The attack on the defenders of that Constitution underlined the injurious consequences which these attitudes could have, particularly in relation to reform. [24] It is then perhaps worthwhile, having indicated the great changes in the constitution since 1798, and the fact that others lie ahead, also to indicate these enduring attitudes.

ITS DEATH AS A RESULT OF 1832—THE DEMOCRATIC STATE

It would, of course, be absurd to maintain that the earlier period was simply one of complacency and inertia. There were major changes, such

19. p. 3.

20. Kilbrandon Report, para. 674.

21. Cmnd. 2767—the White Paper preceding the Parliamentary Commissioner Act 1967. Dicey wrote in *Law and Opinion* (at p. 83) of this earlier period: " exaggerated satisfaction with English institutions retarded liberal reform long after the panic excited by Jacobinism had passed away."

22. *Constitutional History*, p. 417.

23. See *e.g.* the discussion in Vile, *Constitutionalism and the Separation of Powers*, Chaps. V and VIII.   24. Bentham, *Fragment upon Government.*

as the emergence in 1787 of a true consolidated fund. Nevertheless, real constitutional change had to wait until the decision was taken on Reform. If the Act of 1832 did not substantially alter the character of the House of Commons, what it did was to indicate a chosen course. It would, possibly, have been feasible to restrict the growth of the franchise, but at enormous and probably unacceptable costs of many kinds. The extension in 1867 is for that reason more significant in constitutional terms which are not so fundamental as was the making of the basic choice, but are nevertheless of the utmost importance. Bagehot was, of course, perfectly right when, in his campaign against that Act, he wrote in *The Economist* " If you take power from the upper classes, the others will try to remedy evils which no doubt oppress them sorely, and we will end up with a graduated income tax and the regulation of hours of work." He could put the proposition in a different form. " Any such measure for enfranchising the lower orders as would overpower, and consequently disfranchise the higher, should be resisted on the ground of ' abstract right '; you are proposing to take power from those who have the superior capacity, and to vest it in those who have but an inferior capacity. " [25] In the same vein, he explained this " hinge " of the mixed system just referred to. Dealing with the particular initial period of the reign of Pitt he remarked that " The noblemen and gentlemen who had the greatest influence in the counties and a certain number of whom were proprietors of boroughs, the class which, as we have seen, had a despotic power in the House of Commons as it then was " [26] produced the solidarity of the House against Jacobinism to support Pitt.

THE ARRIVAL OF THE ADMINISTRATIVE STATE AND ITS PATCHWORK CHARACTER

Thus reform starting in 1832 did two things. By opening the door to the democratic process it inevitably killed the system of government as it existed in 1798. It was impossible that the influence of the Crown, as it was then exercised, could ultimately survive. The same opening of the political process to other influences produced, as Bagehot foresaw, other consequences which affected the whole nature of government. Pressures to remedy those evils which were felt to oppress led inevitably to the administrative state. If the structural contrast between the constitution of then and that of now is marked, the content of government is even more strongly marked. It is almost true to say that, in the sense in which we would use the words today, there was no internal government by the central government. What there was of internal government was largely in the hands of local authorities of one sort or another. Maitland, writing

25. " Parliamentary Reform ": Works, Vol. III, p. 127.
26. " The History of the Unreformed Parliament and its Lessons ": Works Vol. III, p. 251.

of the situation at the start of the period under review remarks " It [Parliament] seems afraid to rise to the dignity of a general proposition."[27] Professor Griffith has demonstrated how slowly the change came about, and a legislative programme became a necessity for a government.[28]

Clearly reform could not affect the central government alone. The Municipal Corporations Act 1835 was the necessary counterpart. Often reform can be said to have been forced by events, rather than by idealism. The physical conditions resulting from the industrial revolution, and the dangers which they created, were the obvious causes of reforms in public health. Thus it is difficult to say that there was any governing theory; rather there was a triangular tug-of-war between those who trusted to local autonomy, those who were centralisers and those who retained a distrust of local authorities. Indeed the absence of " government " in a modern sense is indicated by the existence of that tangle of authorities arising each for particular purposes, as a local response to a particular need. Thereafter the struggle has been to impose order on this chaos of authorities, a process substantially hampered in England by the Local Government Act 1888 producing the rift and rivalry between town and country. As late as 1954 Professor Robson was writing " What we are concerned with is . . . the confusion and inefficiency, the waste and overlapping and extravagance which necessarily result from the present imperfect machinery of government."[29] Twenty years later the final attempt is being made to bring order into the system, or indeed to create a system. Even the approach to the reform of local government in the nineteenth century was piecemeal and did not look ahead to predictable problems. Thus there emerged new sets of " tradition "—of patterns of behaviour or of government not related to substance, but which soon became entrenched in thought as being correct. When it is examined in the light of substance the tradition of local government is much more modern than is often thought to be the case. It is though, what is thought to be the case which becomes the real obstacle to reform. By the time that it was possible, at the end of the nineteenth century, to have contemplated a system, too much had already happened on a non-systematic basis to make it easily possible to impose order, until further events had made abundantly clear the inadequacies of what existed.

It was in much the same way that the administrative state arrived. Its arrival was as much a revolution as the arrival of the democratic state. From reforms of the poor law and of public health there was a steady expansion of internal government by or under the central government.

27. *Constitutional History*, p. 383.
28. " The Place of Parliament in the Legislative Process " (1951) 14 M.L.R. 279 and 425.
29. *The Development of Local Government* (3rd ed.), p. 101.

Police fell under nationally determined standards. Education started to become a national concern and activities had to be regulated in new ways. So conditions had to be determined for factories, for the safety of ships, or the safety of mines, or for the registration of patent agents. Sometimes the regulation or administration was direct; sometimes it was indirect through the new local authorities, but the quantity and shape of government provides a marked contrast to the state of affairs at the outset of the period under review. Though finally the volume of this regulation was considerable, it too, or the whole change that it implied, seeped over the community at large. This meant that the shape of the machinery of government had, once again, much more the result of response rather than of design. Because of that, some parts of that machinery were almost taken unaware by what was happening, and other parts, which did change their shape, or evolve, did so as a reaction to current pressures, and hence in ways which were likely to have a limited future validity, since they did not look to the future.

THE NEGLECT BY LAWYERS OF THE CHANGES IN GOVERNMENT

On the one hand there was a refusal by the courts to perceive, at first, what was happening. Thus, a sanitary authority was castigated for producing a general scheme relating to cesspits and closets, with little perception of any of the changes in practice which were necessarily inherent in a sanitation scheme.[30] The uncertainty continued up to the date of what were formative cases for modern law. Clearly, as the reference to the Board of Education as an " arbitral tribunal " in *Board of Education* v. *Rice*,[31] or indeed the fumblings and uncertainties about words which had appeared " only in recent years " in *Institute of Patent Agents* v. *Lockwood*[32] demonstrate, this failure to perceive the essence of change continued for some time. Indeed it continued thereafter. There had already arrived a substantially satisfactory body of administrative tribunals before the Committee on Ministers' Powers, and before the lawyers awoke to the fact. The inappropriateness of private Bill procedure (which, in its adversary character, ran back to those earlier times) in many circumstances remained long after the inconveniences had become apparent. So too with planning procedures. The shadow of the attitudes of *Tinkler* v. *Wandsworth Board of Works*[33] was a long one, and obscured the nature of the governmental process in ways reaching beyond those areas in which the new methods and content affected individuals. As late as 1951 there was evident an attitude of " property " in thought about

30. *Tinkler* v. *Wandsworth Board of Works* (1858) 27 L.J.Ch. 342.
31. [1911] A.C. 179.
32. [1894] A.C. 347.
33. (1858) 27 L.J.Ch. 342.

local authorities which might have been appropriate to the age of the unreformed boroughs, when a charter was rightly so regarded.

On the other hand the essentially short-term solutions which were reached, can, in retrospect, be judged by the form that ministerial responsibility in particular, and parliamentary control in general, took. There were, of course, clear and attractive reasons for that development. The detached administration of Chadwick and the Poor Law Commissioners was bound to fail, in the original form and circumstance in which it existed. It was detached from, but intimately connected with, politics, for not even the simplest form of social security can be regarded as apolitical. Yet political control in operation was lacking. There was no other available and satisfactory form of control. Moreover, the democratic revolution had its effect. Matters which had formerly been accepted as capable of determination by judicial process ceased to be so regarded. There was a deference to democratic institutions and a belief that solutions should only be found by such means. In this judicial attitude to public law there are marked contrasts with the attitudes to private law. In relation to the latter, judges adopted an attitude which was much more positive. This attitude was, of course, reinforced as the doctrine of ministerial responsibility developed. That in itself was efficient and justified the attitude, but its efficiency was related to the quantum of business and to the state of the party systems. By 1881 parliamentary questions, which were effectively only thirty years old, had so increased that restrictions had to be imposed, a threat which continues.[34] Mr. Crossman has underlined how the substance of ministerial responsibility depended upon the existence of that " solid centre of independent and independent-minded members." [35] Thus efficient though the system might be at the outset, it would inevitably collapse when conditions changed, and the two critical changes, the growth of business and the growth of party, were predictable. Nevertheless, such was the respect that that efficiency had generated that that constitutional model became as revered as had been the Blackstonian model.[36]

THE ROLE OF POLITICIANS IN CONSTITUTION-MAKING AND ITS CONSEQUENCES

That situation became serious once the revolution of the advent of the administrative state was followed by that of the arrival of the welfare state. That state was born just as the earlier Constitution had reached its peak at the beginning of this century, and thus inherited machinery evolved for different circumstances. It is an intensification of the difficulties created by that set of circumstances which now face us. One aspect of

34. Howarth, *Questions in the House.*
35. His introduction to Bagehot's *English Constitution.*
36. See *e.g.* the quotation at note 21—also from Mr. Crossman.

the development of the nineteenth-century Constitution deserves particular notice. Holdsworth regarded the key as being the Cabinet system, adding: " It was through this system that the sovereignty of Parliament could be used to give the executive any additional powers which it needed, and to settle the relation between the executive and other parts of the machinery of government, central or local." [37] This is peculiarly a lawyer's formalistic way of putting it. What it really describes is an uncontrolled constitution in which constitutional reform is ultimately decided upon or rejected simply by politicians. If one puts into the proposition the political content of the party system, then this role of the politician becomes clear. In itself that is not entirely, or necessarily, a bad thing, as indeed nineteenth-century history demonstrates. It was the politicians who had accepted reality and by slow degrees changed the relationship of the House of Lords to the House of Commons; for the Parliament Act 1911 should really be regarded as largely declaratory, [38] the enactment being forced by Mr. Balfour. The doctrines of ministerial responsibility and of collective responsibility were their creations, and valid in their time, as was the subtle relationship of one to the other. The technique achieved with remarkable ease the fundamental changes which were necessary in the role of the sovereign, even during the difficult period of the reign of Queen Victoria. Virtue can be admitted, though the machine had its limitations. [39] What is arguable is whether the degree of reliance on this mode of reform was, or will be, justifiable. The Cabinet and its machinery affords an example of grounds for doubt. The Cabinet itself as to style or composition could thus be adjusted, but the struggle to make it efficient, by endowing it with a secretariat, was a struggle with politicians. Their objections were predictable—that such a body was untraditional, [40] that it would enable Ministers to " Hansardise " each other, etc., so that even as late as 1922 the existence of such a body could be questioned, though the need for it had been apparent in practice for over forty years. [41] The organisation of government itself suffers in conditions in which each Prime Minister is accorded the right to re-organise Government as he likes, and in which personality, rather than any sense of logic, is often the most powerful force, as is indicated by the history of the location of economic planning over the last twenty years. There are more serious defects which flow from this reliance and which have marked the evolution between " then and now." That reliance has meant

37. H.E.L., Vol. XIV, p. 140.
38. Even Dicey would have so accepted it: *Law of the Constitution* (9th ed.) p. 427.
39. Compare Jenkins, *Asquith*, even when the Cabinet was dealing with the Featherstone Riots, and Hankey, *Supreme Comment*, Chap. XXI.
40. Which it was not; Aspinall, *Cabinet Councils*.
41. The examples given in Jennings, *Cabinet Government*, pp. 250–251 suffice. The Haldane Committee on the Machinery of Government by implication underlines this point in para. 8.

that structures have rarely been regarded as a whole, nor have new structures been fitted within the framework (or, in the alternative, has the framework been adjusted to take them). The problems of the board system, at a national level, were well known. The history of the nineteenth century had illustrated them.[42] They had been underlined by the Haldane Report, by the Royal Commission on the Civil Service and by the Report of the Gilmour Committee,[43] and indeed as a result of the last-named Report care had been taken to bring the last surviving Scottish Boards of that time within the traditional framework. Yet, when after the War there was once again a strong move to utilise the Board system in relation to nationalised industries, there was little mark in the structures of any of this experience. This has meant then that at the level of central government there has, from this particular cause—that change lay in the hands of politicians—been a repetition of the piecemeal approach which was observable in relation to local government. Moreover, there is under this system the serious risk of confusion between a political and a constitutional crisis. They are different. In relation to that confusion 1974 may be more interesting.

This piecemeal approach can be noticed even in the establishment of major committees or Royal Commissions. The Committee on Ministers' Powers did, it is true, deal both with delegated legislation and with administrative adjudication, but in practice its importance lies primarily in the former field, and then only as a result of later political changes. The Franks Committee had therefore to deal later with the second subject in isolation, and, once again, with too limited terms of reference, because it too emerged from a particular political difficulty which prompted or dictated those terms. Those (and particularly the second head, related to inquiries) prevented any examination of the real problem, which was that of the general control of a modern administration. The inadequacy of the result led directly to the creation of the Parliamentary Commissioner for Administration, and so one partial measure compels another partial one and a total solution is rendered impossible. Inadequacy persists. More recently it is the sequence of events which has ensured a piecemeal approach. It seems probable that the Kilbrandon Commission on the Constitution was established as a response to a particular set of political circumstances. It was preceded by the two Royal Commissions on local government[44] and by the implementation of their reports as far as the main structure of local government was concerned, with regional structures left in the air.[45] There is no reason to think that

---

42. F. M. G. Willson, " Ministries and Boards " (1955) *Public Administration* 43.
43. Cd. 9230, Cd. 7338, Cmd. 5563.
44. Cmnd. 4040 and Cmnd. 4150. One of which was itself fragmentary, Wales escaping Redcliffe-Maud in the Report stage, but not in implementation. They are referred to as Redcliffe-Maud and Wheatley, respectively.
45. Cmnd. 5460, para. 198.

the techniques of making a layer cake are appropriate to the construction of an integrated system of government. That inadequacy is now abundantly clear. The creation of the vast Strathclyde local authority has rendered almost impossible (even were it desirable) the insertion of an intermediate level of authority in Scotland.

There has also been, as a result of that cause, combined with the current nature of politics, an impoverishment of constitutional debate. It is fair to say that the Fulton Committee on the Civil Service will not finally be judged as significant a document as was the Northcote-Trevelyan Report of 1854, yet the disparity in the amount of debate related to the two is not proportionate to such difference as there is between the two reports. It is related rather to the fact that almost concurrently with the publication of the Fulton Report was the announcement of the Government's acceptance of it. Yet, had the general debate opened up, elements of the Fulton Report—among others its evocation of the possibility of " hiving off "—might have received much more attention.

Perhaps the most serious consequence has been our obsession with conventions of the Constitution. There is, of course, no constitutional system in which conventions or practices do not play a part. They exist even within the constitutional life of the European Economic Community, the constitution of which is perhaps more dominated by rules of law than any other, and currently further " conventions " are being proposed by the Commission to strengthen the powers of the Parliament.[46] It is because conventions have, with us, been the predominant means of achieving constitutional amendment by politicians that they have assumed so much importance. In consequence there has grown up a belief in a limited role of law in government. That belief is also related to the influence of Dicey's distinction between law and convention. This has led to too ready an acceptance of a view that political redress is to be preferred to legal redress, a view which finds expression both in the courts' difference to the doctrine of ministerial responsibility and in the adoption of the PCA. As an institution it was thought that it had the great virtue of being consistent with the conventional framework, and of leaving it undisturbed, even though that framework was itself in question.

This influence has contributed to the ways in which constitutional principles of a more detailed type have been dealt with in the years between. On the one hand there is observable a like piecemeal approach, in the sense that there was no attempt made to bring the law as a whole into harmony with the modern state. Emergency measures were taken, and loopholes were stopped. The *Alabama* incident produced the

46. See the communication to the Parliament on *Practical Measures to Strengthen the Powers of Control of the Parliament.*

Foreign Enlistment Act 1870, but once again legislation did not, or was not taken to reflect, the unity of government which exists irrespective of the differentiation of the means of government. The Public Authorities Protection Act 1893 was concerned with only one group of authorities engaged upon an integrated process. Although it was evident that in the new world contact between government and citizen was bound to increase, the Crown Proceedings Act 1947 had to be forced. The failure to consider the reality of government behind traditional worlds led to such paradoxical decisions as that in *Bank voor Handel en Scheepvaart*.[47] In such cases, as in *Burmah Oil Co. Ltd.* v. *Lord Advocate*,[48] the debate became arid, and the purposes of rules as necessary instruments of a process seemed to be lost behind technicality. The limits to their logic were not explored. It is possible even to see an intensification of the technicality of the debate. There was, in many of the earlier authorities discussed in such cases, more of the real substance, just as there seems more of reality in *Stockdale* v. *Hansard*[49] than in *Harper* v. *Home Secretary*.[50] At a yet lower level of detail, which is nevertheless serious for individuals, one has only to consider the lack of generalised principle governing *locus standi* in relation to the remedies for the judical review of administrative actions. Thus Professor de Smith was forced to treat the subject under each of the forms of action,[51] yet the concept of *recevabilité*, of admissibility, is a general problem and one with which in the new setting we will have to come to grips. In effect a variety of causes fed upon each other. Deference to Parliament and reliance on political remedies for long allowed the lawyers to hold back. Holding back produced the consequence that when that was no longer possible, the armoury of thought or of remedy of the law was quite inadequte. Yet the pleas of the Law Commissions, even in the limited field of remedies, remain unheard.

In this of course the dominating position of Dicey, and in particular his attitude to public law, was of particular importance. It was important because of his insistence on the ordinary law and ordinary tribunals read in the simplicity of his original exposition. Too little note was taken of the refinement contained in his introduction to the eighth edition where he raised the question of whether a court composed of a body of men " who combined official experience with legal knowledge " might not finally be the best solution in changing circumstances.[52] The passage was

---

47. [1954] A.C. 584.
48. 1964 S.C.(H.L.) 117.
49. (1839) 9 Ad. & El. 1.
50. [1955] Ch. 238.
51. *Judical Review of Administrative Action.* In the setting of prohibition, he speaks of the law being enveloped in a fog which is not easy to penetrate.
52. 8th ed., Introduction, p. xlviii. The process of withdrawal from an extreme position had started with the Introduction to the 6th ed.

never included in the text. It was also important in the fact that, although other parts of his writing demonstrate his awareness of the relationship of politics and constitutional law, *The Law of the Constitution* itself attempted to separate the bones of the law from the flesh of real constitutional life. That is unhelpful to the student and to the law itself.

THE CHANGES SUMMARISED. THEIR CONSEQUENCES FOR THE ECONOMIC STATE

The argument this far can be summarised as follows. At whatever aspect of the Constitution one looks, there has been a fundamental change. The nature and content of government have changed, and even if, in one sense, the changes can be regarded as a continuum, distinct phases of change can be identified. There was the arrival of the democratic state, the arrival of the administrative state, the arrival of the Welfare State, which last nearly coincides with the arrival of the economic state. The last is as important as any of the earlier stages and marks as great a change. It is the change as a result of which the state is not merely concerned with global economic management, but also with detailed internal management. Each " state " or stage emerged as a consequence of its predecessor, but each poses distinct constitutional challenges. Response to these challenges has overall been piecemeal, and thus inadequate. The reasons why response took that form are varied. They include a belief in past virtues of a Constitution which was no longer appropriate in changed conditions, a belief in pragmatism, which could amount to a refusal to plan a whole system, an over-reliance on constitutional change through politicians, and an under-reliance on law, coupled with an unwillingness to rethink the role of law and courts in government. As it has been painted, the picture is no doubt too dark, but over-emphasis is a necessary corrective to complacency. Moreover it is such attitudes which are now challenged, and above all it is the relationship of a constitution and of constitutional law to the whole surrounding circumstance which is becoming increasingly important. Undoubtedly a constitution reflects and is intended to protect and foster certain broad principles, but the way in which it does so must be continuously adapted. When Marshall spoke of the Constitution as a charter for ages to come he did not mean that it was an unchanging charter, but rather that, within certain guidelines (which were themselves to be reinterpreted in the light of current conditions), it was an instrument which because of its nature had to have flexibility. The ultimate limits of state and federal power were not there precisely defined for all time. Those changes were often responses to economic changes as two periods show. In the later years of the nineteenth century federal power had to grow as a result of the growth in the size and nature of inter-state commerce, railways, pipelines and transcontinental frauds. All these, among many other things, needed to be controlled, thus the prime mover in the shift of federal power was economic change; it was only federal power that could be effective. So similarly at the later New Deal period outstanding among the causes of the then shifts of constitutional doctrine was the fact that within an economic union certain forms of economic crisis can only be managed, if they can be managed at all, by the central or federal powers. One could continue. At a further stage in evolution, certain social ills could only find the start of a solution by other shifts in relationship. Desegregation in schools, and Congressional redistricting increasingly, because of the perception of the central court—the Supreme Court—became matters of federal concern.

CURRENT CHALLENGES AND THE UNCERTAIN RESPONSES

That is not a digression from the main stream of this essay. It was the framework which produced the possibilities of change. Looking at the current scene, one can wonder whether, in the absence of such a charter, the United Kingdom Constitution has not lost its flexibility in many serious ways, whether indeed Meander has not become canalised in a course which is not particularly appropriate. It is such considerations which must be in the forefront when one starts to look at the modern Constitution and the way ahead. There is no reason to believe that somehow the United Kingdom can constitutionally stand aside from, or rather be isolated from, major movements and above all major economic movements.

The international challenge

The present period is marked by the fact that the international economic and monetary scene is slowly reshaping itself. The post-War settlements were useful in their time but no longer correspond to changed conditions. Those have affected the validity of the hypotheses on which those settlements were built.[53] Any United Kingdom response to those changes is bound to have internal consequences. So should the encouraging fact in international relations that it is possible on a regional scale to advance, and to accept, through the European Convention on Human Rights, that this part of the moral and political identity of Western Europe (of which much has been talked) is capable of a new level of international control, enforcement or supervision. Internally the same sort of forces are at work. There is a state of flux, whether or not we will be able to adapt may be unsure, but the changes in the pattern of government should be substantial to meet the change in content.

53. A good summary is in Chap. 2 of Kohnstamm and Hager, *A Nation Writ Large?*

The challenge of the economic state

The fact that, whether it is done well or ill, the management of the economy has become a primary consideration for government, can be neglected neither in the Constitution nor by constitutional lawyers. At the level of the most obvious, this has changed the nature of the budget and it should have changed much of the constitutional thought about " fiscal " legislation, which tends still to be regarded by lawyers in Gladstonian terms. It is in this context curious to observe how slowly and with what difficulty the relationship of the Bank of England and the Treasury were reworked. It is not after all quite beyond living memory when the Bank of England could regard itself as almost autonomous.[54] At a lower, and slightly less obvious level, the final pressures which added urgency to the fumbling post-War moves to reform local government did not come from a sudden realisation of the inadequacies of the system— for that realisation had been present for a long time.

The challenge of devolution

It was after all possible to cajole, bully, persuade and subsidise the whole range of authorities into producing services of a more or less tolerable level. Once, however, planning had become such a major function, the urgency of ensuring the existence of authorities of appropriate size and commanding adequate staffs forced change, since in relation to that function wide disparities of size and efficiency had even greater effects upon the whole than they did in relation to other functions. " Planning " must here be understood not in that over-limited way in which it is understood by the " Planning Bar " but in a sense which embraces both physical and economic planning or management. There was no doubt a time in which these two aspects could be thought to be separate or could not be conjoined because techniques were inadequate or believed to be so. Owen's New Lanark Mills owed nothing to government, but government can no longer stand aside from the implantation of industry or the conditions in which it is implanted.

Professor Beer, a friendly but severe critic, has remarked: " My paradox is complete: a system which by the very extension and centralising of power undertaken to deal with modern problems has set in train political consequences that make it exceedingly difficult to deal with those problems." [55] Two problems are in the forefront of his mind, lack of economic growth, and inflation. Both are economic, but, as he underlines, both are political, and both should concern constitutional lawyers. He remarks, in a related passage

" In so far as resources are diverted to satisfying immediate consumption needs

54. See Blake, *An Unknown Prime Minister.*
55. In *Essays on Reform,* the " British Legislature " at p. 91.

—whether through individual purchase or provision by the Welfare State—
there will be that much less available for enlarging Britain's productive capital.
I do not suggest that the choice is an easy one for a government to make—
especially when its margin of favour with the electorate is constantly threatened
by a competitor bidding for the votes of the same consumer groups in which the
Government itself has found crucial support."

He comments also, as have many of us, " thus the level of secrecy in
British Government is excessively high." [56] Despite what has been said
above of the relationship of constitutional law and politics, the pursuit
of the implications of these quotations could lead too far into the field
of politics. Citing them at this stage is though appropriate. They reinforce
the criticism which has been made of leaving constitutional change
exclusively to those engaged in formal politics. Both the bi-polarism and
the secrecy of which he complains are the result of that process. The
second has flowed from the doctrine of ministerial responsibility.[57] It
leads to an impoverishment of political debate, not only in such examples
as that on the Fulton Report referred to above or on the Rothschild
Report referred to below, but for example in the place in economic
argument of such persons as the Governor of the Bank of England. The
first has flowed from certain conventions, and thence into electoral law
which reinforces these tendencies. Thus, the significance of the economic
state (and its link with the welfare state) is underlined, as is the question
of the adequacy of constitutional mechanisms to deal with this world.
In themselves those mechanisms are hardened formalisations of a
nineteenth-century model. That model depended for its success on
different political circumstances, in particular on the circumstance that
parties were not monolithic, and was designed for a simpler content of
politics. Thus the two issues which are important for the current Constitution are the ways in which present machinery may be forced to change
to meet the internal needs and the impact of the external situation, which
is in many ways totally new, upon the internal scene. Those external
forces resulted in the United Kingdom's Membership of the European
Communities, and thus the future of constitutional law has broadened.

RECENT CHANGES IN CENTRAL GOVERNMENT

Internally some major changes have occurred. Three are perhaps
most noteworthy at the centre and present challenges to current underlying assumptions.

The giant ministries

There is the arrival of the giant Ministries which now seem to be a

56. *Ibid.* at p. 99.
57. As indeed the White Paper, *Information and the Public Interest* (Cmnd. 4089),
demonstrates.

permanent fixture of the scene. They have evolved, with some trial and error, under all governments since the war. Sir Winston Churchill's early attempts at " Overlords " were not a success, but the process continued with the eventual creation of a unified Ministry of Defence, the growth of the Ministry of Technology between 1967 and 1969 and the creation of the new giants such as the Department of Trade and Industry [57a] or the Department of the Environment. These are not just administrative changes. Their emergence posed questions for the Cabinet, for what had formerly been an inter-departmental dispute, and hence fit for a Cabinet decision, became in many instances an intra-departmental dispute and (assuming the right qualities of the Minister) unfit for such a mode of settlement, but to be determined within the Ministry. There were further changes on the job of the Minister, who becomes in such giants, or should become, much more of a manager of a team.[58] There are clear repercussions on parliamentary control, even though, by allocation of functions, some of the difficulties of the " Overlord " solution are avoided. It does not necessarily follow that these automatically increased the " remoteness " of government. Internal arrangements, even in the Department of Health and Social Security, can avoid difficulties and indeed diminish them for individuals. Nevertheless there, too, size has its effect, as probably it has had upon the smaller departments such as the Scottish Office, which is affected by the level and manner in which decisions are taken in giants particularly those concerned with economic affairs and management. The strengthening of the economic and statistical side of the Scottish Office may be one mark of a sense of change. Whatever other justification there was for that development, it had become necessary as a defensive mechanism, as a source of independent information, for the Scottish Office.

The Central Policy Review Staff

The second related change, the consequences of which cannot by its nature, be easily judged from outside, is the creation of the Central Policy Review Staff (CPRS).[59] It too was a necessity, in any event, to strengthen the planning mechanisms at the Centre. It became an essential element (again one in a sense defensive) with the arrival of the giant departments, if the Cabinet were to retain reality. Granted their existence there was a real need for a body which could produce alternative policies, which are neither the favourite sons, nor the fragile com-

57a. That the Department of Trade and Industry is now to be broken up does not affect the substance of the argument.

58. See *e.g. New Trends in Government* by Sir Richard Clarke.

59. The *Reorganisation of Central Government* (Cmd. 4506). If examined with care the thought and the terminology of argument in the White Paper does not in this go far beyond that of the Haldane Report.

promises of the giants. It could indeed help democratic debate, though not in the circumstances in which, as with the Rothschild Report on Research Councils, the debate starts against the background of a governmental acceptance in principle of the policy. (The question " How green is your Green Paper?" is often a real one. Frequently such a paper appears to exist at that nice point on a stick of celery at which green and white merge. Thus the use of Green Papers cannot be rated a significant development.) This invention of the CPRS has importance in relation to a third development in central government, which is the rearrangement of management functions involved in the creation of the Civil Service Department outside the Treasury. (Again this was not the result of sudden inspiration, but rather of evolution.)

Central management of government

It would be inaccurate to assert that there has emerged a Troika, of Treasury, CPRS and Civil Service Department, since the horses are ill-balanced. Nevertheless there has emerged a central machine, capable of planning, which, happily, contains a series of centres of power avoiding, for the moment, the risks of a Prime Minister's Department. The rationalisation of government is all to the good, but it involves, or may involve, both an increase in efficiency and of rigidity. In any event it had changed many traditional habits. The evolution of the techniques of PAR (Programme Analysis Review) and PESC (Public Expenditure Survey Committee) to which this re-arrangement at the centre is in part a response, should not be thought of as mere techniques. Indeed the system, it has been said, " should not be regarded as an addition to the conventional system: for if it survives it must ultimately replace the traditional system, and will be the system of expenditure and manpower administration and control within the departments, at the centre, and between the two." [60] The movement is towards strategy. That in itself is a marked departure from the habits of random response which has continued between " then and now." The process of adaptation is slow, for the challenge of the new age is profound. It has been said that the efforts of the West to bring about governmental and administrative reform shed doubt on all the working methods of received ministerial organisation, the capacity for performance of traditional models of public service, of the decision-making processes in government or Parliament, and of present mechanisms for defining the public will.[61]

While there is adaptation of administrative mechanisms, the political, on the whole, lag behind. There are exceptions. The new Expenditure Committee is clearly a parliamentary advance on both the Public

60 *New Trends in Government*, p. 43.
61. Theiss, " Political Planning in Western Democracies " (1970) 21 *Aussenpolitik* 434.

Accounts Committee and the Select Committee on Estimates and is struggling to act as such—struggling because it is not endowed with all the resources which are probably needed. Nevertheless, it is in tune with these other changes. Yet generally the lag is there. For administrative changes of this order can challenge the constitutional world that politicians would like to make for themselves. Thus what is increasingly in question is political dogma, including doctrines such as that of ministerial responsibility. Clearly Ministers must be responsible. The question is for what? If the mechanisms, forced or accepted, are moving towards the longer term, so that all excitement about an annual budget has become an anachronism, then the content of politics has shifted from detail to basic choices and thereafter to a style of debate for which the bi-polar system is ill attuned. The new systems could enhance public debate, but there are few signs that they will be allowed to.

THE RELATED CHANGES IN LOCAL GOVERNMENT AND THEIR CONSEQUENCES

A similar movement to size has, though to a lesser degree, been apparent in the reforms of local government. Authorities, according to the Redcliffe-Maud Report (para. 256) were to be of such a size as to have the strength and to be able to command the necessary skills, qualities which were lacking for the most part in the older authorities. Above all, size was a means of simplification. Redcliffe-Maud referred to the " complex local Government machinery," Wheatley reported " that the relationship between different kinds of authority is over-complicated, and that in many cases the electors have no clear idea of what their elected representatives do or ought to do on their behalf." [62] Simplification there has been in the two Local Government Acts, though not to the extent urged by the Redcliffe-Maud Report. The two-tier system adopted generally in the Local Government Act 1972 does not preserve that simplicity in the sense of a clear definition between the two tiers (which Redcliffe-Maud attempted to keep in metropolitan areas). This is particularly so in areas such as planning in which individuals feel themselves most exposed. In the final result, logic did not always prevail and hence criticism can be made of the distribution of functions and of the mode of distribution which work against the concept of efficiency which was one of the prime objects.[63] Two related consequences of the changes are already clear. The Report,[64] prepared under the steering Committee presided over by Sir Frank Marshall, emphasised the need for the new countries to establish area committees and to decentralise administration establishing area offices with substantial delegated

62. Cmnd. 4040, para. 7; Cmnd. 4150, para. 100.
63. Buxton, *Local Government*, Chap. 10.
64. *The New Local Authorities: Management and Structure.*

powers. In an interim Report stress was placed upon the need to delegate
power and responsibility to officers, a matter which was taken up and
reinforced in the main Report. Such changes in style of working had
already been foreseen in Redcliffe-Maud (para. 497). To that extent the
reforms in local government, unless these correctives are applied, can
produce the resentment which results from centralisation even on this
minor scale, in the same way as it is said that that resentment exists on the
level of national government. The centres of county administration will
be more remote from areas which are their concern, and there will be
changes in the degree of local knowledge possessed by councillors.

THE PROBLEM OF DEVOLUTION

Hence there has arisen interest in devolution. There are, in the
reforms of local government, few signs of any real change in the relationship of central and local government. The traditional elements of
tutelage remain, and perhaps must do so until it is seen how the new
system works in practice. A period of waiting is equally likely before
thought is given to granting new powers. Meanwhile it is likely that the
process illustrated by the reorganisation of the National Health Service
and of water supplies will continue. Areas are still wrong for certain
services and must remain so, and what are deemed to be the needs of a
service will continue to create pressures in favour of this third stream of
authorities, of *ad hoc* bodies organised essentially on a national scale.
Some of these problems were foreseen in the proposals of Redcliffe-Maud
for provincial councils,[65] to be concerned with the broad economic and
environmental framework on a larger scale (within which the functional
authorities exercised their powers) and at the same time exercising
influence upon the central government. Indirectly elected (even though
supplemented by co-option) these councils might not have been suitably
composed, but in the proposal there was also involved the idea of the
decentralisation of central government, and there could have emerged a
sensible link between central and local government. No consideration
could be given to them because of the creation of the Royal Commission
on the Constitution.

The causes of discontent

There were in the Report of that Commission, the Kilbrandon
Report [66] and in the Memorandum of Dissent two divergent interpreta-
tions of the Commission's terms of reference, and for the most part the
Report held to an interpretation dominated by the idea of devolution.
At the outset the Report identified as the prime causes of dissatisfaction

65. Chapter IX of the Report.
66. Cmnd. 5460.

the over-centralisation of government, and discontent regionally with the rigidity of the allocation of public funds, either between regions or between alternative expenditures. " Regional preferences," it was said, " were subordinated to national policies " (para. 277). There was complaint of the lack of co-ordination between central departments and of the secrecy of government. These resulted in other causes of discontent: congestion at the centre and a devaluation of political life in the regions. Finally there was a weakening of democracy, a down-grading of the back-bencher and a growth of *ad hoc* bodies. This perhaps was summed up by the Dissenters when speaking of " a serious erosion which has taken place in the extent to which we as a people govern ourselves " (paras. 35 and 360). The validity of some of the complaints made by people at large is uncertain, 52 per cent. of those questioned in Scotland either did not know of the office of Secretary of State for Scotland or positively thought it did not exist. The pattern in Wales was similar (paras. 379–380). Moreover, within these general complaints there is confusion. It is facile to speak of the erosion of the extent to which we govern ourselves—without relating that phrase specifically to the content of government. Simple methods of organisation are appropriate to simple things. One could at one stage govern oneself much more fully in a rural parish than in a city. Once the isolation of the parish is diminished even that proposition becomes less sure. No one governed a National Health Service formerly, and the invention of that has perhaps enabled many to have more voice in regard to health. Moreover, all of us are capable of willing the ends but are at the same time capable of profoundly disliking the necessary means. We are all simultaneously able to complain about too much government and to insist on those things which make more government essential. It is false to equate the centralisation of government, at least in the United Kingdom, with " remoteness." Much depends upon how the centralised government behaves. It is even more false to argue that the creation of the new " giant " departments necessarily generates that feeling of remoteness. By simplifying, those new departments could diminish that feeling. Nevertheless, it is reasonable to accept that there is an unease, a dissatisfaction. That dissatisfaction may relate, above all, to failures in communication and failures to win assent by government. Those failures may be more particularly related to the political pattern already referred to and in particular to the sense of the secrecy of the governmental process.

The proffered solutions and their criticism

For this unease the Report proposes a range of cures with differing degrees of support. Separation and federalism were excluded. They all depend upon the non-proven hypothesis that " Devolution could do much to reduce discontent." There is no inevitability about that result.

The converse might well be the case. The clash between regional preferences and national priorities is inescapable and it does not follow that devolution will necessarily provide better means of resolving that conflict. Current experience with some local authorities might suggest the contrary. Be that as it may, one proposed solution is to transfer to assemblies in Scotland and Wales legislative powers over a range of subjects of very uneven weight. They range from ancient monuments to harbours, through education, agriculture, social work with particular powers, *e.g.* in relation to the administration of justice attributable to Scotland. The two Secretaries of State would go. There would be separate civil services. Others would like only a directly elected Welsh Advisory Council. One a differently organised Scottish Council. For England any legislative devolution to the regions was ruled out. Some would have preferred a scheme of executive devolution either generally, or for England only, with an assembly working like a county council (even to the extent of using a traditional committee system which present proposals are trying to remove from the local government techniques on the grounds of their inefficiency). Yet another proposal is for regional co-ordinating councils, part nominated, part indirectly elected, and inevitably there is simply a co-ordinating committee of local authorities. The dissenters are equally generous in proposals. Apart from one main scheme of democratic assemblies for the whole of the regions of Great Britain, the two dissenters also produce an alternative. Their main scheme diminishes to a much greater extent the place of central government than do most of the proposals of the Report. The Assemblies under this scheme would be likely to produce all the faults of *gouvernement d'assemblée*. It is unfortunately true that the act of administration cannot, at any serious level, be a democratic act. It is by its nature an authoritarian one, though capable of democratic and other controls. To carry to extreme, loose ideas of participation or of populist democracy is not in practice a way of providing a satisfactory form of government.

To criticise in detail each proposal would be an unnecessarily lengthy exercise for this essay. Particularly since the major proposals for Scotland and Wales fail, it must seem, on grounds of finance. There would be created an Exchequer Board, independent of all governments, which would recommend what Scotland's total expenditure should be, to finance at United Kingdom standards (to be fixed every five years) all transferred services. Thus the standards would be determined on a United Kingdom basis in the determination of which Scotland and Wales would have a reduced voice. They would be fixed for five years irrespective of the possibility of the advent meanwhile of a new government which radically altered the standard of one service. These determinations would be by a mechanism detached from political or other responsibility. This is Chadwick and his Commissioners carried not into a relatively minor part of government but into its very heart. For lesser proposals there is to be a block grant system, when we have never yet, even in relation to local government, been able to invent one which works. In all of this there is an assumption of economic stability which recent history would suggest is rash. How, under such a scheme, does one use public expenditure as an economic regulator either easily or without excessive friction between the different layers? In short, if one is to make any prophecy about the future shape of the Constitution, one can exclude all the major proposals of the Royal Commission and of the Dissenters. In substance the Report continues nineteenth-century habits of thought.

There are deeper reasons for rejecting the Report. The evidence given to the Commission indicated that there was serious incomprehension of the system of government, that, as Wheatley had earlier said, the system had become incomprehensible to many and this incomprehensibility is one of the main keys to discontent. It would seem that the addition of an intermediate level between the new major local authorities and the true central government will merely complicate once more, particularly if there is no uniformity of pattern. This confusion reaches a high point in the Dissenting report when in paragraph 246 it is said that the inter-mediate authorities will have default powers over local authorities in respect of duties laid upon them by either that level or by the central government which itself would have default powers in relation to the intermediate level. This is a system of government by friction which can do little to ease the causes of discontent. Moreover, to these levels there must be added a further one, that of the Communities. To the main consequences of that one must turn in a moment. These structures will not simplify but confuse. If the annual price review in agriculture was a matter of high mystery, the negotiation of finance under the schemes proposed will be even more so.

THE OBSTACLES TO DECENTRALISATION—THE HERITAGE OF THE NINETEENTH CENTURY

Yet problems exist. There is excessive centralisation, there is excessive secrecy, there is a feeling of remoteness in the sense that the individual cannot satisfactorily hit at the governmental machine. There may be a devaluation of the back-bencher. Curiously, in the reasons for the rejection of certain ideas, the Commission does point to certain major causes. A system of Prefects is rejected (para. 999) although it, admittedly, might be valuable, because " there is no way of overcoming the objection that a civil servant could not serve two or more departments or Ministers in circumstances in which there might be a clash of departmental interests." The stumbling block is the derivative consequences of the particular view of ministerial responsibility. On the decentralisation of

Ministries it is said (para. 986) " limitations have to be placed on regional discretion because the ultimate responsibility rests with the Minister, who is accountable to Parliament for the actions of his officials." Earlier it had been said (para. 279) that civil servants in the region were felt to be inferior and feel themselves disadvantaged in their career because of their lack of discretion and absence from the centre. Sweden it was said (para. 849) had achieved a decentralised system and considerable " hiving-off " (which Fulton hoped for), but the Swedish model was of no help since there Members of Parliament are concerned with general policy, but here it could not be expected that Parliament should divest itself of interest in the details of administration. " Moreover, it [the Swedish system] depends on a fully developed system of administrative law ... which might be thought to be alien to our tradition." Both Report and Dissent are full, of course, of a rush of ombudsmen even though the last Report on the PCA says that rather less than half of the members thought it worth while to refer to him. [67] So far as the Federal Republic of Germany was concerned, experience was, it was said, again of little value, even though the virtues of devolved administration there were recognised, because unlike our statutes, German ones had a generality in the declaration of principle and, again, the system worked because there was a well developed system of public law. That in itself was of course alien, etc. One should add three things. Secrecy in government is, as has earlier been indicated, to a large extent a result of the shape of politics and of our version of ministerial responsibility.[68] Equally of course centralisation is a direct result of reliance on a centralised control system. If there is a debasement of the back-bencher that is because Parliament is no longer, as Bagehot put it, living in " a state of perpetual, potential choice." [69] Those are, however, consequences of letting politicians make the Constitution.

ALTERNATIVE MEANS OF CHANGE AND THEIR RELEVANCE TO THE WHOLE SITUATION

Thus did the unchallenged patterns of the nineteenth century Constitution (which in fact emerged much later than the Commission believed to be so) force the Commission into making unworkable proposals when ready solutions were at hand. If those patterns are challenged, it is perfectly possible to decentralise government, to create valid regional centres of decision (which in their turn would help to re-create regional political life). It is also possible to open up government and to bring it nearer to the citizen when it affects him. Realistically that is what he wants and feels the need for. For the most part he is not interested in

67. Report of the Select Committee on the PCA, 1972–73, H.C. 379.
68. See text at note 57.
69. *The English Constitution* (Fontana ed.), p. 158.

theories of structure or else there would have been much more public heat about the changes in local government. Heat there has been, but it has largely come from those with one form or another of vested interest. The only changes which are essential to achieve this are changes in the concept of ministerial responsibility which are long overdue. It had become unreal and has become even more so with the emergence of the giant Ministries. The other is to create an alternative system of responsibility through public law. (For nobody would dream of suggesting that practical government should be subjected to the present incoherent and uninformed system of law.) Not only would such changes help the regions, they would also help the centre in aiding the new mechanisms to work efficiently, and in forcing Parliament to talk of policy and thus decongest itself. The help to the regions would come, not only because of the location of centres of power and decision with them, but also because this alternative mode of control impedes the tendency to uniformity which dominates an administration subjected primarily to political controls. Uniformity is the easiest thing to defend politically, but it may be bad administration. Variance can thus be defended under this alternative system. Moreover, unlike anything proposed by the Royal Commission such changes produce a simpler and thus more comprehensible system of government and one in which, granted the legal framework, there could be some reality in the talk of the autonomy of local authorities. The new authorities might then be more attractive to candidates. It can be said that these changes could not be discussed because of the narrow view taken in the Report of the interpretation of the terms of reference. Yet legal change and some version of public law was inherent in the major proposals. It is unreal and unreasonable to set up such a distribution of legislative powers as is proposed in the Report without making provision for the legal determination of disputes. Even the Ireland Act 1920 did that. On the other hand, such changes were not discussed at all by the Dissenters who took a broader view of their remit. When one reads the whole Report, what is striking is the limited range of ideas. More important than the narrow interpretation was the shadow of tradition, of that " constitution which had served us so well for some hundreds of years "—even if it had not so served, nor had it so long existed. It was a constitution that had never as a whole taken account of changing conditions. To urge that it should is not to fall into the trap of holism, but to assert that the framework is only a part of social engineering.

THE CHALLENGE OF EUROPE

Thus finally internal and external conditions join, and it may in fact be happy that there should at this time be uncertainty about the Constitution. Uncertainty produces the possibility of helpful change. Essentially the external change, membership of the European Communities, challenges precisely the same things. That that change is a constitutional one cannot be doubted. This is not some new treaty relationship. There is a transfer of power which affects national constitutions. Of that the European Court of Justice has had no doubt.[70]

THE LEGAL CHARACTER OF THE COMMUNITIES AND THEIR CONSTITUTIONAL CHARACTER

The constitutional world which we enter is not an amorphous one, it is one which exists within a designed framework established by the Treaties. It is moreover a highly legal one. In it and by it the citizen is expected to have effective legal remedies either against Community organs, or against the government of the member state. When the court speaks of the direct effect of certain rules of Community law, it means that that law has created rights in individuals which are part of their legal patrimony [71] which national jurisdictions are bound to respect and to enforce. If it be said that this system of government is remote, it should be remembered that, on the contrary, as far as the individual is concerned, it is a system which produces more directly enforceable rights (and thus diminishes remoteness) than does our own. It is a system based upon the concepts of public law, as all the arguments on *recevabilité* in the cases under Articles 173 and 175 of the Treaty of Rome demonstrate. We are then, for certain purposes, going to have to work such a system. It is difficult to see why we should not do so for our own purposes, when the advantages of directness are clear. It is simply irrelevant in many cases to put the Intervention Board for Agricultural Produce within the ambit of the PCA. No German merchant would dream of using that device. He will sue (as should his British counterpart) for he has the right to an effective jurisdictional remedy. It is no longer discretionary for a number of public authorities to open up a range of contracts to open competition. Although their attention had been called to this merely by circulars, there is clearly a legal obligation upon them and probably a legal right in prospective contractors.[72] The contrast with the situation under the Stockholm Convention is clear. One could continue. It is by no means certain that sections 21 and 43 of the Crown Proceedings Act 1947 remain valid in the new circumstances. When a Crown servant is bound by superior law to give effect to certain rights, there is no clear reason why he should not be enjoined from obstructing them or obliged to give

70. Case 26/62, *Van Gend en Loos*, IX Rec. 1; Case 6/64, *Costa* v. *ENEL*, X Rec. 1159; Case 11/70, *Internationales Handelsgesellschaft*, XVI Rec. 1125.

71. Case 13/67, *Salgoil*, XIV Rec. 661. For breach of its obligations, the member state may under Community law be liable to compensate individuals, Case 39/73, *Commission* v. *Italy*.

72. See *e.g.* Directive 71/304 EEC: J.O. L. 185 of 16.8.71. It is unsatisfactory to execute, as has been tdone, such Directives merely by circulars.

effect to them. It suffices thus to indicate that we have entered a system of public law, a system designed for individuals and a system which challenges many recent traditions. It need not be feared, since it merely gives reality to the rule of law.

It is nevertheless a legal order of which account should be taken in any changes which we now contemplate. Its importance is realised when it is remembered that proceedings under Article 177 for questioning the validity or interpretation of Community acts have in substance become, obliquely, the means of ascertaining whether national rules, or even administrative behaviour, are consistent with Treaty obligations. Once the meaning of a Community rule, which is directly applicable and which has primacy, has been made clear, the denial of validity to a national rule which conflicts with it must follow. Thus the scope for the challenge of administrative or legislative acts is greatly increased, and there is an obligation upon member states to make effective challenge possible. These two propositions merge in a more general one. The Communities are peculiar, though not unique, in having an extremely limited administration. On the one hand the administration of justice is on a highly decentralised basis and national courts become the instruments of Community law. It is because they are such that all courts must take seriously their obligation under Article 177 (EEC) and their obligation to provide practical results to those rules which have direct effect. So equally the character of " national " administrations changes. In the fullness of time the Customs service will be performing exclusively Community functions collecting the " own resources " of the Communities. Such changes must be reflected in a reconsideration of rules. Indeed fresh thought will be required generally. What, for example, is the precise status of a Statutory Instrument which exists to complete a Community Regulation which has authorised its making only within the limits of that Regulation? The operation as well as the existence of the Communities is a challenge to thought.

The same act of entry raises more general constitutional points. It is convenient to start with the aspect of ministerial responsibility. Clearly that doctrine is affected. The not very informative Report from the Select Committee on Procedure remarked that " The rule as to Ministerial responsibility for answering Parliamentary questions may have to be reviewed in view of the role of United Kingdom ministers as members of the Council of Ministers." [73] The Second Report from the Select Committee on European Secondary Legislation [74] speaks of the difficulty of adapting existing parliamentary devices to the new needs, and continues:

73. Third Special Report (1971–1972), H.C. 448.
74. (1972–1973) H.C. 463, para. 45.

" There is however one notable exception—the doctrine of convention of Ministerial responsibility. The part played by the United Kingdom in this new form of law-making is played by Ministers in their capacity as Ministers of the Crown. . . . The doctrine may therefore be readily adopted and in so far as may be necessary adapted to the purpose in hand."

The Report continues to urge that the Government should accept, " as any Government must, that it will not cause or permit the law of the United Kingdom to be changed contrary to a resolution of the House." [75] These phrases show clearly that that doctrine is in question in its traditional meaning. They also show a failure to comprehend the working of the new system or its needs—dogma is once again dominating reality. For in the first it is clear that whatever the Select Committee may think, the Council of Ministers is, in law, a Community organ, not an intergovernmental body. It is of course true that there is negotiation there. No one can negotiate with their hands bound. The system could not work. The second proposition is also unworkable. If a Council Regulation is made it has effect under Article 189 of the Treaty of Rome, whatever the House has resolved, and no court could, as *Stockdale* v. *Hansard* shows, place that resolution above the law. It is unreasonable to look to a system of regular use of vetoes. Nor does the Committee appear to consider that there is not just one Parliament involved, there are nine. If an intergovernmental system (which the Communities are not) is one which is impossible to work satisfactorily in economic affairs, an inter-parliamentary one is even more unworkable. Yet one joins the Communities for results, those are the purpose of government. The terms of the Report are comprehensible if one reads the tenor of the questions asked in evidence. These extracts were worth quoting, even though they may have a short lived importance, because at least they demonstrate that doctrines are in question and should change. In themselves the extracts are in fact instances of politicians trying to make rules for their own convenience, without looking to the larger scene. The whole Report would in fact make matters worse for many members of the Committee. The attitude it discloses would reinforce the tendency in the Communities to resort to regulations rather than Directives,[76] though that tendency may be inevitable in any case.

THE CHANGES THAT CAN HELP

What is important is to avoid past errors and make the changes in order to help the new system of which we are now part, rather than to change by reinforcing rules which were invented in other circumstances.[77]

75. *Ibid.* para. 80.   76. See the very clear evidence of M. Noel, qq. 723 and 724.
77. Para. 36 of the Report is perhaps the key to the whole. It shows the Committee looking back to a past, which in part never was, and steadfastly refusing to look ahead. It demonstrates too the refusal of the Committee to conceive that some part of truth might have been found by others.

These are changes that should flow. A restructuring of the Committee system of the House is one. Within those Committees it might also be asked whether in fact they would not be better informed (as those of the European Parliament can be) if they abandoned verbatim reports of evidence. A Member of the Commission or of its staff can speak freely before a Committee of the European Parliament but could not under the present rules do so before one at Westminster. In this new situation the attitude of the Kilbrandon Report of rejecting out of hand ideas that are alien to a tradition is an inadequate response. Those ideas may have merit. The problems are not however purely technical, some of them are deep rooted. There is the problem of creating appropriate links between a multi-polar system, which is that of the Communities, with a bi-polar system, which is our own. Such problems cannot be overcome without thought. There are others which are less philosophic. Of course there is a real need to inform Parliament, but just as important is the creation of connecting links between parliaments. Solutions must be sought which are related to the whole system and which produce new connections. With the growth of economic and monetary union, forms of inter-parliamentary relationship will be of the utmost importance, far beyond anything now required by Directives, if there are not to be serious breaks in communication. Those breaks are not to be avoided by sulking in one's tent. There is a new situation and an emerging constitution of the Communities. The internal and Community sides must be related. Thus there is a problem of the democratic control over Community acts, but part of the solution must be found through the evolution of the Community constitution and in particular of the role of the European Parliament, which is not going to be one which will behave just like Westminster. (It may be noted that evidence was being taken until the end of July 1973, the deliberations of the Committee continued until October 22, 1973, but there is no hint of what the Commission had proposed [78] in May 1973 for strengthening the European Parliament and for links between that and national parliaments.) Even here the nine-teenth century experience is relevant. The two situations are so different that no longer, as then, can a constitution simply " grow like Topsy." A far greater element of design is needed, and thus the exclusive control of its development should no longer belong to politicians. That experience is also relevant to teach that, in a situation in which the Communities' constitution is nearly all for the making, we might avoid earlier mistakes and avoid random change which makes more difficult coherent change.

At the intermediate level there will also be changes. It is in the long run, assuming the existence of a regional policy, inconceivable that the relationships between the Commission and the areas concerned can

78. Cmnd. 1000 of June 6, 1973.

exist on a basis on which all is canalised through the central government. Direct links will become inevitable and should be acceptable. It is not unreasonable to think that the new authorities will be of adequate size and capacity to meet this demand, but this prospect reinforces the argument for limiting the number of levels of government. That debate is for the future. Yet the point is worth making for it is of the same kind as the points earlier made of the subtle change which comes over certain national institutions. This time it could be said the permeation is in the opposite direction, from the ground up. On the large scale, the change that has happened (in contrast to the changes which still have to come or are coming) is of course that one branch of the formulation of the Diceian doctrine of the Sovereignty of Parliament has gone. Its passing is marked by the combination of sections 2 (1), 2 (4) and 3 (1) of the European Communities Act 1972. It is that branch which asserts that " no person or body is recognised by the law of England as having a right to override or set aside the legislation of Parliament." Courts now have the obligation to set aside in the sense of declaring inapplicable, the legislation of Parliament where that legislation conflicts with a Community rule. The obligation exists under Community law,[79] it has been incorporated, for greater certainty, in section 2 (1) of the European Communities Act by the direction to give effect to Community law which has direct effect " as in accordance with the Treaties." In accordance with the Treaties the supremacy of Community law had already been declared. Thus courts are left no option.[80] In one sense the legislative competence of Parliament remains untouched, for it can still legislate on any subject it wishes to, and the legislation is valid, it is merely inapplicable in any set of circumstances in which it conflicts with a Community rule. Thus all the circularity of arguments about self-limitation are avoided. The matter can be dealt with this briefly, not because it is unimportant, but because it is obvious. The old rules, in so far as they were valid, related to another situation, one in which there were no superior norms, in which there were no overriding constitutional rules. The situation has changed. We have entered a Community and thus have entered into a situation in which there are constitutional rules, and one of them is the supremacy of law made for the whole. The logic expressed by Marshall C.J. but sufficiently obvious not to need authority, then carries the end result.

79. Case 6/64, *Costa* v. *ENEL*, X Rec. 1159 and Case 77/69, *Belgium*, XVI Rec. 233.
80. I state this bluntly having argued it at length elsewhere. It does not appear to me that other accounts take adequate note of the new situation. See Mitchell, Kuipers and Gall " Constitutional Aspects of British Membership of the EEC " (1972) 9 C.M.L.Rev. 134. I am unmoved by Wade " Sovereignty and the European Communities " (1972) 88 L.Q.R. 172, or by de Smith " The Constitution and the Common Market " (1971) 34 M.L.R. 597, or by his *Constitutional Law*, pp. 79-82.

CONCLUSIONS

This comes as a shock to some. It need not and it should not. Constitutions do not have an eternal virtue. They exist for a day and a generation. The day of the then Constitution was passing in 1798. Thereafter there have been shifts, more or less adequate, to adjust the Constitution to events. Now adjustment comes more sharply. On the one side it must come because finally the Constitution must relate to circumstances, and the adjustments which we have so far made to the demands posed by the welfare state and the economic state have been inadequate. On the other, the abruptness comes since finally we have accepted the changes in the world scene and have joined the European Communities to protect ourselves and to gain results. Over the years that step will have many constitutional consequences, but it is then important to remember that constitutions are after all functional things. No one ever earned a living out of constitutional dogma. Within this new system the European Court has itself said that it and its law will protect fundamental rights,[81] and thus at that level there is no cause for fear. Beyond that there must be room for a rational response to events. As was said above, State/Federal relationships changed in the United States of America as a response to the changing economic and social conditions. The direct effect and direct applicability of certain Community rules were principles which were not simply invented to tease constitutional lawyers. They were invented in order that the intended economic and social results should be realised by ordinary people. If constitutional rules do not have that contemporary quality they are of little value. Constitutional lawyers are not the masters of all human endeavour. Within the limits set by certain fundamental principles they are indeed the servants of others. Over the next few years, if only they will realise that, they will again have an interesting life.

---

81. Case 11/70, *Internationaleshandelsgesellschaft*, IX Rec. 1. In itself this is an advance for us, for the European Convention on Human Rights has no direct effect in our system. This problem will have to be faced in due course.

V

Criminal Law

Crime and the Criminal Law

BRIAN HOGAN

IT would be interesting to know what Mr. Sweet, who opened up shop in 1799, and Mr. Maxwell, who began business two years later, would make of English law and society today. What would first strike them, no doubt, would be the apparent dissimilarities, but once they had got over their wonder at the technical innovations of our times—the motor-car, television and after-shave lotion—it may be that what would strike them most tellingly are the similarities between their times and ours. 1799 was no more propitious a year for opening up new business than 1974, for then, as now, the country was deep in political, economic and social crisis. Since 1793 we had been at war with France and it was not going at all well. The Navy, it is true, had scotched all threats to our supremacy at sea but otherwise the French had the better of it and in the autumn of 1799 the Army, after a dismal campaign in the low countries, returned home with its tail firmly between its legs.

There was little enough to cheer them, or anyone else, on their return. Since 1790 there had been few good harvests and many poor ones, and the harvests for 1799 and 1800 were both disastrous. The effect of this, coupled with the war, was a dramatic rise in prices. Within the decade the price of bread, meat, butter, cheese, vegetables and ale doubled or more than doubled, and "fuel of every description had risen considerably from the same general causes."[1] But if the malady of rising prices was much the same then as now, the remedies applied were quite different. Pitt's Government followed, and here there is an obvious parallel, a policy of cautious inaction, but the employers firmly kept the lid on rising wages. Samuel Whitbread, to his eternal credit, intro-duced a Bill in December 1799 for fixing a minimum wage but this proved to be an embarrassment even to his own party and was easily defeated on second reading. In this period few employees managed to improve their earnings by better than 10 per cent. and those workers who combined to raise their wages could run into serious trouble. In February 1799, for example, two bootmakers were charged with conspiring to advance their wages in seeking an extra 6d. for boots and 3d. for shoes. Lord Kenyon C.J. said the prosecution was of infinite

1. Tooke, *History of Prices*, Vol. 1 at p. 190.

importance to the public; the prosecutor said the real question for the jury was whether the masters were to be under the control of the journeymen. Put that way there could be only one answer and the defendants were speedily convicted.[2]

This is not to say that those who had were entirely indifferent to those who had not. The rich were recommended to make no soups or gravies, to take only the prime cuts of meat and leave the others so that the poor might buy them.[3] In 1800 the Archbishop of Canterbury moved a resolution in the House of Lords calling on his fellows to curtail their consumption of bread and to use some convenient substitute. In England, it seemed, it was the noblemen who were enjoined to eat cake.

At the close of the eighteenth century the conditions existed for revolution. The Government knew this well enough and had passed a series of repressive measures and instituted a number of oppressive prosecutions in order to curb political opposition and the nascent trade unions. It is certain that these measures affected the situation very little, but there was no revolution. Although rioting was almost endemic, the nation survived. This may be attributed to the character of the British—and certainly the British themselves have a high vanity about that character—or it may be attributed to sheer good luck. Historians often say that it is our institutions, and not least the common law, which hold us together in times of stress. To do so they must of course command general, if not universal, respect. That respect, so far as the criminal law is concerned, if it existed in 1800 was not deserved; and if it is deserved today we cannot always be certain that it exists.

THE STATE OF CRIME

It is difficult to make any precise comparison between the state of crime in the community of 1800 and that of today. Nowadays we carefully collect and record statistics and, though statistics can never tell the whole story, the tale which they tell is not one in which we can take any great pride. In England and Wales, with a combined population of some fifty four millions, indictable offences known to the police now exceed one and a half million a year. Since the comparable figure for 1950 stood at under half a million anyone might be forgiven for thinking that we have at least begun the decline if we are not already into the fall.

There are no official statistics for 1800 but a private estimate of the state of crime at the close of the eighteenth century has been provided by Patrick Colquhoun in his *Police of the Metropolis*.[4] Quite where Colquhoun got his figures from does not appear and modern statisticians

---

2. *Leeds Intelligencer*, Feb. 25, 1799.
3. Traill and Mann, *Social England*, Vol. V at p. 672.
4. First published 1795.

might well question his estimates. But there can be no denying his style and our own *Criminal Statistics* would surely be enlivened by adopting Colquhoun's graphic classifications. In his survey of crime in London, the population of which was then about 800,000, Colquhoun estimated that there were some 115,000 who lived by crime. These included:

> " Spendthrifts—Rakes—Giddy Young Men inexperienced and in the pursuit of criminal pleasures—Profligate, loose and dissolute Characters, vitiated themselves and in the daily practice of seducing others to intemperence, lewdness, debauchery, gambling and excess; estimated at..............................3,000.
> Grubbers, Gin drinking dissolute Women and destitute Boys and Girls, wandering and prowling about in the streets and by-places after Chips, Nails, Old Metals, broken Glass, Paper, Twine, etc. who are constantly on the watch to pilfer when an opportunity offers.......................................2,000."[5]

In fact Colquhoun appeared to regard as criminal anyone who was not gainfully and honourably employed so that we need not conclude that one in eight of London's population at the close of the eighteenth century lived exclusively by crime.

In any case statistics, precise or estimated, do not tell us very much on their own. What they do not, and cannot, tell us is of the very considerable difference between the England of then and now, a difference probably most marked in London. In 1800 there was no efficient, disciplined and well organised police force and this single factor makes for the most signicant difference between their social order and ours. It was just not safe to be abroad in urban areas after dark except in bands organised for defence; whatever the hazards of our own times we do not have to consider as a daily risk the activities of highwaymen and footpads. On the other hand it may be that their highwayman was a cut or two above our contemporary mugger—

> " The English highwaymen were an altogether different class from the savage and half-famished brigands who found a refuge in the forests of Germany and among the mountains of Italy and Spain. They were in general singularly free from ferocity, and a considerable proportion were not habitual criminals. . . . Favourite actors and other popular heroes, when stopped by highwaymen, sometimes allowed to pass unmolested as soon as they were recognised; and if the robbed person asked for sufficient money to continue his journey, the request was generally granted."[6]

Be that as it may, it is preferable to be free of highwaymen, however courteous they may be. Our cities are safer places to live in and we must be grateful for that.

THE CRIMINAL LAW

In his *Pleas of the Crown* Edward Hyde East provides us with a state-

---

5. *Police of the Metropolis*, x, xi.
6. Lecky, *History of England in the Eighteenth Century*, Vol. VII at p. 340.

ment of the criminal law as it stood close to the time when Sweet and Maxwell first went into business. Both presumably sold the book but neither had a hand in its publication in 1803. East's work, Peter Glazebrook tells us,[7] acquired immediate authority and had no rival until the appearance of Russell's *Treatise* in 1819.

There is still a lot to be found in East's *Pleas of the Crown* with which the lawyer of today is perfectly familiar. And yet what is most striking on looking through East again is how the last twenty years have put more distance between the criminal law of today and that of East's time than the previous one hundred and fifty. East never did produce a second edition of his work but he might fairly have claimed that much of what he said about homicide, stealing or damage to property remained tolerably good law down to the mid-1950s. But, and all of a rush, the reforms introduced by the Homicide, Theft and Criminal Damage Acts have left East describing a markedly different law. Before the Theft Act 1968, for example, and notwithstanding the Larceny Acts of 1861 and 1916, East was still a perfectly respectable authority on taking and carrying away, the distinction between larceny and embezzlement, breaking and entering, the element of force in robbery and so on. Before the Homicide Act 1957 and the Criminal Law Act 1967 East could still have been cited on constructive malice and on the use of force in support of law and defence of property.

The break with the past brought about by the legislation of the last twenty years has been considerable but not total. Even on homicide East still has something to say. He had no doubt, though on this he seems to have been doing little more than echo the opinions of earlier writers, that the malice aforethought of murder included recklessness as to the taking of human life:

" Thus, if a person, breaking an unruly horse, wilfully ride him among a crowd of persons, the probable danger being great and apparent, and death ensue from the viciousness of the animal, it is murder. For how can it be supposed that a person wilfully doing an act, so manifestly attended with danger, especially if he showed any consciousness of danger himself, should intend any other than the probable consequence of such an act. But yet if it appear clearly to have been done heedlessly and incautiously only, and not with intent to do mischief, it is only manslaughter." [8]

No doubt East would have agreed with the Court of Appeal's recent decision in *Hyam*[9] and the only thing that might have surprised him was that the problem of recklessness in murder should go so long without an authoritative ruling.

But if East would have approved *Hyam* it is doubtful whether he

7. Introduction to East P.C., *Classical English Law Texts*, 1972.
8. 1 P.C. 231.
9. [1973] 3 All E.R. 842.

would have had a good word to say for that variant of malice afore-thought which found favour with the House of Lords in *D.P.P.* v. *Smith*.[10] While in the passage cited East shows some uncertainty about proof of intent and inference of intent, the last sentence shows that he was well aware of the important distinction between negligent and reckless action: between what was foreseen and what was not. Although East held to the view, finally dispelled by *Woolmington*,[11] that on proof of the fact of a killing by the defendant the onus was on the defendant to prove justification or excuse,[12] he never made the mistake of elevating the so-called presumption of intention into an irrebuttable presumption of law.

East's treatment of provocation is in some respects still extraordinarily fresh. The reasonable man—that uncompromising phantom who has done so little to grace our criminal law—had not yet made his appearance in this branch of the law, and the cases cited by East show a common sense and humanity that have only recently been restored to our law. Of course we might see it as less than humane that in *Manning's Case*,[13] where the defendant had killed a man he found in the act of adultery with his wife, the court ordered that he should be burned in the hand. But the court did direct that the burning should be " gently inflicted " and in those days you could not ask for fairer than that.

A notable change in emphasis which has taken place in the last two hundred years is that offences against religion and morality were ostentatiously given pride of place then. East begins his treatise with these offences and the very first case to be discussed is that of Sir Charles Sedley, who, it will be recalled, behaved so disgracefully at Covent Garden. On this case East observes:

" Offences of this kind sap public morals, the necessary foundation of good government; and are therefore properly cognizable by the temporal magistrates, who may punish the offenders by fine, imprisonment, and such other corporal punishment as the circumstances may require." [14]

The decision of the House of Lords in *Shaw* v. *D.P.P.*,[15] holding that a conspiracy to currupt public morals is an offence at common law, would have caused no dismay to East and his contemporaries: it upholds values which it would never have occurred to them to question.

Overall the changes which have taken place in the substantive criminal law since the end of the eighteenth century have, until the last few years, been evolutionary rather than revolutionary. The law as

10. [1960] A.C. 290.
11. [1935] A.C. 462.
12. 1 P.C. 224.
13. 1 East P.C. 234.
14. 1 P.C. 3.
15. [1962] A.C. 220.

stated by East was tidied up over the next one hundred and fifty years but never altered in any fundamental respect. Even the great consolidation of 1861 changed little of substance and was, of course, not intended to do so. Only in the last quarter of a century have reformers really been given their head, and now the pace of change has suddenly quickened and a gap is opening up.

One other marked difference between the criminal law of East's time and our own lies in the use which we make of it. In the last hundred years the criminal law has been employed to regulate conduct in almost every sphere of social activity. It would surely astonish East to learn that what is said about an hotel in Paris might result in a prosecution in London. The criminal law is much more all-pervasive than it was.

TRIAL AND SENTENCE

" If a lawyer of today could be transported back to the English Courts of the eighteenth century," wrote Sir F. D. MacKinnon in 1933,[16] " he would be best able to understand what was going on at a criminal trial at Assizes or at the Old Bailey. There, although he would be indignant at the unfair treatment of the accused, shocked by the indecent haste of the proceedings, and horrified by the sentence, the substance of the procedure would be that of today."

The unfair treatment of a person charged with felony in the eighteenth century, and for some years into the nineteenth, began with arrest and continued throughout the whole of the trial process. He was likely to be incarcerated in a prison where living conditions posed a threat to his health, where he might be terrorised by fellow prisoners, and where gaolers had it in their power to deny him the necessaries of life unless he had the wherewithal to pay his way. If he was to be interrogated this would be done by a magistrate and without the benefit of the formal safeguards now provided by the Judges' Rules. It is unlikely that anyone would have troubled to remind him that he was under no obligation to say anything. If his case caught the public imagination he ran the risk of highly prejudicial press comment for it was to be some years into the nineteenth century before the law of contempt was used to restrain the press.[17]

The trial itself was hardly calculated to restore his confidence in the certainty of justice. If charged with felony he had no right to be represented by counsel except to argue a point of law. By the beginning of the nineteenth century this rule, which had few defenders, appears to have been generally relaxed to the extent of allowing counsel to stand by to examine and cross-examine witnesses on behalf of the defendant, but counsel was not allowed to make a closing speech, or otherwise comment

16. *Johnson's England*, ed. by A. S. Turberville, Vol. 3, p. 301.
17. See, *e.g.* the *Trial of Henry Fauntleroy* (1824), Notable British Trials Series; *Trial of Thurtell and Hunt* (1824), Notable British Trials Series.

in a general way on the evidence, until the law was changed in 1836. For many, if not most, defendants the matter must have been academic since few of them were in a position to afford the services of counsel. Perhaps it was this factor as much as anything else which contributed to the expedition of criminal trials at this time. On the civil side a trial could be prolonged over the years; the will was always there if the money could be found, but there were no rich pickings to be taken from criminal cases. Indeed, the defendant on a criminal charge has been the Cinderella of the legal system until the fairy godmother of legal aid came to his rescue in our own times.

Sir Henry Hawkins has left us a well known account of an early nineteenth century trial for theft of a handkerchief which he timed at two minutes, fifty-three seconds and which resulted in the defendant being transported for seven years.[18] It was not at all untypical either for its brevity or in the trial judge's confident expectation of a verdict of guilty. And this was not necessarily all:

" A cause of much evil is the trying of prisoners after dinner, when from the morning's adjournment all parties have retired to a hearty meal, which at assize time is commonly attended . . . with a good deal of drink. . . . Drunkenness is too frequently apparent where it ought of all things to be avoided. I mean in jurymen and witnesses. The heat of the court, joined to the fumes of the liquor, has laid many an honest juryman into a calm and profound sleep, and sometimes it has been no small trouble for his fellows to jog him into the verdict, even where a wretch's life has depended on the event. This I myself have seen."[19]

It is only necessary to add for the sake of completeness that a convicted defendant had no right of appeal though, on rare occasions, a point of law might be reserved by the judge for the Court for Crown Cases Reserved. One of the least creditable actions in the history of the judiciary was their opposition to a properly constituted system of appeals in criminal cases which they successfully resisted into the twentieth century.

At the beginning of the nineteenth century more than 150 offences carried the death penalty. A man might be hanged for picking pockets, for cutting hop binds, for concealing the death of a bastard child, for sending threatening letters, for forgery, for sheep stealing, for cutting down trees and for much else besides. It could be said, even then, that things were not as bad as they used to be. The burning of women was abolished in 1790, the procession to Tyburn was ended in 1783 and thereafter executions took place immediately outside prisons. Also in 1783 the drop was made general which was something humanitarian in a barbarous business. More important, and more hopeful, there was by 1800 a noticeable decline in the number of capital executions.[20] Less

18. *Reminiscences*, Vol. 1, p. 33.   19. Madan, *Thoughts on Executive Justice*, 1785.
20. See generally, Radzinowicz, 1 H.C.L., Chap. 5.

than half those capitally convicted were actually executed and in the early years of the nineteenth century the proportion executed to those convicted had fallen to about one sixth.

But whatever the improvements the reality was still awful. No doubt contemporary attitudes were different but it is difficult to believe that a reader of *The Times* on July 31, 1799, could have been any less horrified than we are by the following item:

" The execution of Mary Nicholson, for poisoning Elizabeth Atkinson, took place on Monday last, pursuant to her sentence, at the usual place near Durham; and we are sorry to say, that in this discharge of the fiat of justice, the poor creature suffered much torment, for very soon after her suspension, the rope broke, and upwards of an hour elapsed before another was procured to put an end to her misery. In the interim she recovered her faculties and conversed with her unhappy relatives till a rope was brought, when she was launched into eternity amidst the shrieks and cries of the surrounding spectators."

There is nothing we can learn from the penal code of this time except that we are well rid of it.

But in a curious way the scales which were so heavily weighted against the defendant were in other respects weighted in his favour. In the eighteenth and early nineteenth centuries the criminal process was something of a national game of chance for those with the stomach for it. It resembled nothing so much as Russian roulette where the chances of getting away with it are always better than fifty-fifty while the consequences of failure are irreversible.

The lack of an efficient police force meant, it may be fairly supposed, that the risk of detention and capture was much smaller than it is today. But assuming that the defendant was unfortunate enough to be apprehended and charged, all was far from lost. Patrick Colquhoun, anticipating the Criminal Law Revision Committee and Sir Robert Mark by nearly two hundred years, complained of " disreputable practitioners of the Law "[21] and saw how the professional criminal sought to avoid justice:

" If bribes and persuasions will not do, the prosecutors are either intimidated by the expence, or softened down by appeals to their humanity; and under such circumstances, they neither employ counsel nor take the necessary steps to bring forward evidence: the result is, that the Bill is either returned *ignoramus* by the Grand Jury; or, if a trial takes place ... an advocate is heard for the prisoner, availing himself of every trifling inaccuracy which may screen his client from the punishment of the law, the hardened villiain is acquitted and escapes justice; while ... the novice in crimes, unskilled in the deficiences of the law, and unable, from the want of criminal connections, or that support which the professed thief receives from the Buyers of stolen Goods, to procure the aid of counsel to defend him, is often convicted! "[22]

21. *Police of the Metropolis* 1795, at p. 4.
22. *Op. cit.* at p. 23.

Just how a trifling inaccuracy might screen the defendant from the punishment of the law is shown in the following trial in 1799:

" James Austin, Richard Raymert and John Keefe were tried for stealing a ham . . . but it appeared that a considerable part of the ham had been cut off, which made the thing stolen only part of a ham; and as it was charged in the indictment as a ham, the Recorder directed the jury to acquit the prisoners." [23]

Then, as Colquhoun, Romilly and others saw clearly enough, the very severity of the law often led to the defeat of justice. The victims of crime were fearful of instituting prosecutions for minor offences lest the defendant should be hanged for it. Juries would acquit, or reduce the charge to misdemeanour, in the teeth of the evidence. Witnesses would fail to turn up. The result of all this, on Colquhoun's figures,[24] was an acquittal rate in trials at the Old Bailey of over 50 per cent. In this odd way the inequalities of the trial system and the ferocity of the penal laws were to some degree counterbalanced.

CONCLUSION

What any comparison of crime and the criminal law then and now serves to show is that things have very much taken a turn for the better. While it would be arrogant for us to assert that we are better or more law abiding than our forebears, it is clear that in our public conduct we are more tolerant. Our own procedures may not be beyond the reach of criticism but they ensure an incomparably fairer trial to a man accused of crime than was the case in 1800. While punishment can still be severe the response of the courts is neither unthinking nor unfeeling. If the answers to crime are still unknown, we at least ask ourselves the questions. There is, however, no cause for complacency. If Sweet & Maxwell produce another collection of commemorative essays one hundred and seventy-five years from now it may be guessed that the contributors will find much in us that is wanting.

23. *The Times*, Nov. 5, 1799. " It is scarcely a parody to say," said Stephen (1 H.C.L., 284) " that from the earliest times to our own days, the law relating to indictments was much as if some small proportion of the prisoners convicted had been allowed to toss up for their liberty."
24. *Op. cit.* at pp. 90, 91.

VI

Law Publishing

The Development of Law Publishing 1799-1974

M. W. MAXWELL

THE FOUNDERS

When Stephen Sweet started his business at the end of the eighteenth century there was no such thing as a Law Publisher. There were only law booksellers. The title page of Sweet's first published work, Parker's *Reports of Cases in the Court of Exchequer*, published in 1800, bears at the foot the words " Sold by S. Sweet, Law Book Seller, 3 Chancery Lane, Fleet Street." Joseph Butterworth on the title page of *Woodfall on Landlord and Tenant*, published in 1802, also describes himself as a Law Bookseller. The use of the term " publisher " does not seem to have evolved until somewhere around 1820, and even then it was not used except in conjunction with the words " Law Bookseller." In those days it was common for copyrights to be held in varying shares by a number of booksellers and shares in copyrights were freely bought and sold. The title pages of books often bore the imprint of several booksellers. As we shall see, booksellers in those days were accustomed to financing their publications by long credit from the printers and the splitting of copyright was a means of sharing the risks involved.

Alexander Maxwell, who was born in 1776, was not at first a law bookseller. He started around 1800 at the corner of Fetter Lane, and moved first to Charing Cross and then to Snow Hill where he was in partnership with Walter Wilson as book auctioneers and booksellers. It was not until 1811 that he moved to 21 Bell Yard, and it was probably the proximity to the Inns of Court that led him into the publishing of law books. He had been particularly interested in religious matters and both wrote and published books on religion. Among the books in which he had an interest was *Sarratt on Chess* of which he purchased a one-eighteenth share from John Murray for £3 6s. 8d. in 1821. It is not known when he first published a law book, but by 1820 or so he must have been predominantly interested in law books because he was one of the founders of the Associated Law Booksellers, about which more will appear later. He issued with other law booksellers what is described as a " Catalogue of Law Books Ancient and Modern " in 1825 and on the title page this is described as " Printed for A. Maxwell, Law Bookseller and Publisher, 21 Bell Yard."

In fact this was clearly a co-operative effort because other copies of the same catalogue bear the names of Sweet and of Stevens & Sons on the title page.

Alexander Maxwell moved to number 32 Bell Yard around 1830 and in 1831 was granted a Royal Warrant as law bookseller to His Majesty. His son William joined him about this time.

THE ASSOCIATED LAW BOOKSELLERS

In 1822 there were at least eight law booksellers in business and six of them formed themselves into an association denominated " The Associated Law Booksellers." [1] The Minute Book of this body starts with the Rules and Regulations and the object is stated to be as follows:

" That the object of this Association at present is to print and publish New Term and Nisi Prius Reports and such other works in the different branches of the law, as may from time to time be considered by them prudent and necessary and promote each other's success in trade by mutual advice and friendly co-operation." [2]

The Rules then go on to set out the conditions on which publications were to be financed and to be accepted for printing by the Association. No member was to be permitted to have a preponderating share and every work was to be regularly and equally divided. Copyrights were not to be sold except by unanimous consent. No additional member was to be admitted without the approbation of every individual member. The name of the Projector or Manager of a work was to stand first in the imprint and the names of the other members according to seniority.

The Minute Book shows that the first meeting was held on February 6, 1822, but it does not state who were the members nor are the minutes signed. The sole business recorded was the appointment of Mr. Brooke to be the printer. This was presumably Samuel Brooke who subsequently became a publisher and whose business was eventually acquired by either Sweet or Maxwell.

That the number of members was six is evident from the minutes of the second meeting which record that " Mr. G. Wilson proposed Messrs. Whittaker's being admitted as members which was put to the vote and negatived by 5–1." It seems probable that the members were Sweet, Maxwell, Stevens & Sons (who had started in business in 1810), Robert Pheney, Brooke and Wilson, but from the title-page of a catalogue issued in 1823 (the forerunner of the 1825 catalogue mentioned above) printed " for " Sweet, Stevens, Pheney, and Maxwell, it is evident that

1. The odd men out were the Butterworths: see below p. 126.
2. The reference in the objects to the *New Term Reports* is curious. From internal evidence the association was formed in 1822 yet the *New Term Reports* did not start publication until 1835. It may be that the Association did intend to start publication on its formation but that it was unable to obtain the agreement of the reporters.

Brooke and Wilson were, by that time, not active. One further meeting is recorded in March 1822 and there were no minutes after that until a meeting on January 15, 1829, at which were present Sweet, Maxwell, Pheney and Stevens. At that time it is evident that William Benning was a member, as it is recorded that at a meeting of January 24, 1829, Mr. Benning was not present.[3]

Mr. Benning's name does not subsequently appear in the minutes as having attended any meetings and he gave the members of the Association a great deal of trouble in subsequent years.[4]

What caused the Association to be reactivated in 1829 is not recorded. The first meeting in that year records only an agreement that " in future the settlement of half-yearly accounts should be by acceptance or promissory note at a period not exceeding ten weeks from the beginning of the following six month period." In all nine meetings are recorded during 1829 all of them except one being concerned with the publication of a new edition of Blackstone's *Commentaries*. It appears that a Mr. Davies had undertaken to edit this work and was delinquent in delivering his copy. A memorandum by Mr. Stevens dated February 7, 1829, records that

" a person waited upon Mr. Sweet and stated that he came from Mr. Davies with some copy for Blackstone's Commentaries and that Mr. Davies will prepare some more which Mr. Sweet should have sent him from time to time as it was ready. Mr. Sweet stated that he should take no more copy from Mr. Davies having entered into an engagement with another gentleman whose name was not advertised and that Mr. Davies need not trouble himself to get any more copy ready as four years was a long period which time Mr. Davies had had to get the work done and the loss which would now be sustained in cancelling what was printed would be great enough without waiting any further length of time for Mr. Davies in whom no dependence could be placed Mr. Davies having received notice several times that if he did not proceed much faster that the work would be taken out of his hands and given to some other gentleman." [5]

It is also recorded that Mr. Sweet's eldest son was present. This was Henry Sweet who succeeded to the business on the death of Stephen in 1841.

---

3. In that year he had published the first edition of Chitty's *Statutes*.

4. See *e.g. Sweet* v. *Benning* (1855) 16 C.B. 459, 139 E.R. 838. In 1838 Benning attempted to obtain an order against John William Smith and Alexander Maxwell restraining further publication of Smith's *Leading Cases in the Common Law*. He failed in the Chancery Court and on appeal to the Lord Chancellor. The solicitor's bill of costs, amounting to £111 16s. 8d., records that Benning was ordered to pay in costs £58 3s. 10d. The suit is recorded by Samuel Warren in his *Miscellanies*, he having been one of counsel engaged by Maxwell.

5. This sort of difficulty is not unknown to modern publishers, but it is seldom recorded in such eloquent language. The person referred to by Mr. Sweet as having been entrusted with the work was a Mr. Hovenden and it appears that this must have been the nineteenth edition of Blackstone's *Commentaries*, which completed publication in 1836. The editor was paid £150.

On January 1, 1845, Alexander Maxwell took into partnership his son William. The indenture conveys one-half share of the partnership in consideration of " natural love and affection." The value of the partnership assets is stated as £16,000, and the partnership accounts at December 31, 1845, show the value of a half-share as £8,362. The profit and loss account shows a surplus for the year of £1,716. In 1848 Alexander retired and sold his share to William for £7,000, payable by instalments of £500 a year. He died in 1849.

Stephen Sweet had died in 1841. He is buried in Highgate Cemetery, and in Dobby's *Memorials* of that cemetery, published in 1845, it is said of him: " The law bookseller of Chancery Lane, whose death was awfully sudden. Being awoke in the night by an ordinary street riot, which he mistook for an alarm of fire, on running out of the room to arouse his family, he fell and almost instantly expired." He was succeeded by his eldest son, Henry, who at the time of his father's death was travelling in America, laying the foundations of the cordial relations which happily exist today between his successors and the American Bar and Law Schools.[6]

Only one meeting of the Association was recorded in 1830 and one in 1832 at which it was noted that Mr. Sweet and Mr. Maxwell and Mr. Stevens gave Mr. John Richards four bills of £116 13s. 4d. each at six, twelve, eighteen and twenty-four months for the purchase of Mr. Richards' entire right in the stock and copyrights of his business. Mr. Sweet and Mr. Stevens at the same time purchased Mr. Richards' one-eighth share of the copyright of Archbold's *Criminal Pleadings*. After this the Association fell into abeyance until November 1851.

At the first meeting of the re-activated Association in 1851 there were present, in addition to Sweet and Maxwell, Vivian and Robert Stevens and G. S. Norton. Norton remained a member of the Association in his own right for some years and subsequently joined Stevens & Sons, having married into the Stevens family.

Meetings of the Association are recorded thereafter continually until the end of 1856 and from that date the Minute Book records only estimates, prices, decisions as to the number of copies to be printed of various publications and decisions to waste stock. The Minute Book ceases to record in January 1868.

Various topics recur in the minutes throughout this period. At the first meeting in 1851 it is recorded that " a discussion ensued in respect of under selling and the importance of either endeavouring to put an entire stop to it or of opening the trade." At a subsequent meeting Mr. Sweet

6. His brother George Sweet, Q.C., became a well known conveyancer. Between 1836 and 1850 he wrote altogether seven books which were published, as well as editing the third edition of Bythewood and Jarman's *Conveyancing Precedents*. His son Charles in 1882 published a *Dictionary of English Law* which was the forerunner of Jowitt's *Dictionary*.

Stephen Sweet's original premises. (From a contemporary print.)

These are to Certify to whom it may Concern that by Virtue of a Warrant to me directed from The Duke of Devonshire Lord Chamberlain of His Majesty's Household I have Sworn and Admitted Mr Alexander Maxwell into the Place and Quality of Law Bookseller in Ordinary to His Majesty To have hold exercise and enjoy the said Place together with all Rights Profits Privileges and Advantages thereunto belonging

Given under my Hand and Seal this 5th day of July 1831 In the First Year of His Majesty's Reign.

Gent: Usher to His Majesty

Royal Warrant appointing Alexander Maxwell as Law Bookseller to King William IV.

First and current editions of Archbold's *Criminal Pleadings* (1822), Woodfall's *Landlord and Tenant* (1802) and Chitty's *Contracts* (1826).

Directors and editors, with executives representing production, marketing and finance, meet monthly to decide the future publishing programme.

promised to call a meeting of the Law Publishing Trades respecting under selling. It is not recorded who the offending booksellers were and the topic does not recur until February 1853 when it is recorded that it was agreed that the reduced stock (*i.e.* stock which was being sold at a reduced price) should " only be sold to Messrs. Wildy, Davis & Amer, Robertson and Bond at the prices sold to gentlemen." The name of Bond [7] turns up about one year later when it appears that he had somehow acquired some copies of Chitty's *Equity Index* from an overseas bookseller and was selling them at a price lower than the members of the Association. That this sort of thing was not confined to this country is evident from an entry in March 1855 where it is recorded that " the sum of £5 should be allowed to a correspondent of Messrs. Stevens & Norton in Canada, he having taken six copies of Chitty's *Index* and was undersold by Messrs. L. & B. of Boston." [8]

The chaotic condition of law reporting in the 1850s, and the discontent of the profession with the reports, are well known. The discontent of the publishers is reflected in these minutes. In December 1851 Mr. Maxwell reported that the publication of Volume 1, Part 5 and Volume 2, Part 1, of Lowndes, Maxwell and Pollock's *Bail Court Reports* had showed in the half year a loss of £77 4s. 5d. and the *Exchequer Reports* Volume 4, Part 5, and Volume 5, Parts 1 and 2, showed a profit of £22 17s. 10d. only. The meeting resolved that the reporters should be informed that " unless they would continue them at a price that would prevent a loss they should be discontinued." The *Bail Court Reports* were in fact discontinued in 1851 and the *Exchequer Reports* continued only until 1855.

In January 1851, Mr. Sweet brought forward

" a plan for publishing the reports at a cheaper rate by issuing a sheet or half a sheet of cases decided in each court at the commencement of every month and to sell them separately—the idea was warmly received by Messrs. Stevens and Norton who thought the reports would come to that at last."

It appears that this plan came to nothing, for in February 1853 the Minute Book records that it was unanimously agreed that " unless some radical change takes place with regard to publishing the Reports, they will all be annihilated " and it was proposed that there should be a meeting of all the reporters in an endeavour to bring about a new system. This produced a proposal first mentioned in March 1853 to publish what are called *Coalition Reports*. In May Mr. Hare (Editor of the *Chancery Reports*) sent a circular to about fifty barristers proposing a new plan of publishing the reports entirely independently of the booksellers. Mr. Maxwell was deputed to see Mr. Hare who gave him a copy of the prospectus of his

---

7. This was Charles Bond, who had married a Miss Shaw, of the family which owned Shaw & Sons, who had been law stationers since 1750. He entered that business in 1852.

8. Messrs. L. & B. were probably the predecessors of Little, Brown & Company (founded 1837) with whom considerable trade was undertaken at a later date.

scheme. Mr. Maxwell also saw Mr. Scott [9] who said that none of the other reporters fell in with Mr. Hare's views. It was then agreed that each of the publishers see their respective reporters and " show them the accounts of Sales and Expenses of their different reports for the last three years together with their plan for the future publishing of the reports." A meeting of the publishers and reporters was subsequently held at the Chambers of Mr. DeGex at which a new scheme was proposed and the principal feature of which was that " the reports should be published in their present style at the risk and cost of the publishers, the reporters to receive their present amount of remuneration." This decision may have satisfied the publishers and the reporters but it clearly did not satisfy the profession and it is recorded in March 1855 that a Mr. Ewart had given notice in the House of Commons that he intended making a motion respecting an established series of the authorised reports and an article on the subject was mentioned as having been written in the *Standard* and *Post*. At a meeting in May it is recorded that there was a short discussion respecting a memorial to the Lord Chancellor with regard to the state of the reports. Tantalisingly no further reference is made to this subject but the eventual outcome is well known.[10]

The troubles of Mr. William Benning form another recurring theme during this period. He had gone into partnership with a man named Saunders and acquired the business of J. Butterworth and Son,[11] and at sometime early in 1852 he must have got into financial difficulties. This led to the assignment of the assets of the business to a new firm called Benning and Co. which in turn itself eventually foundered.

In October 1852 it was agreed that

" all proposals for new editions of any works published by the house of Benning & Co., Saunders & Benning and Joseph Butterworth and all proposals for any new works by authors, who had been at any previous time connected with the said house, shall be deemed to be matters in which the said R. Stevens, G. S. Norton, H. Sweet and W. Maxwell shall have a joint interest and neither of the said parties shall be at liberty to enter into any such engagements without having previously notified such new edition, new work or reports to the consideration of the said parties."

The problems that arose for the Association were largely due to the fact that the firm of Saunders and Benning had had some shares in the copyrights of some of the books published by the Associated Law Booksellers and when the assets of the partnership were finally offered for sale they included considerable stocks of books published by the members of

9. Editor of the *New Reports, Common Pleas* 1842–1845.
10. See Holdsworth, H.E.L., XIII, pp. 426–428, XV, pp. 248–254, and Lord Lindley in 1 L.Q.R. 137.
11. This was Joseph Butterworth whose nephew Henry, after being apprenticed to his uncle, set himself up in business in 1818. He was succeeded by his son Joshua, on whose death the business was bought by Charles Bond. See *post*, p. 133.

the Association. In order to protect themselves against these being sold off cheaply the members of the Association jointly decided to make an offer for the assets and they eventually acquired them for a sum which appears to have been around £6,700. By so doing they acquired some useful copyrights such as *Coote on Mortgages, Russell on Crime, Arnould on Marine Insurance* as well as the copyrights in a number of reports published by Benning and Saunders. They also bought themselves a lot of trouble with authors. A number of entries refer to difficulties with Mr. Sergeant Stephen who was satisfied neither with the validity of the assignment of the copyright of his two-volume work on *Clergy Laws* nor with the amount which he had received as his share of the proceeds of sale. Mr. Benning himself managed to get back into business as a publisher and some of his former authors remained loyal to him and refused to produce new editions of their works unless they were removed from the Association back to Mr. Benning. Mr. W. T. Pritchard, author of a *Digest of Law and Practice of the Court of Admiralty*, first published in 1847, was particularly incensed and threatened legal action. Mr. Justice Williams, author of the *Law of Executors and Administrators*, also was concerned in some way although he did not appear in any way antagonistic to the members of the Association. Eventually all matters were settled by a final assignment of all the remaining shares of copyright which had been personally held by Mr. Benning, or by paying to the authors the full half-share of the profit on the remaining copies sold by the Association of existing works, on which they had received nothing from the assignee.

THE MERGING SWEETS AND MAXWELLS

William Maxwell was joined in business by his son William Alexander around 1865, and they continued the business at No. 32 Bell Yard until the house was pulled down for the Law Courts when they removed to 29 Fleet Street. At that time they were trading under the name of W. Maxwell & Son and they commenced rebuilding of 8 Bell Yard in 1882 when William Maxwell died. It was completed in 1883 and the business was carried on there until the amalgamation with Sweet in 1889.

Henry Sweet had meanwhile carried on at No. 3 Chancery Lane and had been joined by his sons Herbert George Sweet and Edward William Sweet. When Henry died in 1885 his son Herbert carried on the business under the title Henry Sweet & Sons until 1889.

William Maxwell admitted his son to partnership in 1877. The partnership deed records the value of the business as £21,600. William Alexander was to pay his father interest of 5 per cent. per annum on the value of his half-share, and each party was to draw £600 a year. William died in 1882 and the Revenue Affidavit shows the value of the business as £28,087. William left his half-share of the partnership to be divided between his children, of whom there were ten. By 1887 William Alexander had eight children of his own, and having to share the profits with his brothers and sisters put him in great difficulty, particularly as only one of his brothers was helping in the business. This led him to approach Sweet and to the merger of the businesses and the foundation of Sweet & Maxwell Ltd. on April 1, 1889. Discussions took place at this time with a view to bringing Stevens & Sons into the new company, but these failed to get agreed terms. Valuations were made of the three businesses and produced the following figures:

Sweet & Sons	£30,000
Maxwell & Son	£28,352
Stevens & Sons	£81,595

Sweet and Maxwell each included a figure of £6,000 for goodwill, Stevens £15,000. The Stevens valuations of other items were thought by the others to be excessive, and this, combined with Stevens' insistence that the business be carried on at 119–120 Chancery Lane instead of at Sweet's more commodious premises at 3 Chancery Lane, led to the breakdown of the negotiations.[12]

PRODUCTION, ROYALTIES AND SALES

Much of the minutes is taken up with production matters. It is evident that the publishers were heavily dependent on long credit from the printers. In 1852 it is recorded that Sweet had settled an account for £282 10s. for printing the reports by a bill at fifteen months. In the same year a quotation by Spottiswoode is recorded as " 3 months account and a bill at 12 months or 5 per cent. discount for cash."

Spottiswoode's name recurs right through to 1913.[13] Other printers who regularly did work for the publishers are Roworth (who went out of business in 1952) and Bradbury & Evans, who subsequently became Bradbury, Agnew & Co. William Bradbury was a friend of William Alexander Maxwell, and when Sweet & Maxwell was formed he took up shares in the company and became one of its first directors. When he died his shares were acquired by Bradbury, Agnew & Co., who remained shareholders until quite recently.

A striking aspect which emerges from these records is the astonishing stability of manufacturing costs. This applies to both printing and paper charges, and is best shown in tabular form.

12. When Stevens & Sons was incorporated as a limited company at the same time the figure for goodwill had swollen to £30,000, and it was neatly balanced on the other side of the balance sheet by a 5 per cent. Perpetual Income Debenture, of the same amount, some of which is outstanding to this day.

13. In that year they lost the contract to print the *Law Journal Reports* to The Eastern Press, which has ever since specialised in law book and journal printing.

Year	Work	Printer	Qty.	Price per sheet	Paper
1822	Law Reports	Brooke	N/A	£2 16s.	N/A
1852	Law Reports	Spottiswoode	1,250	£2 15s.	N/A
1853	Law Reports	Spottiswoode	1,500	£3 3s.	N/A
	Smith's *Mercantile Law*	Cox	1,500	£3 3s.	23s. 6d. the ream
1855	Williams' *Executors*	Bradbury	1,500	£3 12s.	24s. 6d.
1868	Burne's *Justices* (5 vols.)	Bradbury	2,500	£5 15s.	16s. 0d.
1889	Mews' *Annual Digest*	Roworth	2,500	£7 0s.	16s. 9d.

Paper is of course sold by weight and the earlier entries do not record this. In 1893 the paper for the *Annual Practice* cost 3⅛d. per lb, in 1895 2⅞d., in 1904 2⅛d., and in 1912 2⅞d. In 1916 it had risen to 5d., to fall back to 4⅛d. These levels prevailed until the outbreak of war in 1939.

The minutes are of course much taken up with relationships with, and payments to, authors. It was usual up to the end of the nineteenth century to pay a lump sum, or some variation thereof, and the royalty system did not come into use to any extent until the 1890s. Some idea of what authors and editors received may be got from the following examples.

1830 *Collyer on Partnership*. The author to be paid £100 in bills of £50 each at three and six months after day of publication and £50 at three months after date when the expenses are paid.

1852 Smith's *Mercantile Law*, 5th edition. Mr. Dowdeswell to be paid the sum of £175 if published in June 1853, but if not published until after that time the sum of £150 only.[14]

1852 It being observed that a loss of £3 2s. 6d. had been incurred on Vol. 3, Part 3, of De Gex & Smale's *Chancery Cases*, it was resolved that the Reporters be paid at the rate of £10 instead of £12 a sheet (of sixteen printed pages). Similarly it was reported that the *Exchequer Reports*, Vol. 6, Part 3, had produced a loss of £10 8s. 0d., and it was resolved that the rate of payment to the Reporters be reduced from £11 to £9 a sheet.

1853 Chitty's *Index to Equity, Privy Council and House of Lords Cases*, 3rd edition in 4 vols. The editor Mr. Macourlay was paid £330.[15]

1857 *Trower on Debtor and Creditor*. Author to be paid £25 on day of publication, £25 when 250 copies are sold, and £25 when 500 copies are sold and £100 for every future edition.

1865 *Russell on Crime*, 4th edition in 3 vols. The editor was paid £850.[16]

References to royalty agreements start with Stroud's *Judicial Dictionary* in 1890, and Dicey's *Conflict of Laws* in 1893, but the fixed-fee basis con-

---

14. Ten years later the editor of the seventh edition was paid £210.

15. The fourth edition was published in 1883–89 in nine volumes, for which the editor, Mr. Hirst, was paid £1,382. This was the foundation for Mews' *Digest*, first published in 16 volumes in 1898, for which Mr. Mews was paid £3,500.

16. Mr. Horace Smith was paid only £500 for the sixth edition, in 1896.

tinued for many years. Indeed it was not until the middle thirties that royalties became the rule rather than the exception for new works. It is now the accepted practice except in the case of works commissioned by the publisher, and for the editing of existing works which is normally done on a fee basis.

Selling methods in the early days appear to have been limited to advertising in newspapers. In 1852 the minutes record agreement to advertise Wordsworth's *Railway Law* in *The Times, Daily News, Morning Chronicle, Morning Post, Railway Times, Law Times, Legal Observer, Jurist* and *Globe*. Advertising rates must have been low in those days.

It would appear that the trade was hit by a depression in 1852, for the minutes record long lists of books to be sold at reduced prices.

It was in that year that the first reference is found to circulars. In March 1852 the minutes record that " the propriety of forwarding a circular to the county court judges respecting the new edition of Saunders on Pleading and Evidence was discussed when it was resolved that Mr. Sweet should draw up a circular for approval." In January 1853 permission was sought and granted by the Post Office to publish as a newspaper *The Law Publisher's Circular*, which was a list of all the books offered at a reduced price. The number of stamped circulars sent out was 14,000. If, as seems likely, one circular was sent to each practising barrister and solicitor, the equivalent number today would be 32,000.

The principal method of selling today remains the mailing of circulars. From time to time use has been made of travelling representatives, but never very effectively. The nature of the company's list is not suited to this kind of selling, in contrast to Butterworths, whose encyclopedic works could not be sold solely by mail order. The use of travelling representatives was indeed one of the innovations introduced by Stanley Shaw Bond[17] and for a long time it was not too well accepted by the profession.

OVERSEAS

It is appropriate here to make a brief diversion to the influence of the Sweets and Maxwells overseas.

The export of books was important from early days. As recorded above, Henry Sweet had been visiting the United States in 1841 when his father died. English law books had been in use in the United States from very early times, sometimes in pirated editions. An American edition of Blackstone's *Commentaries* was published in 1771. The Minute Book records a number of visits to the United States by Mr. Sweet and others and some of these included visits to Canada. In that country Robert Carswell had set himself up in business in 1865, at first as a second hand law bookseller, but he subsequently started to publish books on the local

17. See *post*, p. 133.

laws. He also developed a considerable trade with Sweet & Maxwell, and in 1889 it is recorded that he ordered 1,000 each of Smith's *Mercantile Law* and Roscoe's *Criminal Evidence*. Around this time there developed considerable competition on the other side of the Atlantic for some of the English books, and the minutes record offers by the Boston Law Book Company, Little, Brown & Company and Banks Brothers to take copies of Talbot and Fort's *Index of Cases*. It was at about this time that the United States Copyright Law required that books be printed in the United States if copyright was to be secured in that country and, in 1892 it was decided to print *Russell on Crime* in the United States in conjunction with Little, Brown & Company, to secure copyright. Two volumes were printed in Cambridge, Massachusetts, by Wilson, and one by Houghton, Mifflin. American cases were incorporated in the footnotes of this edition. When Dicey proposed to write his work on *Conflict of Laws* in 1893, he suggested that there should be an American editor who would insert the appropriate American case references, and suggested the name of Professor Moore for that purpose. This was agreed to and the Boston Law Book Company obtained estimates for printing in that city. Both books were in fact published in 1896 and in each case the American publisher eventually resiled from the agreement to take half the edition. The same thing happened in 1903, with the second edition of Stroud's *Judicial Dictionary*, and the experiment was not repeated. For the next fifteen years the names of Carswell, Canada Law Book Company, Little, Brown & Company, and Boston Law Book Company are repeated in the minutes frequently, each one of them taking copies of new books or new editions. By 1913 it seems clear that Carswell were taking more books than any of the other companies and a close relationship had been built up.

William Alexander Maxwell's son Percy had joined the Carswell Company in 1909, and in 1913 Mr. Carswell, being in need of more capital, offered Sweet & Maxwell the opportunity to take shares in his company. A substantial proportion was taken up and Carswell became the sole agent for Sweet & Maxwell for North America. The reasoning behind this investment was that the growth in local publishing combined with the increasing divergence of the local law from English law would inevitably lead to a considerable reduction in Sweet & Maxwell exports to Canada and that a share in the profits of the local company would compensate for this. In fact this did not prove to be the case for a very long time, and Canada and the United States continue to be an important market for English books.

The earlier minutes say nothing about Australia, but it presumably must have developed into an important market by 1869, when William Alexander Maxwell's brother, Charles Frederick Maxwell, went to Australia to set up in business distributing his brother's books. After a voyage of 177 days, graphically recorded in his Diary, he set up in Chancery Lane, Melbourne. He quite soon started publishing for the local market and established quite a substantial business. His first major publishing venture was the *Australian Law Times*, which was first published in 1879 and ran for fifty years. A year later he commenced publication of the *New South Wales Law Reports*. In 1889 he died while his wife and children were on a visit to England and the business fell into other hands. It subsequently became part of the Law Book Company of Australasia Limited, in which Sweet & Maxwell took a substantial interest in 1913. The Law Book Company opened an office in New Zealand, but on the outbreak of War in 1914 the manager closed the office and joined the Army. The business was acquired by Butterworths, and Sweet & Maxwell did not re-establish a presence until 1950, when in conjunction with the Law Book Company they acquired a company which formed the basis of what is now Sweet & Maxwell (N.Z.) Ltd. These overseas companies continue to form an important part in group activities today and to provide substantially for the needs of the legal professions in the countries concerned, both by local publishing and by the supply of Sweet & Maxwell's books and periodicals.

THE PUBLISHERS AT THE TURN OF THE CENTURY

Between 1868 when the original Minute Book of the Association of Law Publishers ceases and the time of the formation of the companies there had continued to be close collaboration in the publication of Associated Books. Also during that period there had been acquired by Sweet & Maxwell the old houses of William Clarke & Sons, Samuel Brooke and Richard Pheney. A new Minute Book was opened in April 1889 to record the meetings between Sweet & Maxwell Ltd. and Stevens & Sons Ltd. about associated publications.

By this time publishing was the major activity of the companies. They continued to be booksellers and indeed it is still the practice today for law publishers both to be booksellers and to sell their own products direct to the profession. There were now in addition to Sweet & Maxwell and Stevens & Sons three other law publishing houses, Butterworth, Shaw & Sons [18] and Stevens and Haynes.[19]

Sweet & Maxwell had a good list of copyrights and good living authors, and the company had on its formation received an injection of additional capital from various sources but in particular from Mr. William Bradbury of Bradbury, Agnew & Company (the publishers of *Punch*). Competition

18. By this time this business was wholly owned by the Bond family, and was run by Charles Bond's sons Charles and Richard. From being a law stationery business it had developed into a substantial publishing business as well.

19. So far as is known this had no family connection with Stevens & Sons. It was bought by Sweet & Maxwell in 1919.

was not immediately very great and they were able to embark on a fairly considerable publication in the *Revised Reports* which were edited by Sir Frederick Pollock and started publication in 1891. In 1897, on the suggestion of Charles Green of Edinburgh,[20] they started the publication of the *Encyclopedia of the Laws of England* in 12 volumes, the first modern work of its kind.

In 1895 Mr. Maxwell's eldest son, William Harold, joined the company, and in 1899 Herbert Sweet died, leaving no son. His son-in-law William Frederick Laurie joined the company in 1901 to represent the Sweet family interests.

The picture, however, was radically changed in 1895 when the business of Butterworth & Company was purchased by Shaw & Sons. Charles Bond and his son Stanley Shaw Bond set about turning what was a fairly sleepy company into an extremely enterprising and forward-looking one, and they had all the resources necessary for this purpose. The first real effect of those activities became evident in 1899 when Butterworth issued the *Yearly Supreme Court Practice*. The *Annual Practice*, known as the *White Book*, had started publication in 1882 under the title of the *Annual Chancery Practice*. In 1898 3,700 copies of the *Annual Practice* were sold and the number was reduced to 3,433 by 1903 and 3,126 by 1907. It did not reach this figure again until 1946. The publication of the *Yearly County Court Practice* had a similar effect on the sales of the *Annual County Courts Practice*.[21]

In 1905, when Charles Bond retired, Butterworths was separated from Shaw & Sons, and most of Shaw's law books went to Butterworths.[22] Stanley Shaw Bond was now in sole charge of the business and he proceeded with the programme of encyclopedic works which had begun with the *Encyclopedia of Forms and Precedents* in 1902. Halsbury's *Laws of England* followed in 1904 and the *English and Empire Digest* in 1919.

Stanley Shaw Bond introduced professionalism into law publishing, and it took the other law publishers nearly half a century to catch up with him in this respect. The main reason for this was that they simply did not have the resources to match Bond. Both Sweet & Maxwell and Stevens & Sons had a preponderance of family shareholders, many of whom were largely dependent on dividends, and though they were reasonably profitable, the profits were distributed on a scale which by today's standards was generous.

Despite the increase in competition, however, the company did make slow but steady progress. There was a steady demand for the already

---

20. Proprietor of W. Green & Sons, which was acquired by Sweet & Maxwell from his widow in 1956.
21. Publication of these competing works continued until 1944, when the shortage of paper led to the discontinuation of the *Yearly Practice* and the *Annual County Courts Practice*.
22. Including notably Stone's *Justices' Manual*, which still bears both imprints.

existing practitioners' textbooks and more of these were produced. The size of the market does not seem to have expanded very substantially over a period from the beginning of the century to the middle twenties, to judge by the printing numbers recorded. Prices remained remarkably stable although the impact of conditions in the First World War naturally did affect prices. The period from 1914 to 1918 was a rather thin one in terms of the return to the shareholders, but, all things considered, the company survived this difficult period well.

There were one or two abortive projects which were affected by the outbreak of the War, in particular an attempt to revive the *English Reports Annotated*. Behind this project was an organisation known as the Reports and Digest Syndicate which comprised Sweet & Maxwell, Stevens & Sons and The Canada Law Book Company. The Syndicate was formed at the instigation of the owner of the Canada Law Book Company, a man named Cromarty, who was a colourful figure with a somewhat remarkable ability to finance his business with other people's money. The Syndicate, which was formed in 1913, was also to undertake the publication of the *Law Journal Reports* and Mews' *Digest*. Exactly what caused its demise in 1915 is not clear, but it seems probable that it was as a result of the wartime conditions.

THE INTER-WAR YEARS

No discernible change in the pattern of publishing can be seen for the period up to the depression of 1929, the impact of which did not really begin to make itself felt until around 1931.

When the present writer joined the company in 1928 it was still essentially a family company. The Managing Director was William Harold Maxwell and he had working with him his brothers, Stanley and Leslie. Mr. Theophilus Sayle (the son-in-law of W. F. Laurie) was the Company Secretary and the Director representing the Sweet family interest.

At this time a substantial and very profitable[23] trade was being done in antiquarian law books, and indeed in secondhand materials as a whole. Through the 1920s some of the major American University libraries had been steadily building up their collections of early English law books, and a large trade was done with some of them, in particular Harvard and Yale, and to a lesser extent Minnesota. This was to continue, but on a reduced scale following the depression, and really only ceased at the outbreak of the Second World War. During the 1930s the prices of these books had risen to very high levels indeed and they had become too expensive for the average law library to buy. The reason for this was that they were now being collected as examples of early printed books, rather

23. On one occasion a copy of Magna Carta, spotted by Harold Maxwell in a bin of old books outside a second-hand bookshop in York, was bought for 9s. and subsequently found to be an unrecorded edition. It was sold to an American library for £900.

than as early law books. At the same time a considerable trade was done in portraits of judges and in legal prints. All these activities came to an end at the outbreak of the War in 1939 and were not resumed.

No editorial organisation of the kind which is seen today then existed. It was the practice to consult friends in the Inns of Court about proposals for new books and the quality of authors coming forward. The first formal appointment of an editorial nature was that of Dr. Harold Potter who in 1932 became consultant to the company. His broad knowledge of the field of both students books and of the requirements of the practitioner as a former practising solicitor were most valuable and he continued as the company's adviser until his untimely death in 1951.

A further step was taken in 1935 when John James, a great-great-grandson of Stephen Sweet, joined the company. He had been called to the Bar and first went to work with the Australian company, returning to set up the editorial organisation for the third edition of the *Encyclopedia of the Laws of England* which started publication in 1938.

TODAY'S FOUNDATIONS

The first step in setting up a really professional editorial organisation was taken in 1942 when John Burke joined the company. He had been a law publisher all his working life, first with Butterworths and then with Hamish Hamilton (Law Books). Under his guidance the standard practitioners' works were modernised and many innovations were made. The most notable perhaps was *Current Law* which was first published in 1947 and became an immediate success. This was followed by the looseleaf encyclopedias, starting with the *Encyclopedia of Planning and Compensation* which was the forerunner of the many such works now published. He laid the foundations for the highly professional editorial approach on which the company now prides itself.

Throughout there had been collaboration with Stevens & Sons on the books which had always been published in association. This had from time to time not been without its frustrations. The management of Stevens in the 1920s and 1930s had been less than enterprising, and through its inertia had permitted Butterworths to establish works which competed with some valuable associated properties despite Sweet & Maxwell's desire to be more aggressive. Examples are Chitty's *Statutes*, of which Sweet & Maxwell had wanted to do a new edition in 1925, and the *Law Journal Reports*, which Sweet & Maxwell had for many years wished to publish on a weekly basis. It would perhaps be going too far to suggest that a different policy would have stopped the publication of Halsbury's *Statutes* and the *All England Reports* but at least Butterworths could have been made to work harder for their success.

During this period Stevens & Sons had been managed by people who were not members of the Stevens family. Just before the outbreak of the

Second World War Robert Hilary Stevens, a great-great-grandson of the founder of the business, joined the company in a junior capacity. During the War and the immediate post-War period he had endeavoured to revive the fortunes of the company which were at a low ebb, and for a time was quite successful, particularly in developing the publication of books on international law, a subject in which he took a close personal interest. Unfortunately these publications were not very profitable and by 1950 the company was in some financial difficulty. Sweet & Maxwell therefore proposed that a merger should take place of the interests of the two companies and this took effect on July 1, 1950. Hilary Stevens joined the Board of Sweet & Maxwell and remained a director until his death in 1961.

Following the merger a programme of consolidation and rationalisation of the publishing of the two companies was carried out and this led to the position today which is dealt with in the next chapter.

PERSONAL NOTE

It should perhaps be explained that any apparent bias in this account towards the Maxwell side of Sweet & Maxwell is not deliberate but is the result of circumstances. There is remarkably little documentation of the Maxwell business but none at all appears to have survived of the Sweet or Stevens businesses. Such Minute Books as are available are fairly cryptic and frequently there is no background whatever for decisions recorded. Much of what is said above is the result of personal knowledge gleaned from my father, who could not be persuaded to set his recollections down in writing.

I wish to thank Mr. H. Kay Jones of Butterworth & Company and Mr. Alban Carey of Shaw & Sons for information about their respective companies. Any misstatements are mine alone.

Law Publishing Today

JOHN BURKE & PETER ALLSOP

SWEET & MAXWELL's law publishing at the present day requires to be looked at in the light of its development over the past three decades.* In 1943, Sweet & Maxwell were what they had been since the beginning, a family concern publishing a number of solid textbooks whose names were household words—in legal households at any rate. Sweet & Maxwell possessed, in addition, some long-established major works which had been relied upon by generations of lawyers and which constituted a solid base for the firm's publishing.

The late Field-Marshal Sir William Slim (afterwards Lord Slim) gave to his book describing his campaign in Burma the title *Defeat into Victory*. In some ways this would be a not unfair description of Sweet & Maxwell's law publishing. The period under review starts with a melancholy chapter, which may be entitled " The Demise of the Major Works."

MAJOR WORKS AND OLD FAITHFULS

The major works published by Sweet & Maxwell included Mews' *Digest of English Case Law* in some fifty volumes, Chitty's *Statutes of Practical Utility* in a similar number of volumes, and the *Law Journal Reports*, begun in 1823 and comprising 127 volumes. All these works had been losing ground to more modern competitors and one by one they died lingering deaths.

In addition, Sweet & Maxwell had been first in the field, in 1897, with the *Encyclopedia of the Laws of England*, the second edition of which, in 1908, ran to seventeen volumes. A third edition of this work had been begun shortly before the Second World War and five volumes had been published. Enemy action destroyed the whole of the sheet stock, the manuscript copy and the paper stock, and publication was perforce suspended. After the war was over it was decided to abandon the project.

As a result, the period under review saw Sweet & Maxwell denuded of virtually all profitable major works and forced to rely on their periodicals and textbooks.

* During this period Stevens & Sons merged with Sweet & Maxwell and brought with them some very important publications and authors but, for simplicity, all books and publications are lumped together as Sweet & Maxwell's.

The first and greatest of these periodicals was the *Law Quarterly Review*. This had commenced publication in 1885 and had achieved the highest reputation among practising and academic lawyers all over the English-speaking world. The standard was set once and for all by its creator and first editor, Sir Frederick Pollock. It has been maintained in all its integrity by Professor A. L. Goodhart, Q.C., K.B.E., who has been Editor-in-Chief since 1926. He has been assisted by Mr. R. E. (now Mr. Justice) Megarry and Mr. Paul Baker. It now runs to eighty-eight volumes and has had to be reprinted to meet continuing world demand.

Two much younger periodicals were the *Conveyancer and Property Lawyer* (New Series), commenced in 1936, and the *Modern Law Review*, first published in 1937.

The new series of the *Conveyancer and Property Lawyer* was begun under the editorship of the late Dr. Harold Potter as a quarterly and taken over on his death in 1951 by Mr. Edward George. It is now, owing to pressure of material, published six times a year and in 1970 showed its vigour by giving birth to a collection of looseleaf conveyancing precedents edited by Mr. Ernest Scamell.

The *Modern Law Review* is centred on the Law Faculty of the London School of Economics, where it was started by Lord Chorley, who edited it for thirty-five years. It comprises thirty-five volumes. Its success is underlined by the fact that it also has had to be reprinted to meet continuing demand.

Two works essential to all practitioners are the *Law List* and the *Supreme Court Practice*. The *Law List* was first issued in 1775 and is an annual publication. So far as relates to certificated solicitors practising in England and Wales it is published by the authority of the Law Society. The *Supreme Court Practice* (the " White Book ") was first published in 1882 as the *Annual Chancery Practice*, and later as the *Annual Practice of the Supreme Court*. The *Supreme Court Practice* is now published every third year with supplements bringing it up to date in the intervening years.

The criminal lawyer's bible remains Archbold's *Pleading, Evidence and Practice in Criminal Cases*, or, more shortly, *Archbold*. This was first published in 1822. Now in its thirty-eighth edition, frequent new editions are necessary and it is kept up to date in a very sophisticated manner with cumulative supplements and a noter-up service issued three times a year.

In addition to these essential volumes Sweet & Maxwell were fortunate in that although their major works had perished they had a number of textbooks of established reputation on all subjects of the law, as will be seen below. These were not however enough and whatever could be done with them was no more than a stout holding operation. Sweet & Maxwell, like Alice and the Red Queen, were running hard to keep in the same place. Something more was necessary to fill the yawning void left by the loss of the great major works.

CURRENT LAW

The break-through came with *Current Law*, published in 1947. *Current Law* has the virtue of extreme simplicity. Its purpose was expressed in its first advertisement which read:

If you had a learned clerk who read and digested all the reported cases and all the statutes and statutory rules and orders and everything else of legal interest and presented them to you classified every month and at the end of the year in a year book—
Would you think him overpaid at two guineas a year?

On the cover of *Current Law* this was expressed succinctly in the simple boast " ALL the law from EVERY source." And whilst the price has altered, the purpose and its fulfilment remain, twenty-seven years later, the same.

Current Law achieved an instantaneous success especially among the younger lawyers who derived some satisfaction in occasionally being able to bring a senior up to date. Harman J. (later L.J.) said " It must not be assumed that Equity is beyond the age of child-bearing." Sweet & Maxwell had demonstrated to the profession that they were live, up-and-coming law publishers. Two years later Sweet & Maxwell re-entered the major works field with *Current Law Statutes*.

PLANNING

The second break-through came in 1948. The Town and Country Planning Act 1947 effected a revolution in the method of land use control. It was large, complicated and rather frightening. The Act was due to come into force on July 1, 1948, and the legal profession and the owners and managers of property were in a state of some uncertainty as to its effects. At exactly the right moment there appeared the *Journal of Planning Law*. Its team of experts in all aspects of planning law, headed by Mr. (now Sir) Desmond Heap, proceeded to lead its bemused public, month by month, through the maze of the new legislation. The *Journal* had an even more immediate success than *Current Law* and confirmed in the minds of the profession the impression of liveliness at Sweet & Maxwell. The *Journal* continues today in a larger format under the title of the *Journal of Planning and Environment Law*. By its specialist approach the *Journal of Planning Law* made a break-through in more ways than one, since not only were many more specialist journals to follow in later years but also it provided a regular and frequent service by providing monthly digests of cases, Acts, orders, circulars and planning decisions. This service element soon required backing up with full annotated texts of the multiplicity of statutes, orders, circulars etc. and these found their place in the looseleaf Encyclopedias.

THE LOCAL GOVERNMENT LIBRARY

The first work published in 1949 was the *Encyclopedia of Planning and Compensation* which became an essential tool for anyone involved in the web of planning law. It is hardly too much to say that anyone appearing before the Lands Tribunal without the *Encyclopedia* in his hands found it difficult to get a patient hearing. Planning and compulsory purchase law continued to grow and, under successive governments, to suffer convulsive changes. In 1959 the *Encyclopedia* was replaced by two—the *Encyclopedia of Town and Country Planning* (in three volumes) and the *Encyclopedia of Compulsory Purchase* (in two volumes), both of which, incidentally, promptly doubled the number of their subscribers, and which together started the Local Government Library.

On the sound military principle of reinforcing success planning law was reinforced by the publication in 1950 of *Planning and Compensation Reports* (subsequently to widen its scope and become *Property and Compensation Reports*). Successive governments also frequently added subjects requiring the treatment provided by looseleaf work and a number of new Encyclopedias were launched in the Local Government Library: *Housing* (1958), *Road Traffic* (1960), *Factories, Shops and Offices* (1962), *Highways* (1965), *Betterment Levy and Land Commission* (1967 for the period whilst this aberration lasted, essential at the time and as a lasting monument), *Public Health* (1968).

TAXATION

Another area in which Sweet & Maxwell had practically no established textbooks was taxation and this too was one in which the law changed so rapidly that a looseleaf Encyclopedia provided the best service to the profession. With a consolidated Income Tax Act passed in 1952 the opportunity was taken to launch *Current Law Income Tax Annotated Service* (Clitas) covering income tax, surtax (two volumes) and profits tax (one volume). Even these volumes were not enough and the subject showed signs of becoming unmanageable so that the work was relaunched as the *British Tax Encyclopedia* in five volumes in 1962. Today these volumes are crowded and three bound volumes have been added to cover income tax and surtax, capital gains tax and corporation tax, and a further separate *Encyclopedia of Value Added Tax* was published in 1973.

The need to provide an even more frequent service together with informed comment was met by the periodical *British Tax Review*, started in 1956, which appears six times a year.

Taxation now forms such an important part of personal and business affairs that its effect must be taken into account before, rather than after, transactions are entered into, and this fact inspired *Tax Planning with Precedents* by Mr. D. C. Potter and Mr. H. H. Monroe, which lifted the veil and showed the non-specialist practitioner how to arrange his client's affairs so as to avoid unnecessary depredations by the state. First published in 1954, it was an instant success and as the rules of the game change with appalling frequency and suddenness, it has reached its seventh edition in 1974.

PROPERTY AND CONVEYANCING

Modern taxation shattered the old mould of conveyancing precedents and such multi-volume works as *Key and Elphinstone* and *Prideaux* achieved their final editions in the 1950s.

In many other ways conveyancing has been profoundly affected by economics and Mr. V. G. H. Hallett, from a wide and intimate experience of modern problems, produced in 1965 a one volume set of conveyancing precedents which embodied the new ideas and yet were acceptable to a highly conservative profession.

In this area of the law Sweet & Maxwell can present such well known names as *Lewin on Trusts*, *Tudor on Charities* and, the longest lived of them all, Woodfall's *Landlord and Tenant*, first published in 1802 (twenty-seventh edition 1968). These three have been collected with other titles into the Property and Conveyancing Library, together with such new works as Ruoff and Roper. *The Law and Practice of Registered Conveyancing* (first edition 1958, third 1972). The Library is not exclusive and many important titles such as *The Law of Real Property* by Megarry and Wade (first edition 1957, third 1971) have been added in this area of law. This book immediately took its rightful place as a classic; perhaps unusually for a large work, finding a market amongst students as well as the practitioners for whom it was intended. Mr. Justice Megarry's other major work, on the Rent Acts, although originally published in 1939, went into nine further editions between 1946 and 1967.

COMMON LAW AND COMMERCIAL LAW

The grouping of books into Libraries was only one of the activities necessary to revitalise the list and present it in an attractive form to the market. All the standard texts had to meet the challenge of the winds of change through drastic adaptation in style, content and format to comply with modern requirements, often amounting to complete rewriting, as many showed clear signs of age and decay. Their names still command respect, and unlike the old major works they had few rivals.

In the Common Law Library two of the grand old survivors from a former era were *Chitty on Contracts* and *Clerk and Lindsell on Torts*. *Chitty* had run into twenty-one editions when, in 1960, it was put into the hands of a team of academic lawyers from Oxford University led by Dr. J. H. C. Morris of Magdalen College. At about the same time *Clerk and Lindsell* was entrusted to a team from Cambridge University headed by Dr. A. L. Armitage then of Queen's College. The two works were largely rewritten and the experiment was a complete success. The work of the academic lawyers proved to be wholly acceptable to practitioners and has helped to bridge the gap between the world of the academic lawyer and that of the practising barrister and solicitor. Other titles in this library have owed their survival to rewriting: Chitty's *King's Bench Forms* (1834), which became Chitty & Jacob's *Queen's Bench Forms* in the twentieth edition in 1969, and *Mayne on Damages* (1856) was so completely rewritten as to become *McGregor on Damages* in the thirteenth edition in 1972.

This process of revitalising has been carried through all the standard Sweet & Maxwell textbooks, notably such as Dicey and Morris, *The Conflict of Laws*. The book was first written by Dicey in 1896. The ninth edition was published in 1973.

One other Library was created, the *British Shipping Laws,* and the principle adopted for this differed from that applied to other Libraries, which were groupings of books in certain areas. *British Shipping Laws* was prepared to a scheme with volumes arranged in alphabetical order taking in such well known titles as Carver, *Carriage by Sea* (1885, twelfth edition 1971), Marsden, *Collisions at Sea* (1880, eleventh edition 1961) and others, and adding to them entirely new titles, such as *Admiralty Practice* by McGuffie, Fugeman and Gray (1964).

In the general commercial field such old titles as Palmer's *Company Law* (1898, twenty-first edition 1968) and *Byles on Bills of Exchange* (1829, twenty-third edition 1972) still provide up-to-date works for the practitioner. The wind of change in company law was reflected by a new work, *Weinberg on Takeovers and Mergers* (1963, third edition 1971). The old law of master and servant disappeared beneath a welter of legislation, particularly since 1959, so that the looseleaf *Encyclopedia of Labour Relations Law* was published in 1972 largely as a result of the Act of the previous year. This was complemented by the *Industrial Law Journal,* also published in 1972, absorbing the *Industrial Law Society Bulletin.*

The whole area of commercial law has been supported by the quarterly *Journal of Business Law,* first published in 1957.

OTHER PRACTITIONER WORKS

In other fields new texts were published to fill the gaps and to meet the challenge presented to many distinguished authors by new subjects for example *Restrictive Trade Practices* by Lord Wilberforce, A. Campbell and N. P. M. Elles.

When one considers the famous works published by Sweet & Maxwell and Butterworths in the criminal field it is perhaps surprising that there has been no great expansion here. A major service has been provided monthly since 1954 by the *Criminal Law Review* and larger and larger issues of the *Criminal Appeal Reports* (first published in 1908), have reflected the increasing interest in this branch of law. But of major new titles there have been few, Professor Glanville Williams' *Criminal Law: The General Part* reached a second edition in 1961 and the profession will surely be deprived of a great scholar's contribution to the law if it is not completed and further editions produced.

In the international law field there has been expansion and contraction. Whilst the regular annual volume of *The Year Book of World Affairs* increases regularly in popularity, the market for books in this field has remained consistently small, and although the works of Professor Georg Schwarzenberger maintained their important position, only one major work has been added in this field of law, Professor D. P. O'Connell's work *International Law*, the second edition of which was published in 1970.

SOME IMPORTANT SERIES

A regular contribution to legal learning has been provided by the annual volume of lectures given at University College, London, and published since 1948 in the series *Current Legal Problems*.

British International Law Cases started in 1964 has now reached Volume 9, with the supplementary volume 1966–70.

A series of a different nature which has contributed many important titles has been the *Hamlyn Lectures* created under the will of the late Miss Emma Hamlyn of Torquay, who was concerned to provide lectures for the common people so that they may appreciate the privileges they enjoy from the common law. It is perhaps invidious to single out the names of only a few of the eminent authors, both from home and overseas, who have lectured for this series, but the volumes provided by Lord Denning, Lord Devlin and Professor Glanville Williams have, with others, become part of the vital literature of this period having been most frequently re-edited or reprinted.

EUROPE

This commemoration year is almost identical with what may be one of the greatest major influences upon the law of the United Kingdom, entry into the European Common Market. A whole new body of law now applies to this country and although by performing an act of faith the *Common Market Law Review* was launched in 1963, it is now that new books are really needed for the profession. Translations of outstanding works from France and Holland have already been published, but the main contribution Sweet & Maxwell will make will be contained in the *Encyclopedia of European Community Law*. This area of law has all the features of volume and rapid change, which are best covered by a looseleaf Encyclopedia, and at the time of going to press the first three volumes in what is likely to be a multi-volume major work have been published.

STUDENTS' BOOKS

Sweet & Maxwell have always been strong in their list of students' textbooks. The wish of many teachers to produce their own books has meant that only a few of the titles now published have a long history. The company has been fortunate in being able to find eminent editors to continue these older works. Mr. Justice Megarry took the old established Snell's *Principles of Equity* (1868) and made of it a new and vital thing (twenty-seventh edition, with P. V. Baker, 1973). During the same period he found time to set out the ancient and complex English Law of Real Property in attractive lucidity in *A Manual of the Law of Real Property* (1946, fourth edition by P. V. Baker, 1969).

Two other titles which are leaders in the higher levels of legal education are Salmond's *Torts* and Winfield's *Tort*. Both were recognised when first published as authoritative, each the result of a lifetime of teaching. But academic thinking on this topic has shown much development and it was fortunate that each work has found an editor who has given a new brilliance to the original—*Salmond*, sixteenth edition 1973 by Professor R. F. B. Heuston, *Winfield & Jolowicz*, ninth edition, 1971, by Mr. J. A. Jolowicz, assisted by Dr. T. E. Lewis and Dr. D. M. Harris.

There have been many outstanding contributions in the textbooks for students, but a few should be singled out. Professor L. C. B. Gower's *Principles of Modern Company Law* (1954, third edition 1969) made a somewhat daunting subject exciting. It also persuaded a slightly stunned body of practitioners that an academic saw further into their mysteries than was wholly decent. The law of contract has been restated by Mr. G. H. Treitel (1962, third edition 1970) and Dr. J. H. C. Morris, having edited the major practitioner's work for some years, produced an entirely new book on *Conflict of Laws* in 1971 for the student reader.

The subjects taught for university degrees have not remained static, though most of the subjects we have dealt with above have been in most university courses. One, however, which, as in the practitioner world, has grown in importance has been *Revenue Law* and Mr. Barry Pinson's work, first published in 1962, is now in its seventh edition, having become an annual publication since 1970.

Whilst textbooks have maintained a vital place in law teaching, there has been a steady growth in supplementary volumes, which, by their sales, have shown how much they are appreciated by students whose access to library volumes may be difficult. The particular area of importance has been the case book or volume of cases and materials. The first (1957) in Sweet & Maxwell's list was *Smith & Thomas* on *Contract*, the fifth edition of which appeared in 1973. *Criminal Law* (Elliott & Wood), *Tort* (Weir) and other subjects have had their case books, but the recent volumes published in 1973 were wider in scope and entitled *Cases and Materials in Revenue Law* (A. J. Easson), *English Legal System* (Geoffrey

Wilson) and *International Law* (D. J. Harris). Even more basic materials have been provided in the volumes of Statutes on Property, Family Law and Estate Duty, which have, in some universities, now taken a place in the examination halls.

Many thousands of students will have had their initial introduction to law through Professor Glanville Williams' *Learning the Law* (1945, ninth edition 1973), and their steps will have been guided further by Professor O. Hood Phillips' *A First Book of English Law* (1948, sixth edition 1970). Having moved deeper into the study of law, Professor Lord Lloyd's *Introduction to Jurisprudence* (1959, third edition 1972) will have taken many in this country and overseas into new realms of legal thinking.

These substantial and learned textbooks are primarily designed for the university student and those taking the examinations to become members of the legal profession, but many other students study law for different professions or none, and whilst often their standards must be as high as those of the professional lawyer, there are many cases where the concise textbook or case book gives all they require. Sweet & Maxwell have therefore launched (1968) the *Concise College Texts* and (1973) *Concise College Casenotes*, which cover not only such traditional subjects as contract and tort, but also such esoteric fields as hotel and catering law.

The standard textbooks designed to give an overall coverage of a subject are frequently felt to give insufficient discussion on some topics, and a new series, entitled *Modern Legal Studies*, was launched in 1973 to cater for the more selective and individual approach that is gaining favour. Such untraditional titles as *Economic Torts* and *Human Rights and Europe*, accompany *Registered Land* and *Settlements of Land* in the first batch.

All the popular students' books are now published in paperback form at much below the price of the hardback editions, both authors and publishers making their contribution to achieve this result. Sweet & Maxwell were early in the field with this venture into cheaper editions and have been repaid with very greatly increased sales. An odd side effect is that there is now virtually no market in secondhand students' textbooks, a fact which does not dispirit publishers of new editions.

THE PUBLISHING MACHINE

Law publishing, like almost everything else, has changed in the past three decades. It has become markedly more professional, with budgets, computerised accounting and sophisticated costing. Behind the editor, and tending to breathe down his neck, stands the accountant with advice, criticism and, occasionally, grim approval.

In 1944 a lawyer with an editorial assistant and secretary were the editorial department. Today the department consists of twelve lawyers assisted by a production manager and a team of assistants with varying degrees of experience, but all acquiring the special skills of law book editing, making a total of twenty-eight in all. In addition the writers of this article and other senior management brood over the publishing process from a more or less detached position.

During the thirty-year period, and indeed since 1913, the editorial department have been well served, not only by the readers of The Eastern Press, but also by all the staff of that printing house. Punctual publication of journals, particularly the monthlies, has been achieved only with their willing and helpful co-operation.

THE COST OF BOOKS

Like everything else there has been a great increase in the price of law books, particularly since 1959, when a six-week strike in the printing industry heralded what has proved to be an annual increase in printing and binding costs. Successive devaluations have had their effect on paper which used to be the cheapest item in the making of a book. Within a short time it has risen by nearly four times and recently, type ready for the machine has been sitting at the printers waiting for paper to be printed on.

A significant factor in cost is the increase in the volume of law. In 1822 the first edition of *Archbold* consisted of 403 closely printed pages of text 7 ins. $\times$ 4 ins.; in 1973 the thirty-eighth edition ran to 1,573 pages, $8\frac{1}{2}$ ins. $\times$ $5\frac{1}{2}$ ins. In 1943 Chitty's *Contracts* sold for £2 10s. 0d. for one volume. The price of the twenty-third edition is £18·50 for 1,656 pages in two volumes.

But the price which, economically, must be charged for a book depends very much on the printing number. The unit cost of a book costing £5,000 to produce is £5·00 if the printing number is 1000, but only 50 pence if the printing number is 10,000 (not now an unusual printing number for a law book). What has helped to keep the price of books from shooting into the stratosphere is that the market for law books has increased and widened. There are more practitioners, many more law students, more law libraries in new universities, polytechnics and technical colleges throughout the English-speaking world. And the market for law books is not confined to lawyers—architects, accountants, company secretaries, officials of government departments, state institutions and local government bodies need law books and as they usually do not have to dig into their own pockets they are more likely to buy what they need. The solid core of the market for law books remains the country solicitor, who has to rely on himself and his own library to a greater extent than his brethren in the cities and at the Bar. The Bar are excellent customers, but barristers have a distressing habit of sending their clerks to borrow a book which they have not got in chambers. And, of course, the libraries of the Inns of Court are close at hand. Nothing has changed here.

Legal aid and advice have made a very big difference to the legal profession. That figure of fun, the briefless barrister, has practically disappeared. In addition, the very great rise in the prices at which land and houses change hands has made run-of-the-mill conveyancing a much more profitable exercise. All this results in an appreciable strengthening of the traditional market for law books.

THE WRITERS

The other side of the medal is not so gratifying to the law publisher. Books have to be written or edited and this is best done by practising lawyers or by academics. So far as practising lawyers are concerned there are two kinds of potential authors. First the lawyer, usually a barrister of experience, who is willing to make that experience available to the rest of the profession and somehow finds time to do so. He has always been a rare bird and the passage of years has not made him commoner. Secondly, there is the able young man with time on his hands, waiting for his practice to grow and eager to do some writing to earn some money and keep himself usefully occupied. His name on a book is the only form of advertising available to the young barrister and he may, with luck, find himself sought after as an expert in a particular branch of law; Sweet & Maxwell's list can show several examples. But, largely due to legal aid and advice, this category of author has become difficult to find. Fortunately, some lawyers have what the late Lord Justice Harman (in the litigation arising out of George Bernard Shaw's will) termed the *cacoethes scribendi* and are willing to turn their talent to the writing and editing of law books. In America the dearth of practising lawyers willing and able to write has driven the larger publishing houses to set up huge editorial departments, which churn out enormous publications by a form of internal combustion. It is to be hoped that such a development will be a long time coming in England. On the other hand, the considerable increase in the number of law faculties in new universities has added largely to the number of academic lawyers, and it is from these that some of the most useful contributions to legal literature have come. In their case the imparting of knowledge in one form or another is not merely a sideline, it is their business.

The function of a publisher can be stated with a terrible simplicity: to publish the right book at the right time at the right price. In this respect law publishing today is the same as law publishing yesterday. It is perhaps not wholly true of law publishing tomorrow. As has been pointed out above, the price at which a book can be sold is largely governed by the printing number. It follows that, if the publisher can see only a very small market for a book or other piece of writing, he has to decide whether there will be any buyers at all at the price that economics would force him to put upon it. It too often happens that he decides that the book, paper or what have you is unpublishable when that test is applied to it.

"*FUTUROLOGY*"

A different problem is presented by the growing bulk of legal publications—law reports and periodicals in particular—where each year sees additions to the series and more pressure on the space available for their accommodation. One answer to both these problems possibly lies in the use of the new techniques of micro-film and micro-fiche: modern photographic devices which can be stored in small spaces, but which require special " readers," although the cost of producing both is very much less than that of setting up type and printing from it. In the case of original work such as a thesis the micro-film or micro-fiche can be prepared from clean typescript. " Readers " are liable to be expensive and not very portable objects (but these objections are being rapidly overcome) and few today would own or use one if he had an alternative. It is possible to prepare prints of the relevant pages, but this requires further apparatus or a more sophisticated " reader." In the United States of America, where 30,000 new decisions are handed down each year to be added to the colossal number already in existence, some lawyers are being forced to use these devices, but in many libraries the " readers " sit unused. These and other more advanced methods of storing and retrieving legal material are being continually investigated and experimented with, but they are not yet available on an economic basis.

It is possible that new generations of lawyers will be trained in new methods so that law books cease to be the essential tools they are in 1974. Sweet & Maxwell's editors keep their eyes very much on these new creatures of the future, but the writers are deeply grateful for the fact that age will prevent any of this " futurology " having an effect upon them.

VII

Local Government

Local Government—The Evolving Story; or, What Next?

DESMOND HEAP

This year of grace, 1974, sees the 175th anniversary of the House of Sweet and Maxwell, Law Publishers. One hundred and seventy-five years is a long time; if we call it one and three-quarters centuries it sounds even longer. Over that extensive period Sweet and Maxwell have been hard at work publishing all sorts of law books, including books on local government and its many facets, and including what is today probably its most important facet of all—planning control over the development of land.

It is a long, long look backwards to the days of 1799 when Sweet and Maxwell began. The French Revolution had started ten years earlier—the fall of the Bastille in 1789 was to have a notable effect upon (amongst a thousand other things) local government—but the first train out of Euston (for Birmingham) was not to steam off until forty years later (in 1839) when Mr. Hardwicke had finished building the Euston Arch (not really an arch at all) and the equally famous Euston Great Hall, that splendid memorial to the proportional beauties of the double-cube lately removed to make way for the horizontal-functionalism of " New Euston."

In 1799 Sweet and Maxwell was some six years ahead of the death of Nelson and sixteen years ahead of the fall of Napoleon; Queen Victoria was not yet born (and it would be thirty-nine years before her coronation); the Industrial Revolution was getting under way and the rush to the towns was about to begin. In short, the times were, as usual, changing. In the next one and three-quarters centuries, that is to say, in the lifetime (to date) of Sweet and Maxwell, they would change more fundamentally than they had ever previously done since, one would think, the invention of the wheel.

FIVE CENTURIES WITHOUT CHANGE

And where stood local government at the confluence of the eighteenth and nineteenth centuries? The answer is that it stood very much where

151

it had been standing for the previous 500 years. There was county local government and there was borough local government. The ancient and pervading cleavage between these two systems dates from about the middle of the fourteenth century. It was a cleavage that was much alive and kicking in 1799. It has continued to kick enthusiastically and, at times, almost violently right down to the last decades of the twentieth century for this double-headed format for local government came to its ultimate end only on April 1, 1974—but more of this anon.

Returning to 1799 again one saw local government in the counties being discharged (as it had been for some five centuries) by Justices of the Peace (those enduring creations of King Edward III) sitting in quarter sessions but at informal meetings of the sessions summoned for the discharge of " County Business."

Entirely outside this system of county local government stood the chartered boroughs, some of them very ancient indeed. As units of local government the boroughs sprang into being for a variety of what (in those early days) were good and sufficient reasons. There were many and differing reasons why people in given areas should feel the urge to congregate. Sometimes it might be the needs of trade and sometimes the needs of defence as, for example, the need to " watch out " for the French—hence the Cinque Ports.

The boroughs were incorporated by royal charter and their powers and duties relating to local government depended on what sort of a charter they could win from the royal hands. Charters varied greatly, some were freer than others in which event the boroughs had less control " from above." It has been well said that " there can hardly be a history of the English borough for each borough has its own history."

There was one thing—and just about one thing only—that county local government and borough local government had in common. Neither of these two forms was in the least bit " democratic " (as the expression goes today)—that is to say they were not manifestations of local *self* government even though they did constitute local government of a kind. In the counties the justices were not popularly elected—on the contrary they were royal nominees. In the boroughs, whilst the local constitution depended on the terms of the relevant charters (and charters, as has been mentioned, varied greatly) it was generally true to say that the local folk did not greatly enter into the picture. In 1799 local government had undoubtedly been going in county and in borough for many a century but local *self* government had yet to come.

Thus we return to the fall of the Bastille after which things were never to be the same again. Liberalism was stirring—Lord Byron was shortly to die at Missolonghi demanding freedom for " the Isles of Greece, the Isles of Greece, where burning Sappho loved and sang "—and the Day of the Common Man was drawing nigh.

SHIFT TO THE TOWNS AND EARLY REFORM

Moreover in the early nineteenth century life was getting more complex as the rush to the towns (fired by the industrial revolution) got progressively under way and more responsibilities of a local government nature were being generated by the times. The big question was: Were the instruments of local government as they then existed going to be equal to their new and developing tasks?

It soon appeared that they were not and this led (unfortunately for local *self* government) to the creation of a vast horde of *ad hoc* bodies—local bodies charged with one duty only. Thus there came into being Improvement Commissioners, Boards of Health, Sanitary Authorities, Turnpike Trustees and so on and so forth with the result that the middle of the nineteenth century was described as " a chaos of areas, a chaos of franchises, a chaos of authorities and a chaos of rates." It was all very complicated and, worst of all, it was getting increasingly inefficient.

The new Liberalism, blowing over from Europe, poised itself for action as soon as it got securely ensconced in the corridors of power and the seats of authority, that is to say, in Parliament. Central government was reformed first and this came with the Reform Act of 1832. Next the municipal corporations of the ancient chartered boroughs were put through the legislative hoop by the Municipal Corporations Act 1835 which made them all a good deal more responsive to the popular will.

Further reforms for the boroughs came in 1882. In the meantime county local government was grinding to a halt as it saw more and more local government responsibilities vested in the hands of an ever growing number of *ad hoc* bodies. But in 1888 came the biggest change—a positive upheaval—of all.

The Local Government Act of 1888 stripped the justices of the peace of their local government functions. In their stead the Act created a new style of local authority for county local government. It created the administrative counties (sixty-one of them) each with its county council elected by popular vote. At the same time it elevated a large number (ultimately there were eighty-three) of the chartered boroughs to the status of county boroughs.

A county borough and an administrative county were mutually exclusive. The county borough was an all-purpose authority totally independent of any adjacent or surrounding county and within the borough boundary it discharged *all* the functions which fell to local government.

In the administrative county there was a sub-division of the county into three different types of county district, namely the non-county borough, the urban district and the rural district.

Thus was created in 1888 that great and abiding cleavage (earlier mentioned) in the styling of local government in the counties (where it was split-level or two-tiered) and the county boroughs (where it was single-level). The counties and the county boroughs had to learn to live side by side and this was not easy. Naturally each claimed their own type of local government to be the better. The debate was continuous and frequently vehement. As more and more people left the countryside to live in the towns the county boroughs sought to expand. But, alas, they could never expand one iota except at the expense of the counties.

Thus the atmosphere of pervasive belligerency developed and continued and Parliament was, ever and anon, called upon to do something about it. Boundary extensions were handed over to boundary commissions—statutory bodies established to see fair play between the competing interests of the counties and the county boroughs. All action dried up with the outbreak in 1939 of the Second World War. At the conclusion of hostilities further boundary commissions came and went without anything much being done.

POST THE SECOND WORLD WAR

However, in 1963 local government in London—London had always been " special "—was reformed by the London Government Act of that year. The area of " London " was greatly expanded into " Greater London " (at the great expense of Middlesex—which for local government purposes totally disappeared—Surrey, Kent and Essex) and the two-tiered system was established with the Greater London Council functioning at one level and thirty-one London boroughs plus the City of London Corporation functioning at another level.

Local government outside the capital had to wait a little longer before being changed and that quite radically. After three years' deliberation a Royal Commission reported that the future of local government in the provinces should be based generally on the unitary system exemplified by the county boroughs though an exception could be made for the two-tier system in certain heavily urbanised areas. Thus, after some eighty years of disputation, the county boroughs won victory for their own system when the Royal Commission reported in 1968.

Alas for the county boroughs, there is indeed many a slip between cup and lip. In 1970 the government of the day not only changed politically (from a Labour to a Conservative administration) but it also changed the (general) acceptance by its predecessor of the Royal Commission's recommendations. The Government decided that in future there was to be local government at split-level (or two-tier) right across the board. The Local Government Act 1972 established this new format across the entire face of England and Wales and the counties (after the aforesaid eighty years of disputation) came at long last into their own.

THE NEW BEGINNING OR THE GREAT UPHEAVAL

The new beginning dates from April 1, 1974, after which things in local government will (once again) never be the same. On that date all the county boroughs dissolved and the proud and independent towns of Bristol, Manchester, Liverpool, Kingston-upon-Hull, Birmingham, Cardiff, Plymouth and many others ceased to exist as independent local government authorities.

Before April 1, 1974, there were (outside London) fifty-eight administrative counties in England and Wales and there were some 1,000 boroughs (county and non-county), urban districts and rural districts. From April 1, 1974, all this changes into (outside London) fifty-three New Administrative Counties from which will stem 369 New Districts. Local government functions are divided between county level and district level.

How will it all work? This remains to be seen—we must wait and see. Undoubtedly it is a great upheaval and undoubtedly there will be a generating of dust which will need time to settle. By way of example it may be stated that before April 1, 1974, there were some 145 local planning authorities (county councils and county borough councils) each carrying the authority for anything done in the planning field in their respective areas. On April 1, 1974, there were born some 340 local planning authorities. The appellation local planning authority disappears and it becomes necessary to speak of " County Planning Authority " or, as the case may be, " District Planning Authority."

At the moment planning functions are uneasily divided between these two different types of authority—the district planning authority being given what is probably the greatest share of the planning function but the county planning authority being responsible for structure plans and for what are veiledly called " county matters." What are " county matters " when it comes to town planning? What indeed; " there's the rub;" again, we shall see.

One thing can be stated for sure. One of the reasons for the upheaval on April 1, 1974, was the need to make local government more interesting and attractive to people of merit and intelligence. Will it do so? Again, that is the question. Local government, certainly since 1888, has sought to be local government " of the people, by the people, for the people." It has never been the idea that local people should be governed by experts but by themselves. The words of Lord Salisbury, way back in 1877 but still highly relevant to the current scene, come to mind.

" No lesson seems to be so deeply inculcated by the experience of life as that you should never trust experts. If you believe the doctors, nothing is wholesome; if you believe theologians, nothing is innocent; if you believe the soldiers, nothing is safe. They all require to have their strong wine diluted by a very large admixture of insipid common sense."

The elected representative knows best what the electors (the people, the citizens) will stand and expert advice often needs to be tested in the light of what the people *want*. The people may not know what they want but that cannot be helped—that is one of the tricks of democracy!

Well, will the new system attract all the eager and enthusiastic and imaginative people it was (and is) intended to do? As has been said, *that* was one of the motivating factors behind the Great Upheaval of April 1, 1974. The answer to this question depends on what local government is all about. Is it today about anything interesting? Is it about anything important? Indeed, what is it about anyway?

Local government was at the peak of its heyday in 1930. All the duties of the *ad hoc* authorities of the nineteenth century had been successively handed over to the local government authorities established in 1888. Here is another reason why 1888 is such an important date. If 1888 is called the beginning then 1930 (if not the end) can be called the beginning of the end. The number of duties which local government has lost to new *ad hoc* authorities and to the central government is astonishing and enormous. Among many which it has lost can be mentioned: (1) gas and electricity; (2) hospitals; (3) transport (tramways and buses); (4) valuation for rating.

Undoubtedly the " sweep " of local government is nothing like so vast as it was. Of the powers that remain today, and are really important and worthwhile, it is submitted that education plus town planning control (including housing) are the only ones outstanding. (As a *local* government function education would seem to be balanced on a knife edge with the central government poised to snatch!)

Moreover, local government seems about to lose more for in the pipeline are proposals (if not, as yet, parliamentary Bills) to remove from local control many existing health functions together with the maintenance of sewers—that most traditional of all local government functions! In addition there is to be an ombudsman for local administration.

Does all this make local government a really worth-while vocation and, if so, what sort of a salary can elected honourable members rightly claim—always assuming we (the people) want professional and local government politicians *at all* (which is doubtful)?

It is a teasing question but a lot more is going to be heard about it—indeed the first murmurs have already been heard. It cannot be long now before the cry is taken up by the new councillors who, with less duties to perform than ever before (this is incontrovertible) take so much longer about their business. (*Quaere:* Whatever happened to the *officers* of local government authorities?)

In all of this one thing is certain, Sweet and Maxwell with 175 years of experience, watching and reporting the passing local government scene, will be more than ready to deal with all the vicissitudes of the future!

VIII
Procedure

Civil Procedure since 1800

I. H. JACOB

THE administration of civil justice plays a role of crucial importance in he life and culture of a civilised community. It constitutes the machinery or attaining what Lord Brougham called " justice between man and man."[1] It manifests the political will of the state that civil remedies must be provided for civil wrongs, that is, that infringements of private rights in the enjoyment of life, liberty and property must be made good so far as practicable by compensation and satisfaction or restrained if possible. It responds to the social need to give full and effective value to the substantive rights of members of society, which otherwise would be diminished or denuded of worth or even reality. It complements the system of criminal justice, the political and social necessity for which is perhaps more obvious and compelling, since it provides the machinery for the conviction and punishment or correction of offenders against the code of criminal wrongs. So it is that the administration of justice, both civil and criminal, lies at the heart of the law,[2] and the quality of justice, which is the touchstone of a civilised society, depends in large measure upon the arrangements provided for its administration.

For these reasons a survey of the system of the administration of civil justice since 1800, covering the organisation of the civil courts and their practices and procedures, could be both important and rewarding. At the outset, however, it needs to be stressed that, while the system prevailing at the beginning of the nineteenth century was itself the product of a long and continuous historical development stretching back to Anglo-Saxon times,[3] so the system prevailing today is not the last word on the subject, for we still have the inescapable duty and responsibility of reforming our own system to meet the changing needs of modern society and indeed to meet the needs of a changing society. In this respect, we may perhaps profit from some of the lessons of the history of changes in civil procedure and law, and particularly the changes made during the period under review, that the main directions in which such changes require to be made point towards the elimination, or at least the reduc-

---

1. *Speeches of Lord Brougham with Historical Introduction* (1838), Vol. 2, p. 324.
2. See Sir Maurice Amos, " A Day in Court at Home and Abroad " [1962] 2 C.L.J. 340.
3. See, e.g. Sir Frederick Pollock, " English Law before the Norman Conquest " (1898) 14 L.Q.R. 291–306, reprinted in *Select Essays in Anglo-American Legal History* (1907), Vol. 1, pp. 88–107.

tion, of vexation, delay and expense which Jeremy Bentham long ago characterised as " the burthens of judicial procedure," or in more specific terms, towards providing almost unhindered access to the courts and tribunals to all persons for the resolution of their civil disputes, whether large or small, removing the sense of fear and alienation of the masses of people at the prospect of resorting to legal machinery and lawyers, lifting the nightmare burden of the costs of litigation, freeing the procedures and practices of the courts from the fetters of technicalities and formalities, and increasing simplicity and flexibility in judicial administration in place of complexity and rigidity. At the same time we may perhaps also learn the need to deal with and to overcome some of the other lessons of this history, that changes in civil procedural law have been made slowly and with difficulty in piecemeal and fragmentary fashion and generally when they were long overdue,[4] that the legal profession was prepared to tolerate gross anomalies and archaic procedures and was in large measure resistant to changes in procedure,[5] and that only vigilant and informed public opinion, with whatever professional legal assistance which may be available, can accelerate the pace and ensure the proper changes of reform in civil procedural law.

It may be useful to begin by a general view of civil procedure in 1800, next to inquire what was the impetus for reform and what were the mechanics of change, and then to examine in a brief, panoramic view the changes made throughout the whole system, the organisation of the civil courts, their practices and procedures at all stages of proceedings, including the systems of remedies, appeals, enforcement of judgments and costs, and lastly to glance at the prospects for the future.

GENERAL VIEW OF CIVIL PROCEDURE IN 1800

From the vantage point of 175 years on, it may be said without exaggeration that in 1800[6] the system of civil justice in England appeared

4. See R. W. Millar, *Civil Procedure of the Trial Court in Historical Perspective* (1952), Chap. 1, " Procedural Evolution and the Anglo-American System."

5. See Edson R. Sunderland, " The English Struggle for Procedural Reform " (1925–26) 39 *Harvard Law Review* 725, and see W. S. Holdsworth, " The Development of Written and Oral Pleading " in *Select Essays in Anglo-American Legal History* (1908), Vol. 2, p. 640. " English law suffered at the close of the eighteenth century from a development too exclusively professional . . . . The unrestrained efforts of a hierarchy of professional lawyers are apt to produce results similar to those attributed by Maine (*Ancient Law*, pp. 19, 20) to the unrestrained efforts of a hierarchy of priests—' usage which is reasonable generates usage which is unreasonable.' "

6. This study has already been partly sketched, see Lord Bowen, " Progress in the Administration of Justice during the Victorian Period," published in *The Reign of Queen Victoria: A Survey of Fifty Years of Progress* (1887), Vol. 1, pp. 281–329, edited by T. H. Ward and reprinted in *Select Essays in Anglo-American Legal History* (1907), Vol. 1, pp. 516–557; W. Blake Odgers, " Changes in Procedure and in the Law of Evidence," published in *A Century of Law Reform* (1901), pp. 203–240; Augustine Burell, " Changes in Equity ,Procedure and Principles," *ibid.*, pp. 177–202; Lord Chorley, " Procedural

to be in a state in which there was very little system and precious little justice. It presented an incredible picture of institutional and procedural complexities and technicalities, anomalies and absurdities, archaic and even feudal practices, which operated in large measure to produce gross and palpable injustices in the sense that meritorious claims were delayed or denied or inhibited from being brought, and many meritorious defences went unheard. Apart from the fact that access to the courts was in practice out of the reach of the great majority of the people of the country, those who were able or were compelled to resort to the courts were subject to endless delays, fruitless wrangling, burdensome expense and mortifying vexations.

Law and equity

The broad features of the system of the administration of civil justice prevailing in England in 1800 may be briefly sketched.

The outstanding feature was the existence of two separate and distinct systems of judicature, the Court of Chancery administering equity in Lincoln's Inn, and the courts of common law administering law in Westminster Hall. The two jurisdictions had no common historical origin and administered justice on principles which were essentially unlike and which went far beyond the requirements of a rational division of labour. " The remedies they afforded to the suitor were different: the procedure was unreconcilable; they applied divers rules of right and wrong to the same matters."[7] " In the year 1800, what was right at law was wrong in equity. Judgment would be given on the same facts for the plaintiff in Westminster Hall and for the defendant at Lincoln's Inn." [8] The common law treated as untenable claims and defences which equity allowed, and conversely an injunction would frequently issue out of the Court of Chancery to restrain the plaintiff from enforcing the judgment that he had obtained at law. The Court of Chancery whose procedure was little adapted for the determination of controverted issues of fact was constantly compelled to have recourse for that purpose to the assistance of a court of law,[9] and conversely the suitor was often driven to equity to assist him in the prosecution even of a legal claim for

---

Reform in England," published in *David Dudley Field Centenary Essays* (1949), edited by Alison Reppy; and see also Sir William Holdsworth, *A History of English Law* (7th ed., 1956), Vol. 1, Chap. VIII, " The Reconstruction of the Judicial System," pp. 633–650, and *ibid.* (3rd ed., 1944), Vol. IX, Chap. VII, " Evidence, Procedure and Pleading," pp. 245–411. For a fuller treatment of the subject, see R. W. Millar, *Civil Procedure of the Trial Court in Historical Perspective* (1952); Samuel Rosenbaum, *The Rule-Making Authority in the English Supreme Court* (1917) (a valuable work not easily obtainable in England).

7. Bowen, *op. cit.*, p. 517.   8. W. Blake Odgers, *op. cit.*, p. 207.

9. The Court of Chancery also sent parties to law " whenever a legal right was to be established, when a decision on the construction of an Act of Parliament was to be obtained, a mercantile contract construed, a point of commercial law discussed," *op. cit.*, p. 518.

" the common law had no jurisdiction to prevent a threatened injury, could issue no injunctions to hinder it, was incompetent to preserve property intact until the litigation which involved the right to it was decided, and had no power of compelling litigants to disclose what documents in their possession threw a light upon the dispute or to answer interrogatories before trial." [10]

Theoretically the two jurisdictions were well-defined, but in practice there was often uncertainty as to the proper forum. Suits in Chancery were constantly dismissed because it appeared at the hearing that there was a remedy at law, while plaintiffs were non-suited at law because they should have sued in equity, and thus the bewildered litigant was driven backwards and forwards from law to equity and from equity to law.

" The conflict between the two systems, and their respective modes of redress, was one which, if it had not been popularly supposed to derive a sanction from the wisdom of our forefathers, might well have been deemed by an impartial observer to be expressly devised for the purpose of producing delay, uncertainty and untold expense." [11]

The superior courts of common law

The three ancient superior courts of common law were the Court of King's Bench, the Court of Common Pleas and the Court of Exchequer, each with a different history and originally different functions. In 1800 they flourished side by side and sat in Westminster Hall. By various devices, including the use of legal fictions, they had gradually acquired equal and concurrent jurisdiction over personal actions. By 1800, " no practical necessity was left for the maintenance side by side of three independent channels of justice, in each of which the streams ran in similar fashion and performed the same kind of work," [12] but there still remained some important differences between those three courts.

First, the Court of King's Bench still maintained jurisdiction of civil and criminal cases alike and exercised supreme supervisory authority over all inferior tribunals including civil corporations and public bodies and the justices of the peace, as well as over the Admiralty and ecclesiastical courts, with its two great weapons of mandamus and prohibition. The court consisted of the Chief Justice and three puisne judges.

Next, the Court of Common Pleas, which was historically the most ancient of the three, still retained, " with no particular benefit to society," [13] jurisdiction over the surviving forms of real actions though it also exercised general authority over personal actions. The court consisted of the Chief Justice and three puisne judges. Its practice, however, was marred in two ways: first, it enforced the restrictive practice of

10. Bowen, *op. cit.*, p. 518.
11. Bowen, *op. cit.*, p. 518.
12. *Ibid.*
13. *Ibid.* p. 519.

giving exclusive audience to serjeants-at-law during term time[14] and, secondly, the attorney had to advance out of his own pocket a proportion of the fees much earlier than was customary in the other courts.[15]

The Court of Exchequer still retained exclusive jurisdiction over revenue cases and some other matters, though it had power over all personal actions as well, and it also was a court of equity and assisted in Chancery business. The court consisted of the Chief Baron and three Barons of the Exchequer.

The procedure at common law as compared to the wants of the country had become antiquated, technical and obscure.

" From the beginning of the century, the population, the wealth, the commerce of the country had been advancing by great strides, and the ancient bottles were but imperfectly adapted to hold the new wines. At a moment when the pecuniary enterprises of the Kingdom were covering the world, when railways at home and steam upon the seas were creating everywhere new centres of industrial and commercial life, the common law courts of the realm seemed constantly occupied in the discussion of the merest legal conundrums which bore no relation to the merits of any controversies except those of pedants and in the direction of a machinery that belonged already to the past." [16]

Notwithstanding the pressure of a rapidly increasing volume of litigants, these courts in accordance with an antiquated system, sat during only four short terms of three weeks each, after which they dispersed to the Guildhall or the Assizes to try jury actions at *nisi prius*. Their procedure was based upon the system of special pleading, which, however admissible as a species of dialectic, inevitably promoted excessive technicality and absorption in mere forms. Just claims were liable to be defeated by trivial errors in pleading, by infinitesimal variances between pleading and proof and by the non-joinder or misjoinder of mere nominal parties. The arbitrary classification of actions into " forms of action " was another pitfall into which the most wary sometimes fell. If a surprise occurred at *nisi prius*, the court was unable to adjourn the proceedings a single day. And, as a crowning paradox, a fundamental rule of evidence excluded absolutely the testimony of the parties and of all witnesses who had the remotest interest in the result.[17]

The above summary indicates only very broadly what were the cumbrous procedures and pedantic technicalities, the anomalies and absurdities, which caused litigants in the common law courts expensive delay, vexation and disgust[18] and perhaps a description of some of

14. It was not till 1847 that this vexatious and injurious monopoly was finally abolished. See *The Serjeants' Case* (1839) 6 Bing. N.C. 187 for a desperate last-ditch struggle of the serjeants to preserve their monopoly.

15. Brougham, *Speeches*, p. 327.

16. Bowen, *op. cit.*, p. 520.

17. V. V. Veeder, " A Century of English Judicature 1800–1900 " in *Select Essays on Anglo-American Legal History* (1908), Vol. 2, p. 731.

18. Odgers, *op. cit.*, p. 212.

these features might help to savour the full flavour of the archaic, antiquated, and in some respects harsh, inflexible and harassing system of
civil procedure prevailing at common law in 1800.

The action of ejectment is a familiar and conspicuous example of the
survival of one of the legal fictions which, however useful when first
devised, had long outlived their absurd procedure. The normal parties
to an action to recover possession of land were two wholly imaginary
characters called John Doe and Richard Roe, personages who had no
more existence than Gog and Magog. The action was brought by John
Doe who averred that the true owner of the land had given him a lease
of the property in question but that Richard Roe had wrongfully ejected
him " with force and arms, that is to say, with swords, staves and knives,
entered the said tenement with the appurtenances and ejected the said
John out of his said tenement and other wrongs to him did." For his
part Richard Roe, being only a " casual ejector " notwithstanding his
apparent violence, advised the real defendant to appear in court and
procure himself to be the defendant in his place and this he was allowed
to do on the condition that he would not deny the existence of the lease
to John Doe or the forcible entry of Richard Roe; and this tissue of
invention of unreal persons and non-existent leases preceded every
investigation of the claim to possession of land.

In personal actions there were several different technical methods of
commencing proceedings, taking out process for bringing the defendant
to court,[19] which could be either a mesne summons or an attachment or
distringas against his property or a *capias* against his person, and which
could be common or special, bailable or not bailable, and upon a bailable *capias* the defendant would be either taken or stood out to the process
of outlawry. The right to arrest a defendant on mesne process, simply by
swearing an affidavit that the defendant owed the plaintiff £10 or
upwards and put him in prison, was a serious infringement of the freedom
of the person, but was tolerated as one of the methods of exercising
jurisdiction over the defendant. If he was served with the writ, the
defendant put in as sureties for the future appearance " common bail "
by the imaginary figures of John Doe and Richard Roe, but upon the
plaintiff's affidavit the defendant could be arrested and kept in prison
unless and until he put in a " special bail," *i.e.* until he found two real

19. The First Report of the Common Law Commissioners (1829) summarised these
as follows: In the King's Bench by Original Writ adapted to the Action or by Bill which
could be by (1) Attachment of Privilege, (2) Bill of Middlesex, (3) *Latitat*, (4) Bill and
Summons, the first three methods being either Bailable or not Bailable; in the Common
Pleas (1) by Original Writ adapted to the Action, (2) by Original Writ of *Quare Clasum
Fregit*, (3) by common *Capias* which was Bailable or not Bailable, (4) by Bill of Attachment of Privilege or (5) by Bill and Summons; in the Exchequer by (1) *Venire ad
Respondendum*, (2) *Subpoena ad Respondendum*, (3) *Quo Minus Capias*, (4) *Venire* of Privilege,
(5) *Capias* of Privilege and (6) Bill and Summons.

and substantial sureties for his appearance at the trial.[20] There was no machinery for the court to give judgment in default of appearance,[21] and there was no method of obtaining summary judgment without a trial in actions in which there was no defence.[22]

The plaintiff was bound at his peril to choose the right " form of action "[23]: if he selected the wrong one, he would be non-suited and would have to pay the defendant's costs though he could then begin again, making a second choice. Moreover, the plaintiff had to confine his action to one ground of claim, for he was not allowed to join in the same action two or more causes of action or complaint,[24] nor was he allowed to join in one action another plaintiff, or to bring one action against two or more defendants, to raise separate claims by the plaintiffs or against the defendants arising out of the same transaction.[25] The common law had no machinery to avoid multiplicity of proceedings, and did not allow the defendant to raise a counterclaim against the plaintiff or bring a third party into the proceedings.

The next stage of the proceedings, the stage of pleadings, was encrusted with technicalities and formulae, verbal refinements and subtleties in the statement of the case which too often defeated justice,[26] but nevertheless the highest praise was showered upon the system of pleading.[27] It was raised to the level of a " science " and the experts in this occult science were called " special pleaders." Their task was to formulate propositions of law, which the party whose pleading it was undertook to prove at the trial. " The old system of pleading at common law was to conceal as much as possible what was going to be proved at the

20. Tidd's *Practice* (9th ed., 1828) dealt with the subject of *Process* in over 150 pages.

21. See Preface to Vandervilt, *Cases and Materials on Modern Procedure and Judicial Administration*.

22. " Merchants were hindered for months and years from recovering their just due upon their bills of exchange," Bowen, *op. cit.*, p. 520.

23. The forms of action upon contract were Account, Assumpsit, Covenant, Debt, Annuity and *Scire Facias*; the actions for wrongs were Case, Detinue, Replevin and Trespass *vi et armis* (see Tidd's *Practice*, *ibid.*, p. 1).

24. So an action on a bond could not be joined with a claim on a bill of exchange, and an action on a covenant could not be joined with a claim for a simple contract debt. " A man who had been assaulted and accused of theft in the market-place of his town was obliged, if he wished redress for the double wrong, to issue two writs and to begin two litigations which wound their course through distinct pleadings to two separate trials " (Bowen, *op. cit.*, p. 520).

25. If two persons were injured in the same accident, separate actions would have to be brought by each of them (see Odgers, *op. cit.*, p. 213).

26. See W. S. Holdsworth, " The Development of Written and Oral Pleadings," in *Select Essays in Anglo-American Legal History* (1908), Vol. 2, pp. 614, 640.

27. See Co.Litt. i, 303a: " And know my son, that it is one of the most honourable, laudable and profitable things in our law to have the science of well pleading in actions real and personal "; and see Hobart, p. 295: " Cases arise by chance and are many times intricate, confused and obscured and are cast into forms and made evident, clear and easie by good and fair pleading, so that this is the principal art of the law."

trial."[28] The issue that emerged from the pleadings[29] had to be a single issue in law or in fact. The common law had no general power to allow the amendment of pleadings except under the Statutes of Jeofail which permitted variances between pleading and proof at trial to be corrected and, as observed above, there was no power to grant the discovery and inspection of all relevant documents save the limited right to crave *oyer* of deeds and copies of written instruments referred to in the pleadings or to order oral discovery by requiring specified interrogatories to be answered on oath. The result was that the parties would proceed to the trial of the issue of fact very much in the dark and subject to whatever surprise may be sprung by the opposite party.

The issue of law could of course be determined by the court and the pleadings would show whether, if the issue was of fact, it was triable by the court or at the Bar or at *nisi prius* by a jury, which could be a common or special jury. The jury trial was conducted in public, orally in open court when the witnesses of the parties would be called before the jury in turn and orally examined, cross-examined and re-examined, and the verdict would follow immediately after the speeches of counsel and the summing-up of the trial judge. As previously mentioned, however, the outstanding feature of the common law trial was that the parties themselves and anyone remotely interested in the result of the case, including members of their family, were rigorously excluded from giving any testimony before the court.

The remedies at common law were very limited and consisted in the case of the successful plaintiff in giving judgment for the recovery of money, goods or land or, rarely, for an account, and the costs of the action. The common law courts were powerless to grant any of the equitable remedies, such as injunction, specific performance, declaration, rectification, rescission.

28. *Per* Cotton L. J. in *Spedding* v. *Fitzpatrick* (1888) 38 Ch.D. 410.
29. The sequence of pleadings began with the Declaration of the plaintiff, which could be common or special and consist of one or more counts and could be in chief or by the bye or filed absolutely or *de bene esse*, and this was followed by the Plea of the defendant, who could plead to the jurisdiction of the court or in abatement or in bar or who could raise a demurrer to the Declaration, which could be either to the whole or part of the pleading and either general to the substance or special to the form, and he could raise one or more pleas, whether general as by pleading " the general issue " (which gave no indication as to what he admitted and what he denied and no indication what was the special ground of defence) or special. The Plea in turn was followed by the Replication by the plaintiff, which could be in denial or by way of confession and avoidance or estoppel or new assignment of the injury complained of or which could itself raise a demurrer to the Plea. These pleadings would be followed by the Rejoinder of the defendant, the Surrejoinder of the plaintiff, the Rebutter of the defendant and the Surrebutter of the plaintiff. No wonder that Baron Parke, who " for more than 20 years had bent all the powers of his great intellect to foster the technicalities and heighten the absurdities of the system of special pleading " (see Veeder, *op. cit.*, p. 747), earned the nickname of " Baron Surrebutter."

After trial and before verdict, the unsuccessful party could move the court for a new trial or in arrest of judgment or for judgment notwithstanding the verdict or a repleader or *venire facias de novo*. No appeal lay from the decision of the judge on any of these matters, but " error " would lie to the Exchequer Chamber only if it were apparent on the record or only from a special verdict arranged by the parties or directed by the judge. [30]

The enforcement of the judgment would lie against the goods of the judgment debtor, or his person [31] or his land or, if the judgment were extended, against his goods, person and land.

The Court of Chancery

The Court of Chancery administered a code of ethics which was searching and precise but which by 1800 had crystallised into an almost inflexible system. [32] It gave effect to rights beyond the reach of the common law, recognised equitable claims and defences which were untenable at law, awarded remedies which were unknown at law, gave assistance to the common law courts in the conduct of actions before them by way of the discovery of documents, and dealt with whole classes of transactions over which it had acquired a special cognisance. " But its practice was as dilatory and vexatious as its standard of right and wrong was noble and accurate." [33] The whole of its machinery except hearings in court was on paper and conducted in secret. It had no effective machinery for the examination or cross-examination of witnesses or for deciding matters of conflicting testimony but it had a wondrous machinery by the Bill in Chancery for allowing the plaintiff to " scrape the conscience of the defendant," and for the defendant to do like to the plaintiff by a cross-Bill.

" A bill in a Chancery suit was a marvellous document, which stated the plaintiff's case at full length and three times over. There was first the part in which the story was circumstantially set forth. Then came the part which 'charged' its truth against the defendant or in other words, which set it all forth over again in an aggrieved form. Lastly came the interrogating part, which converted the

30. See Bowen, *op. cit.*, p. 522.

31. " The imprisoned debtors (unless they could afford to pay extortionate sums for slightly better accommodation) were confined in small dark, damp, crowded rooms— rooms with no ventilation and often full of vermin. No bed was provided; the sexes were not separated; moral corruption and physical disease were the inevitable results. The misery which they suffered is powerfully described in the pages of Dickens and Thackeray " (Odgers, *op. cit.*, p. 219).

32. See *per* Lord Eldon L.C. in *Gee* v. *Pritchard* (1818) 2 Swan. 402 at p. 414: " the doctrines of this court ought to be as well settled and made as uniform as those of the common law, laying down fixed principles, but taking care that they are to be applied according to the circumstances of each case. I cannot agree that the doctrines of this court are to be changed with every succeeding judge. Nothing would inflict or give me greater pain in quitting this place than the recollection that I had done anything to justify the reproach that the equity of this court varies like the chancellor's foot."

33. Bowen, *op. cit.*, p. 524.

original allegations into a chain of subtly framed inquiries addressed to the defendant, minutely dovetailed and circuitously arranged so as to surround a slippery conscience and to stop up every earth."[34]

When the defendant made his " answer " on oath assisted by his solicitor and counsel,[35] it often became necessary for the plaintiff to restate his case by drawing an amended Bill which required another answer until at last the voluminous proceedings were completed and the cause was at issue.

The evidence for the hearing would be taken by interrogatories prepared beforehand and administered to the witness in private before an examiner or commissioner sworn to secrecy, and none of the parties was allowed to be present either by themselves or their agents. If the witness was to be cross-examined this could only be done upon written inquiries prepared equally in advance by a counsel who had never had the opportunity of seeing or hearing the witness. After the completion of the depositions, copies would be furnished to the parties at their own expense, and no further evidence was admissible, nor in general could any slip in the proofs be repaired except with leave, when the whole process would have to be gone through again.

The suit was then entered for hearing, but since in almost every case there were on an average two hearings, each destined to be separated by a period of something like two years, it was not uncommon for four years to be wasted in absolute inactivity, over and above any delays that might occur in taking accounts or prosecuting inquiries.[36] These delays were further greatly aggravated by the risk that a party to a suit might die while it was pending, so that it required to be reconstituted by a Bill of *revivor* or a supplemental Bill, and the whole process would have to be gone through again, and this event happened very frequently, since in a Chancery suit all parties interested in the result had to be parties to suit.[37] Moreover, when a decree was made at a hearing, the litigation was by no means over, since the case went into chambers and often accounts and inquiries were necessary under the supervision of a master.[38] Much of the delay of the Court of Chancery was attributable to the masters of the Court of Chancery, their officers and their staff of

34. Bowen, *op. cit.*, p. 524. No wonder that John Wesley described a Chancery Bill as " that foul monster," see Augustine Burell, *op. cit.*, p. 182. The Chancery Bill actually contained nine, not three, parts, *ibid.*, p. 181.

35. " The responsibility for the accuracy of the story shifted, during its telling, from the conscience of the defendant to that of his solicitor and counsel, and truth found no difficulty in disappearing during the operation." Bowen, *op. cit.*, p. 525.

36. Bowen, *op. cit.*, pp. 528–529.

37. See Bowen, *op. cit.*, p. 526. " It was satirically observed that a suit to which 50 defendants were necessary parties (a perfectly possible contingency) could never hope to end at all, since the yearly average of deaths in England was one in 50."

38. If objections were successfully taken to the master's report, the whole long process would have to begin *de novo*.

clerks.[39] There were some twenty-eight to thirty clerks in court, who were said to be the repositories of the practice of the court, and who were in theory nominally attached to or under " the Six Clerks " who each drew £1,000 a year but whom no one ever seems to have seen officially. The payment of these officials was by fees, which may explain why their work was protracted and delayed.

In 1800, the Court of Chancery had only two judges—the Lord Chancellor and the Master of the Rolls.[40] The slow progress of the Chancery business was further aggravated not only because the court was undermanned,[41] but because of the dilatoriness of Lord Eldon, the Lord Chancellor from 1802 to 1827,[42] in formulating his opinions. He also sat singly on appeals from the Master of the Rolls and the Vice-Chancellor and he presided in the House of Lords over the hearing of appeals from himself so that he had little time to bestow on his own duties as a Chancery judge of first instance. Not surprisingly, as Lord Bowen has remarked, " A formidable list of arrears naturally blocked the entrance to the Temple of Equity."[43] The delays were estimated to be of the order of twelve to fifteen years, and it was said that petitions filed in 1810 were still undisposed of in 1825.[44]

A good deal of Chancery business was non-contentious, where there was no real dispute between the parties, and the court was really called upon to exercise powers for the protection and the administration of property, but " though no one wished for war, all the forms of war had to be gone through: the action had to be fought from beginning to end

39. See Bowen, *op. cit.*, p. 529. " The office of the master of the court was one of historical dignity and antiquity. . . . A considerable portion of his judicial and ministerial duties he discharged by deputy. The work was done in private with closed doors, removed from the healthy publicity which stimulates the action of a judge. There was little practical power to expedite proceedings or force on the procrastinating litigant. . . . Much legal literature during the beginning of the reign [of Queen Victoria] was devoted to attacking and defending the institution of masters in Chancery; but when at a later period it fell, it fell with the general assent of the legal world."

40. Some equity work was carried out by the barons of the Court of Exchequer, but this was very limited and intermittent.

41. A Vice-Chancellor was appointed in 1813 to relieve the pressure but with not much success.

42. Bentham referred to him as the " Lord of Doubts," and see V. V. Veeder, " A Century of English Judicature 1800–1900," in *Select Essays in Anglo-American Legal History* (1907), Vol. 1, pp. 733–734.

43. Bowen, *op. cit.*, p. 528. In January 1839, " the total amount of causes set down and to be heard (before the Lord Chancellor, the Vice-Chancellor and the Master of the Rolls) was 859, and it was facetiously observed that a greater arrear would probably never appear in the lists of the Court of Chancery, seeing that it had become wholly useless to enter any cause which was not to be brought on out of its time as a short or consent cause." *Ibid.*

44. Odgers, *op. cit.*, p. 223. Bowen, *op. cit.*, at p. 529, reports the remark of Mr. George Spence, the author of a well-known work on the equitable jurisdiction of the Court of Chancery, made in 1839: " No man, as things now stand, can enter into a Chancery suit with any reasonable hope of being alive at its termination, if he has a determined adversary."

just as though every question of fact was in dispute and the parties were at daggers drawn."[45] Even in such cases, therefore, the whole elaborate Chancery procedures had to be followed, which necessarily involved delay, uncertainty and untold expense.

The system of Chancery procedure could and sometimes did produce ultimate justice, and at its formal stage, when the pleadings had been filed and refiled on amendment, all the interrogatories answered, all the depositions recorded, all the accounts taken, all the inquiries made, all the issues tried, all the objections of the masters' reports rejected, justice was no doubt done with vigour and exactitude, but the cost in terms of time, money and vexation was out of all proportion to what was achieved. " The honest suitor emerged from the ordeal victorious rather than triumphant, for too often he had been ruined by his way."[46] The picture of the Chancery suit of *Jarndyce* v. *Jarndyce* depicted by Charles Dickens in *Bleak House* contains genuine history,[47] and the pathetic cry of " honourable " practitioners to would-be litigants, warning them to avoid entering the portals and suffering the pitfalls of the Court of Chancery, was authentic and heartfelt: " Suffer any wrong that can be done you rather than come here."

Other courts

In addition to the three superior courts of common law and to that of Chancery, there were in 1800 a multitude of other courts in the land, each separate and distinct from the others, each with a different history, functioning with separate sectarian practices, with no uniform procedure, no unifying influences, and no system of common appeals. They presented a bewildering picture of a diffuse, disjointed and fragmented system of the administration of civil justice, with numerous courts exercising specialist or local jurisdiction throughout the country.

Among the more important of these courts were the following. There was the High Court of Admiralty, which sat at Doctors' Commons, and twice a year for criminal cases at the Old Bailey.[48] There were the ecclesiastical courts which also sat at Doctors' Commons,[49] which exercised authority over the personal estates of deceased persons testate and intestate.[50] There was the " Welsh Judicature," consisting of the

45. Blake Odgers, *op. cit.*, p. 226, and Bowen, *op. cit.*, p. 527.
46. Bowen, *op. cit.*, p. 526.
47. Bowen, *op. cit.*, p. 538.
48. According to Lord Bowen, *op. cit.*, p. 534, this court " was rescued from obscurity by the great wars of the reign of George III, by the prize cases for which it was the necessary tribunal, and by the genius of Lord Stowell."
49. A body of advocates and proctors enjoyed a monopoly in Doctors' Commons from which the general legal profession was excluded from audience and practice. The fraternity of Doctors' Commons and the ecclesiastical officials who thronged its purlieus are faithfully sketched by Charles Dickens in *David Copperfield*.
50. These spiritual courts included the courts of the Archbishops of Canterbury and York, the diocesan courts of the bishops, the archdeacons' courts and other tribunals of

Courts of Great Sessions, which had existed since the reign of Henry VIII. There were the three ancient Palatine Courts of the Duchy of Lancaster, the County of Chester, and the County of Durham. There were numerous borough and local inferior courts of record, of which the more important were the Lord Mayor's Court in the City of London, the Tolzey Court of Bristol, the Liverpool Court of Passage, the Salford Hundred Court and the Norwich Guildhall Court[51]; and there were courts held by the sheriff[52] and Courts of the Cinque Ports.[53] There were also some remnants of the ancient county courts or courts of requests established in different localities by separate statutes, which had formerly some limited jurisdiction to collect small debts only, and which were wholly inadequate to the needs of the provinces and were practically obsolete by 1800; and there were Courts Leet and Courts Baron which exercised some civil jurisdiction in cases concerning land. There were then, however, no local inferior courts of general jurisdiction for dealing with small claims or debts such as our present system of county courts. There was no Court of Divorce; and of course there was no system of tribunals exercising judicial functions outside the ordinary courts of law.

GENERAL VIEW OF PROCEDURAL CHANGES SINCE 1800

The present system of the administration of civil justice bears hardly any resemblance to the system prevailing at the beginning of the nineteenth century as described above. The changes made during the intervening period have completely transformed the system almost beyond recognition, and the transformation has taken place in almost the whole area of judicature and procedure. Viewing the entire system across the gulf of 175 years, it is hardly credible that the present system should bear any affinity, still less owe its parentage, to the system prevailing in 1800. But such a telescopic view, while permissible as an exercise in historical perspective, does not necessarily convey a true or accurate picture of the relation between the past system and the present, for it misses out some essential aspects of the middleground, the landscape between the two promontories. The fundamental changes from the old to the new

---

still more limited jurisdiction such as the Court of Arches, a branch of which was the Court of Peculiars (both of which heard appeals from the ecclesiastical courts), a Faculty Court, which granted dispensations to marry and a Court of Delegates for ecclesiastical affairs. " All judges and officers of the spiritual courts were appointed by the prelates; they were sometimes lawyers of position, sometimes lawyers of no position at all, sometimes clergymen, and were usually paid by fees. Many offices were granted in succession and reversion, deputies discharging the duties, of which the emoluments were considerable . . . these tribunals were a soil in which abuses grew and flourished." Bowen, *op. cit.*, p. 535.

51. See Halsbury's *Laws of England* (3rd ed., 1954), Vol. 9, Title, *Courts*, Part 11 " Borough and Local Courts of Record."

52. *Ibid*. Part 12.

53. *Ibid*. Part 13.

system which revolutionised the administration of civil justice, were made in stages, mainly during the period of forty-five years from 1830 to 1875. During this period, there was a slow gradual progression of the old system developing into the new, starting with the Uniformity of Process Act 1832, followed during the middle period from 1850 to 1860 with an accelerated pace by three Common Law Procedure Acts of 1852, 1854 and 1860, and three Chancery Practice Amendment Acts of 1850, 1852 and 1858, and then a great stride forward with the Judicature Acts of 1873 and 1875, after which the system took on the basic features of its modern form which has been continually developing ever since. The old order changed and yielded its place to the new which in time became the old order which changed and yielded its place to the further new; and so there has been and still is a continual process of change, linking the several steps of change each to the other, and thus imparting the sense and flavour as well as the reality of the continuity of the present civil judicial process with the past.

There are, however, two more fundamental features of the present system of civil justice, which indelibly mark its lineage with the past, namely, its adversary character and the role of the court and the orality, immediacy and publicity of its proceedings.

The present system has retained its adversary character, under which the parties play the predominant role in the conduct of the litigation, and the court plays a passive and neutral role until the actual trial itself which then comes under the predominant control of the court. The parties retain the initiative at all stages of civil proceedings; it is left to them to raise by their pleadings the issues and questions in dispute between them, to prepare and present their respective cases on their own, to call what witnesses, including expert witnesses, they want and in the order of their choice, to conduct the examination and cross-examination of the witnesses before the court. As a corollary, the court plays an inactive role throughout the whole of the proceedings except when called upon to decide questions or issues raised by the parties and except to control the conduct of the trial and of the proceedings before it. The court has no power to conduct a preliminary investigation of the case, to call or to examine witnesses before or at the trial, to call for reports by its own expert witnesses or to act of its own motion against the will of the parties, at any stage of the proceedings.[54]

Moreover, the present system has retained the ancient common law features of orality, immediacy and publicity, rather than the Chancery system, which was largely written and the parties and witnesses examined in secret and not orally or openly or immediately before the trial court.

54. See Jacob, " The English System of Civil Proceedings " (1963–64) 1 C.M.L.Rev. 314.

The great virtues of the common law system, distinguishing it from the civil law system prevailing on the Continent of Europe, were thus saved,[55] and they constitute the bulwark of the fundamental right to a fair trial.

It may well be that some other factors, cultural, traditional as well as procedural, have also contributed to imparting the semblance of continuity between the past system and the present. The position of the judiciary, independent of the executive and held traditionally in high regard and esteem by the community at large as the repository of justice under the law, has remained much the same today as it was in 1800, with possibly increased authority and influence. The binding or persuasive force of precedents, which have an almost unbroken sequence from the Year Books, brings the old law and practice very much to the forefront of the present day. The names of some of our present institutions and practices, such as the Chancery Division, the Queen's Bench Division, the Admiralty Court, the terms pleadings, discovery, interrogatories echo similar institutions and practices of the past, and help to clothe them in the garb of the new. And lastly the sense of security is greatly strengthened and comforted by the belief, whether well-founded or not, that however much things may have changed, the basic structure of what was still remains.

IMPETUS FOR REFORM

This belief, however, should not blind us to the fact that the system of civil justice prevailing in 1800 has been completely replaced by an entirely new system, and the question may be asked, what was the impetus for reform?

At the outset, it should be stressed that the impetus for the reform of the administration of civil justice did not come from the general body of the legal profession or the judiciary; it came in despite of them.[56] On the contrary, so far as the Bench and Bar were concerned, they basked in the euphoria engendered by Blackstone's extravagant eulogies of the prevailing system and his resounding phrases extolling " its solid foundations . . . its extensive plan . . . the harmonious concurrence of its several parts . . . the elegant proportions of the whole."[57] " The common law in its substance and procedure was by everybody in England regarded with a veneration superstitious to the point of idolatry. It was declared,

---

55. See Millar, *op. cit.*, p. 36.

56. See W. S. Holdsworth, " The Movement for Reforms in the Law (1793–1832) " (1940) 56 L.Q.R. Part I, p. 33, Part II " The Principal Pioneers of Law Reform," *ibid.* p. 208, and Part III, " Brougham's Speech of 1828," 340; and see especially Edson R. Sunderland, " The English Struggle for Procedural Reforms " (1925–1926) 39 Harv.L.R. 725.

57. 4 *Blackstone Commentaries* 443, and see 3 *Blackstone Commentaries* 268.

and generally believed to be ' the perfection of reason '."[58] The practitioners' books dealt with procedure as though based upon principles of ultimate utility, and as late as 1828, Tidd felt able to remark of the reigns of George III and George IV " that it may with truth be affirmed that in no period of our history has the law been better administered."[59] Above all reigned Lord Eldon, the Lord Chancellor, " who absolutely opposed all change in his own court as well as in the common law courts . . . and resisted reforms in the common law procedure as encroachments upon equity."[60]

The impetus for reform is not a matter of mere chance, for change must be fashioned by human hands and brains. It often and perhaps always requires the conjunction of three factors, the objective social conditions, the theoretical spark, and a sustained and informed public opinion which together call for change. On such a full sea was the administration of civil justice in England in 1800 then afloat.

The objective social conditions in 1800 were fully ripe for change when the rapid growth of manufacturing industry, of trade and of population, coupled with the influence as well of new ideas in the sphere of government as of advances made in economics and social sciences, had shaken men loose from many old traditions or prejudices and had, while rendering much of the old law inapplicable, made a great deal of new legislation indispensable.[61]

The theoretical spark was provided by Jeremy Bentham and his followers including Lord Brougham, Sir Samuel Romilly, Bickersteth (later Lord Langdale M.R.), James Mackintosh, James Mill and John Stuart Mill. Bentham's influence in the field of law reform, particularly the administration of justice, has been immense, pervasive, far-reaching, and it is still operative. His was the almost solitary voice raised against the chorus of professional praise of the judicial system in 1800, but it was a voice crying in the wilderness.[62] He maintained that the existing law, so far from being the perfection of human reason or the product of matured experience was but " a fathomless and boundless chaos, made up of fiction, tautology, technicality and inconsistency, and the administrative part of it a system of exquisitely contrived chicanery which

58. J. F. Dillon " Bentham's Influence in the Reforms of the Nineteenth Century," in *Select Essays in Anglo-American Legal History* (1907), Vol. I, p. 494.

59. Tidd's *Practice* 9th. ed. (1828), Preface, p. ix.

60. J. M. Zane, " The Five Ages of the Bench and Bar of England," in *Select Essays in Anglo-American Legal History* (1907) Vol. I, p. 724, and see Sunderland, *op. cit.*, p. 728. " As the political head of the legal cult, Lord Eldon sat on the woolsack for almost a generation (1802–1827) keen, alert, steadfast, tireless, fearful of innovations, devoting all the resources of a powerful and technical mind to the preservation of the current practice of the day."

61. James Bryce, " A Comparison of the History of Legal Development at Rome and in England," in *Select Essays in Anglo-American Legal History* (1907) Vol. I, p. 336.

62. Sunderland, *op. cit.*, p. 728.

maximises delay and denial of justice." [63] He wished to rebuild the whole system anew, using old materials so far as they were useful and no other. Lord Brougham said of him " The age of reform and the age of Jeremy Bentham are one and the same. No one before him had ever seriously thought of exposing the defects in our English system of jurisprudence." [64] Sir Henry Maine said in 1874: " I do not know a single law reform effected since Bentham's day which cannot be traced to his influence.[65] Bentham did not produce a code of civil procedure, as David Dudley Field produced the New York Code of Civil Procedure, but his influence may be attributed to his theory of utility as a working rule of legislation, and to his tireless and unremitting challenge of the artificial, unsystematic, over-elaborate procedure at law and in equity when it was firmly held by the profession to be in no need of reform.[66]

The third factor which contributed to the transformation of the English system of civil justice prevailing in 1800 was the force of public opinion, expressed through the columns of influential periodicals.[67] As Professor Sunderland remarks,

" the striking characteristic of the British revolt against the apotheosis of legal formalism was its popular origin and support [68]. . . One is amazed by the violence of the attack which the public directed and maintained for at least two generations through the press. It was not only a war against legal abuses, but a class struggle against a profession which was believed to be responsible for them." [69]

The press campaign was further strengthened by the work and publications of the Society for Promoting the Amendment of the Law, and later the National Association for the Promotion of Social Science which Lord Brougham founded in 1857.[70] One of the more important achieve-

63. Dillon, *op. cit.*, p. 496.
64. Brougham, *Speeches, op. cit.*, p. 288.
65. *Early History of Institutions*, Lecture XIII, cited Dillon, *op. cit.*, p. 492. Sir James Stephen said, " Bentham's theories upon legal subjects have had a degree of practical influence for the legislation of his own and various other countries comparable only to those of Adam Smith and his successors upon commerce," cited Dillon, *op. cit.*, p. 492. Macaulay said of him that he was " the man who found jurisprudence a gibberish and left it a science," cited Dillon, *op. cit.*, p. 493. For a comparison between Bentham and David Dudley Field, see Roscoe Pound, " David Dudley Field: an Appraisal " in *Field Centenary Essays (1949)*, p. 1 ; for an account of the influence of Bentham in civil law countries, see R. W. Millar, " Civil Procedure Reform in Civil Law Countries," *ibid.* p. 137.
66. See Roscoe Pound, *op. cit.*, p. 4. See also Zagday, " Bentham on Civil Procedure " in *Jeremy Bentham and the Law* (1948) (Stevens).
67. See Edson R. Sunderland, " The English Struggle for Procedural Reform (1921–26)," 39 Harv.L.R. 725, which sets out a penetrating study of contemporary opinion on the subject, citing the views expressed in the *Edinburgh Review*, the *Westminster Review*, the *London Spectator*, the *Saturday Review*, the *Illustrated London News*, and *The Times*, whose " editorial columns thundered against the abuses of the system and the beneficiaries of those abuses," *ibid.* p. 730.
68. *Ibid.* p. 729.   69. *Ibid.* p. 731.
70. For an interesting light on law reform during the nineteenth century, see Sir Cecil Carr, *A Victorian Law Reformer's Correspondence* (1955), Selden Society Annual Lecture.

ments of the Law Amendment Society was its scheme for the collection and collation of civil judicial statistics about which its report of 1857 stated, " Such statistics afford the best, if not the only means of noting the practical working of laws and tribunals of listing the principles of legal reform, and of estimating the utility of any system of jurisprudence by the testimony of actual fact." [71]

THE MECHANICS OF CHANGE

Given the impetus for the reform of the administration of civil justice, the question arises how was such reform brought about? What were the mechanics of the change from the old to the new system?

The machinery for reform in this field as in many similar areas has followed a fairly regular, familiar pattern. When sufficient interest or pressure was aroused for changes to be made and could no longer be stemmed, the government of the day would decline to form its own political judgment as to whether any and if so what reforms should be made. Such a question would be removed from the area of party politics; and the government would profess to be interested but neutral about the problems of change. It would accordingly set up a commission or committee consisting mainly of judges and members of the legal profession, with an occasional sprinkling of lay members, to inquire into the problem, and to make recommendations as to what changes were necessary or desirable, with terms of reference which were generally limited, though quite often implicitly containing a hint or two as to the general direction of change. The commission or committee would take " evidence " from interested bodies and persons, and then publish its report with its recommendations for changes to be made. The government of the day would consider the report and its recommendations, and would adopt or adapt such of them as it thought fit and would implement such recommendations by proposing the necessary legislation in the form of statute or statutory Rules of Court. Thereafter a pause would ensue, as though the legal profession and the system of civil justice required to absorb the new changes and adapt themselves to the new conditions. The pattern has thus been, commission or committee—report and recommendations—legislation—pause. Almost every single change made since 1800 to this day in the organisation of the civil courts and in civil procedure has followed this pattern.

The movement for the reform of the system of civil justice in England since 1800 may be said to have been definitively inaugurated by the celebrated speech of Henry Brougham in the House of Commons on

71. Cited in the Report of the Committee on Civil Judicial Statistics (1968) Cmnd. 3684, p. 2.

February 7, 1828.[72] At the end of his speech, he proposed the appointment of a commission to inquire into the defects of the law. In fact two commissions were appointed, one of which was to inquire into the practice and procedure of the courts of common law, which issued six reports between 1829 and 1834.[73]

After a pause of about twenty years two further commissions were appointed in 1850, the one to inquire into the practice and procedure of the superior courts of common law, which issued three reports in 1851, 1852–53 and 1860, and the other to inquire into the procedure of the Court of Chancery, and the main recommendations of its Reports were embodied in three Common Law Procedure Acts 1852, 1854 and 1860 and four Chancery Practice Amendment Acts 1850, 1852, 1858 and 1860. There followed another pause, this time slightly shorter, of about fifteen years.[74] The powerful and influential Judicature Commission was appointed, which issued two reports in 1868 and 1869, which led to the passing of the Judicature Acts of 1873 and 1875. These Acts, together with the Rules of Court made thereunder, have firmly laid the foundations of the structure of civil judicature and procedure which has prevailed ever since, and though there have been many changes, improvements, refinements and developments since then, following the Reports of many commissions and committees, the system of civil justice remains today substantially as it was created by the Judicature Acts of 1873 and 1875.

It remains now briefly to sketch the main outlines of the system as it prevails today.

THE ORGANISATION OF THE CIVIL COURTS

The main thrust of the changes in the administration of civil justice since 1800 has been in the direction of establishing a single system of courts administering a uniform code of procedure.

72. See *Speeches of Lord Brougham with Historical Introduction* (1838), Volume 11, pp. 319–486. It was said that he spoke for six hours, during which he exhausted a hatful of oranges—the only refreshment then tolerated by the rules of the House. For a summary of this speech, see W. S. Holdsworth, " The Movement for Reform in the Law (1793–1832) " (1940) 56 L.Q.R. 340. Brougham omitted to deal with equity and commercial law and much of the law of real property, but otherwise the speech set out to give a survey of the main defects in English law and to suggest remedies, and the main subjects he dealt with were the Courts, Procedure, Pleading and Evidence. Nevertheless, Bentham expressed quiet disappointment and disgust, remarking " Mr. Bentham's mountain is delivered, and behold, a mouse. The wisdom of the reformer could not overcome the craft of the lawyer."

73. The members of the commission to inquire into the practice and procedure of the courts of common law were Bosanquet, Parke, Alderson and Stephen, and on the first three of these being raised to the Bench they were replaced by Pollock, Starkie, Evans and Wightman. A commission to inquire into the work of the Court of Chancery) had earlier presented two reports in 1826 and 1828 but no legislation had resulted until 1830.

74. The Judicature Commission was appointed in 1867.

So far as the organisation of the courts was concerned, the changes came in stages. First the " Welsh Judicature " was abolished[75]; a Court of Probate was established in 1857 to deal with the estates of deceased persons testate and intestate, in place of the ecclesiastical courts[76]; and a new court for Divorce and Matrimonial Causes was created in 1858.[77] Following the recommendations of the judicature commissions, the Lord Chancellor, Lord Selborne, with the assistance of Lord Cairns and aided by the law officers (later Lord Chief Justice Coleridge and Sir George Jessel, Master of the Rolls) carried through Parliament the Supreme Court of Judicature Act 1873, which was amended by the Judicature Act 1875, and came into force on November 2, 1875. These Acts took the final dramatic leap forward by creating the Supreme Court of Judicature consisting of the Court of Appeal and one single High Court of Justice in which there were conjoined together the former Courts of Chancery, the three superior courts of common law, the Court of Probate, the Court of Divorce and the High Court of Admiralty. Instead of separate " courts," there were new tribunals under the style of " divisions " of the High Court, consisting of the Chancery Division, the Queen's Bench Division[78] and the Probate, Divorce and Admiralty Division.

The outstanding contribution of the Judicature Acts was not merely in the creation of a single High Court, but above all in the integration, or as it has been familiarly called, " the fusion " of law and equity. Every division and every judge of the High Court is vested with the same plenary powers and jurisdiction, and law and equity must be administered by them in every civil cause or matter equally.[79] The High Court must give effect to all equities of the plaintiff,[80] to all equitable defences,[81] and to all common law statutory rights and duties[82] and the old procedure of filing a Bill in Chancery to restrain the plaintiff from proceeding at law was abolished.[83] The overriding objective of the Judicature Acts was that the High Court and the Court of Appeal, in the exercise of the jurisdiction vested therein, had the amplitude of power to grant all such

75. See 11 Geo. IV & 1 William IV. c. 70 which implemented the recommendations of the First Report of Common Law Commissioners in 1829. " Whether the alteration was in the end a benefit to Wales has been doubted by competent critics," see Odgers, *op. cit.*, p. 231; and see Holdsworth, H.E.L. Vol. 1, p. 131.

76. See Court of Probate Act 1857.

77. See Matrimonial Causes Act 1857.

78. Under the Judicature Acts, the Court of Queen's Bench, the Court of Common Pleas and the Court of Exchequer had continued their separate identities as separate Divisions; but by an Order in Council in 1881, they were amalgamated into a single Division, called the Queen's Bench Division.

79. Supreme Court of Judicature (Consolidation) Act 1928, s.36.

80. *Ibid.* s. 37.

81. *Ibid.* s. 38.

82. *Ibid.* s. 42.

83. *Ibid.* s. 41.

remedies whatsoever as any party may appear to be entitled to in respect of any legal or equitable claim properly brought so that as far as possible, " all matters in controversy between the parties may be completely and finally determined and all multiplicity of legal proceedings concerning any of these matters avoided."[84]

Nearly 100 years later the structure and organisation of the High Court, while retaining the main framework, have nevertheless undergone far-reaching and radical changes. Partly by the Administration of Justice Act 1970,[85] and partly by the Courts Act 1971,[86] the High Court has been reconstituted and its business redistributed, so that it now consists of the following three divisions:

(a) Chancery Division to which contentious probate actions have been transferred and from which matters relating to infants including wardship have been transferred to the Family Division.

(b) Queen's Bench Division, which now includes two separate specialised courts, namely (1) the Admiralty Court and (2) the Commercial Court; and

(c) Family Division, which deals with all matters concerning matrimonial and family relations and property.

The new Admiralty Court constituted within the Queen's Bench Division retained the same judge, registrar and staff as the old Admiralty Division; and the new Commercial Court of the Queen's Bench Division handles the business formerly dealt with in Commercial Court.[87]

The Courts of Assize, whose history stretches back over 700 years to the origins of the common law itself, have been abolished, and they have been replaced, so far as civil actions are concerned by a number of authorised trial centres in the main provincial towns in six circuits into which the country has been divided. The High Court judges still " go on circuit " but no longer to open the Assizes of each of the county towns.[88]

A great advance forward to decentralise the work of the High Court in London was made by the creation of District Registries[89] which are branches of the High Court in the country. There are now nearly 130

---

84. *Ibid.* s. 43.

85. Implementing in part the recommendations of the Second Interim Report of the (Evershed) Committee on Supreme Court Practice and Procedure (1951) Cmd. 8176.

86. Implementing the recommendations of the Report of the Royal Commission on Assizes and Quarter Sessions (Beeching Report) (1969) Cmnd. 4153.

87. See Lord Justice Scrutton, " The Work of the Commercial Courts " (1923) 1 C.L.J. 6.

88. Special provision is made for the hearing of Chancery proceedings in specified trial centres.

89. See Judicature Act 1873, s. 60 as amended by the Judicature Act 1875, s. 13. And see District Registries Order in Council 1899.

District Registries, and between them they deal with about the same volume of common law as the Queen's Bench Division does in London.[90]

The Judicature Acts created the office of " Official Referee "[91] to enable prolonged or detailed inquiries and accounts to be dealt with by separate offices, and so as to relieve the main body of judges from performing their ordinary judicial duties. This office has now as such been abolished,[92] but " official referee business " continues to be conducted by circuit judges appointed to perform this function, both in London and in each of the other five circuits.

In addition to the broad framework of the High Court as described above there are other specialist courts, which should perhaps be mentioned, including the Patents Appeal Tribunal, the Companies Court, the Bankruptcy Court, the Court of Protection and the two somewhat hybrid courts, the Restrictive Practices Court and the National Court of Industrial Relations.

So far as the courts of inferior jurisdiction are concerned, after a long struggle and several false starts[93] in 1846 the county courts were established with a jurisdiction limited to £20.[94] From time to time, the jurisdiction was extended, and the present limit of £750, which was recently imposed[95] looks already very much out of date, and it seems very probably that the jurisdiction will be increased to £1,000, or even £1,500.[96] At the same time, almost all the borough and local courts of record have been or are in the course of being abolished,[97] with the consequence that the county courts will remain almost the sole civil courts of inferior jurisdiction. It is perhaps worth stressing that in fact the great bulk of civil business is conducted in the county courts,[98] whose jurisdiction has been extended to a great variety of matters, including divorce in undefined cases, and to many matters relating to infants.

90. See Civil Judicial Statistics (1972) Cmnd. 5333, Table 7, p. 9.
91. Judicature Act 1873, ss. 56 and 57, and see Roland Burrows, " Official Referees " (1923) 1 C.L.J. 504.
92. See Courts Act 1971, s. 25 (1).
93. See W. S. Holdsworth, " The Movement for Reform in the Law (1793–1832) " (1940) 56 L.Q.R. 37: " In 1820 and 1824, Lord Redesdale proposed to establish efficient county courts for the recovery of small debts; and in 1824, Lord Eldon agreed that some such measure was necessary. In 1828, Lord Althorp, . . . proposed the establishment of local courts. . . . In 1824, a bill to establish these courts was proposed; in 1828 the subject was taken up by Peel, and in 1830 by Brougham " (see Brougham, *Speeches*, Volume II, " Local Courts ").
94. County Courts Act 1846.
95. See Administration of Justice Act 1969, Part I.
96. This was recommended by both the (Beeching) Royal Commission on Assizes and Quarter Sessions (1969) Cmnd. 4153 and the (Winn) Committee on Personal Injuries Litigation (1968) Cmnd. 3691.
97. See the Courts Act 1971, ss. 42 and 43, and the Local Government Act 1972, s. 221 and Sched. 28.
98. In 1972 the number of actions commenced in the county courts was 1,676,722 (see Civil Judicial Statistics (1972) Cmnd. 5333, Table 22, p. 78).

In 1882 the Central Office of the Supreme Court was established to deal with the administrative side of the Chancery Division and the Queen's Bench Division, and it was managed under the supervision of the Masters of the Queen's Bench Division. The administrative work of the other superior courts was managed separately, and the county courts were managed by the Lord Chancellor's Department.[99] In 1971, however, a unified administrative court service had been set up under the control of the Lord Chancellor. The country is divided into six circuits each under the administrative control of a circuit administrator, who, subject to the supervisory control of the presiding judges appointed for each circuit, is responsible for the efficient conduct of business in the High Court, the Crown Court and the county courts in his circuit. Each circuit is further divided into areas containing county courts and a centre or centres of the High Court and the Crown Court, with a courts administrator in each area responsible to the circuit administrator.

RULES OF COURT

At common law, the courts assumed jurisdiction to make general rules for the regulation of the practice before them,[1] and it was said that the practice is the law of the court, and as such a part of the law of the land.[2] But by the Civil Procedure Act 1833, s. 3, power was conferred on the common law judges to make rules which had statutory form, for the reform of pleading.[3] Such power was extended in its scope[4] and also to the Court of Chancery[5]; and the Judicature Acts conferred powers on the Rule Committee constituted thereunder, to make rules to regulate " the practice and procedure " of the Supreme Court.[6] Under these powers, the Rules of the Supreme Court 1883 were made, to replace the Rules of Court which were scheduled to the Judicature Act 1875, and they remained in force with many additions and alterations for about eighty years. As a result of the recommendations of the (Evershed) Committee on the Supreme Court Practice and Procedure made in the strongest terms that a complete revision of the Rules be immediately put

99. See Lord Chorley, " Procedural Reform in England " in *Field Centenary Essays* (1949), p. 109.

1. See *Bartholomew* v. *Carter* (1841) 3 Man. & G. 125. See also S. Rosenbaum, *The Rule-Making Authority in the English Supreme Court* (1917), p. 4.

2. See Tidd's *Practice* (9th ed., 1828), Introduction, p. lxxi.

3. Under this power, the Hilary Rules were made in 1834. See 10 Bing. 453–475. For a criticism of the operation of these Rules, see W. S. Holdsworth, " The New Rules of Pleading of the Hilary Term 1834 " (1923) 1 C.L.J. 261. " Never was a more disastrous mistake made."

4. Common Law Procedure Act 1852, ss. 223–225; Common Law Procedure Act 1854, ss. 97–98.

5. Chancery Practice Amendment Act 1850, ss. 30–32; Chancery Amendment Act 1858, ss. 11–12, by virtue of which the beneficial Consolidation Orders of 1860 were issued.

6. See s. 99 of the Judicature Act 1925.

in hand,"[7] the entire rules were revised and rewritten, first by a partial revision in 1962 and the entire revision completed in 1965. The Rules of the Supreme Court 1965 were published and came into force on October 1, 1966.[8] These Rules, it has been said, provide a landmark in the history of English civil procedure, for not only do they lie at the very foundation of the machinery of justice, but they shape the whole course of civil litigation, and lay down the guide-lines which the parties must follow in the conduct of the proceedings. The Rules are clear, certain, comprehensive, consistent and coherent, and their outstanding achievement is their simple, logical rearrangement, providing the framework of a code of civil procedure.

A change of fundamental importance was made in relation to the effect of non-compliance with the requirements of the Rules. In all such cases, such non-compliance whatever form it takes must be treated, not as a nullity, but as an irregularity which the court will have power to amend or rectify or regularise.[9] This power, together with the extended powers of amendments after the expiry of the current period of limitation,[10] is intended to prevent technical defects or errors in proceedings from being fatal in themselves and to remove some of the blots which " have marred our copybook." [11] They go a long way towards reaching out to the rather exuberant remark made by Lord Bowen [12] that " It may be asserted without fear of contradiction that it is not *possible* in the year 1887 for an honest litigant in Her Majesty's Supreme Court to be defeated by any mere technicality, any slip, any mistaken step in his litigation." This ideal state has yet to be achieved.

PRE-TRIAL PROCEDURES

(a) *Commencement of actions*

Turning now to the actual progress of proceedings, one of the first fundamental changes in procedure made since 1800 was the abolition of arrest on mesne process [13] or the power to seize goods or property before judgment, and the introduction of a uniform method of commencing civil actions, by writ of summons.[14] There are now four modes of com-

---

7. Second Interim Report (1951) Cmd. 8176, p. 46.

8. For a summary of the main changes introduced by the revised Rules, see Jacob (1963) *The Legal Executive*, p. 263; Neane, *ibid.* p. 272; Jacob (1966) *The Legal Executive*, p. 167; Hawkins, *ibid.* p. 181.

9. See R.S.C., Ord. 2, and see *Harkness* v. *Bell's Asbestos & Engineering Ltd.* [1967] 2 Q.B. 729, C.A.

10. See R.S.C., Ord. 20, r. 5.

11. See *per* Lord Denning M.R. in *Re Pritchard Decd.* [1963] Ch. 502 at p. 518.

12. Bowen, *op. cit.*, p. 541.

13. An insignificant survival of this process exists under the Debtors Act 1869, s. 6, and the equivalent process under the writ of *ne exeat regno*, see *Felton* v. *Callis* [1969] 1 Q.B. 200.

14. See Uniformity of Process Act 1832.

mencing proceedings,[15] and some would think it is desirable that these should be reduced to one single mode for commencing civil proceedings of every kind. Generally speaking, original process has to be served personally on an individual defendant,[16] though again some would think the methods of service could be conveniently extended.

(b) *Default judgments*

Another fundamental change in procedure introduced in 1832 was the power of the court to allow judgment in default of appearance to be entered, without the need for the attendance of the defendant or the proof of simple claims.[17]

(c) *Joinder of parties and of causes of action*

The common law rules precluding the joinder of parties and causes of action were greatly modified by the Common Law Procedure Acts of 1852, 1854 and 1860 and were greatly liberalised by the Judicature Acts, and the Rules of the Supreme Court. The overriding principles which now prevail are: (a) that all necessary and proper parties, but no others, should be before the court to enable the effectual and complete determination to be made of all the issues and questions arising in the proceedings, and (b) that all the disputes or questions arising between such parties should be determined, so as to avoid the multiplicity of proceedings.

To this end no action will be defeated by reason of the misjoinder or non-joinder of any party[18] and the joinder of parties is permitted as of right in a wide area of circumstances, or otherwise with the leave of the court,[19] and relief may be claimed by or against necessary and proper parties jointly, severally or in the alternative. Moreover, the court has wide powers to add, substitute or strike out parties as may be necessary, and to allow the intervention of a person not a party, against the wishes of the parties, so long as he is directly interested in the result of the instant litigation.[20] The death or bankruptcy of a party will not cause an action to abate where the cause of action survives[21] and where there has been a change of parties brought about by reason of death, bankruptcy,

15. See R.S.C., Ord. 5, r. 1. These are by writ, originating summons, originating motion and petition, and the same modes are available in the county court.

16. See R.S.C., Ord. 65, r. 1. The court has power to order substituted service in an appropriate form where personal service is " impracticable," see R.S.C., Ord. 65, r. 4.

17. See R.S.C., Ord. 13, rr. 1–4, and see also R.S.C., Ord. 19, rr. 2–6. The power is exercised extensively: in 1972 out of the total number of writs issued in the Q.B.D. in London, amounting to 94,898, there were no less than 33,968 judgments in default. See Civil Judicial Statistics (Cmnd. 5333) Table 8, p. 37.

18. R.S.C., Ord. 15, r. 6 (1).

19. R.S.C., Ord. 15, r. 4.

20. See R.S.C., Ord. 16, r. 6, and see *Gurtner* v. *Circuit* [1968] 2 Q.B. 587.

21. See R.S.C., Ord. 16, r. 7, and see Law Reform (Miscellaneous Provisions) Act 1934, s. 1 (1), under which causes of action in tort survive death, except in the case of defamation.

assignment, transmission or devolution of interest or liability, the action can be reconstituted.

Subject to procedural safeguards, all civil proceedings by or against the Crown may be brought as in the case of ordinary citizens.[22]

Representative actions, or as they are sometimes called " class actions " may be brought by or against one or more persons as representing numerous persons having the same interest in any proceedings.[23]

The joinder of causes of action is also permitted in a wide area of circumstances or otherwise with the leave of the court.[24] The defendant can make a counterclaim against the plaintiff,[25] or against the plaintiff and a person not already a party,[26] or the defendant can bring third party proceedings against a person not already a party, who can in turn bring fourth party proceedings and so on, and claims in the nature of third party proceedings can be made between co-defendants.[27] Where a person is under a liability from two or more adverse claimants in respect of a debt or money, goods or chattels, he may claim relief by way of interpleader.[28]

The whole range of the constitution of an action so far as the joinder of parties and causes of action is concerned is under the control or supervision of the court, which makes orders for the separate trials of issues or questions, or between causes of actions, or parties or as may be necessary,[29] and conversely, the court may consolidate two or more actions.[30]

(d) *System of pleadings*

After what was called the disastrous Hilary Rules of 1834[31] the Common Law Procedure Acts 1852–1854, made some amends by depriving the forms of action of much of their significance, and excluding all fictitious averrments and demurrers for defects in form, and limiting the extent of special pleading. The fundamental change in pleadings, however, came with the Judicature Acts and the Rules of Court, and consisted of requiring the parties to plead material facts only and not the evidence, to support their respective claims or defences. This change from pleading propositions of law to pleading material facts has resulted

22. See Crown Proceedings Act 1947, especially s. 13, and R.S.C., Ord. 77.
23. See R.S.C., Ord. 15, r. 12, but this power has been somewhat restrictively exercised so far, see *Markt & Co. Ltd.* v. *Knight S.S. Co. Ltd.* [1910] 2 K.B. 1021, C.A.; *Smith* v. *Cardiff Corporation* [1954] 1 Q.B. 210, C.A.
24. R.S.C., Ord. 15, r. 1.
25. R.S.C., Ord. 15, r. 2. The procedure by counterclaim was introduced by the Judicature Act 1873, s. 24, now the Judicature Act 1925, s. 39.
26. R.S.C., Ord. 15, r. 3.
27. See R.S.C., Ord. 16.
28. See R.S.C., Ord. 17, which was introduced by the interpleader Act 1831.
29. R.S.C., Ord. 15, r. 5, and Ord. 33, rr. 3 and 4.
30. R.S.C., Ord. 4, r. 10.
31. See p. 181, n. 3, *supra*.

in putting parties on their guard and telling them what they will have to meet when the case comes on for trial,[32] and this prevents " surprise " at the trial. At the same time, extensive powers of amendment have been conferred on the court " for the purpose of determining the real question in controversy between the parties to any proceedings."[33] It is still, however, necessary for a party to plead material facts which will consti-tute a reasonable cause of action or ground of defence, otherwise the pleading will run the risk of being struck out, a procedure which has replaced the old form of demurrer.[34]

(e) *System of discovery of documents and interrogatories*

The Common Law Procedure Acts conferred power on the common law courts to compel the parties to give limited discovery of documents and to answer interrogatories, and this power was of course extended to all divisions of the High Court under the Judicature Acts and the Rules of the Supreme Court.[35] In actions begun by writ, indeed, discovery of documents is required to be made automatically after the close of pleadings, and the documents to be disclosed extend to all those which are or have been in the possession, custody or power of the parties relating to any matter in question in the action.[36] In personal injury actions, discovery of documents may be obtained from a person not a party, as well as before the commencement of proceedings.[37] On the other hand, the use of interrogatories, although much favoured in equity,[38] is nowadays very limited in its use by practitioners.

(f) *The system of masters*

Before 1837, the judges of the superior common law courts attended to all interlocutory applications in chambers. But this system was found most inconvenient. As a result, the Superior Courts (Officers) Act 1837 abolished a large number of the former officers of these courts and created the masters of the common law courts, who were empowered to assist the judges in their interlocutory work. By the Judges Chambers (Despatch of Business) Act 1867, the judges were enabled to make rules empowering the masters sitting in chambers to transact any business which a judge of a common law court sitting in chambers could transact,

32. See *per* Cotton L.J. in *Phillips* v. *Phillips* (1878) 4 Q.B.D. 127.
33. R.S.C., Ord. 20, r. 8 (1).
34. See R.S.C., Ord. 18, r. 19. For the judicial and terminological relation between " a form of action " and " a cause of action," see *per* Diplock L.J. in *Letang* v. *Cooper* [1965] 1 Q.B. 232 at pp. 242 *et seq.*
35. R.S.C., Ord. 24, (discovery of documents), Ord. 26 (interrogatories).
36. R.S.C., Ord. 24, r. 1 (1). These words have been given a wide connotation and extend to any documents that may throw light upon the case *Compagnie Financiere du Pacifique* v. *Peruvian Guano Co.* (1882) 11 Q.B.D. 62.
37. R.S.C., Ord. 24, r. 7A.
38. See *per* Tomlin J. in *Duke of Sutherland* v. *British Dominions Land Settlement Corpora-ion* [1926] Ch. 746 at p. 753.

except in matters relating to the liberty of the subject, and such rules were made in the same year.

As a result, almost the whole of the pre-trial procedures in the Queen's Bench Division is nowadays carried out by the masters, and in the provinces by the district registrars, and the equivalent work in the other divisions is also carried out by the masters in the Chancery Division and the Registrars of the Family Division. In this way, the judges are left to be free for more important work and to come fresh to the trial of actions, and, above all, the system of masters provides a more speedy and more economical machinery for pre-trial applications to be made to the court.[39]

One of the most important applications that come before the master is the Summons for Directions, which is a kind of stock-taking occasion, when the master will give directions for the future course of the action, so as to secure the just, expeditious and economical disposal thereof.[40]

(g) *Disposal of actions without trial*

The Queen's Bench masters exercise power in a number of procedural devices for the disposal of actions without trial. These include summary judgment under Order 14, under which, after appearance by the defendant, the plaintiff is entitled to issue a summons supported by an affidavit verifying the cause of action, and deposing to his belief that there is no defence, and to ask for summary judgment without trial; or the master may dismiss an action for want of prosecution where there has been inexcusable and inordinate delay causing prejudice to the defendant.[41]

SYSTEM OF TRIAL

In the system of trial the earliest changes came in the sphere of admissibility of evidence. First in 1843, interested parties were allowed to give evidence; next in 1851, the parties themselves were admitted to give evidence, and then in 1853, the spouses of the parties were made competent witnesses. In 1937, the Civil Evidence Act allowed hearsay evidence to be admitted in limited circumstances, and this Act has been replaced by the Civil Evidence Act 1968, under which, subject to complying with the machinery there laid down, hearsay evidence may be admitted at the trial in civil actions.

Under the Civil Evidence Act 1972, the court has power to compel the parties to exchange medical and other experts' reports.

So far as the actual mode of trial is concerned, the greatest single change has been the virtual elimination of the jury from civil trials. The

---

39. See A. S. Diamond, " The Queen's Bench Master " (1960) 76 L.Q.R. 504.
40. See R.S.C., Ord. 25, r. 1 (1).
41. See *Allen* v. *Sir Alfred McAlpine & Sons Ltd.* [1968] 2 Q.B. 229, C.A. and see Supreme Court Practice 1973, paras 25/1/3A *et seq.*

first break came with the Common Law Procedure Act 1852, which allowed the parties to dispense with a jury by consent, but the fundamental change was effected not so much by the Administration of Justice (Miscellaneous Provisions) Act 1933, s. 6, which limited the right to a jury to specified classes of action, but more by a series of decisions of the Court of Appeal, which laid it down that the court will only grant a jury in exceptional circumstances.[42] The result is that nowadays only an infinitesimal number of actions are tried with a jury.

SYSTEM OF REMEDIES

The court has power to award any remedy, whether legal or equitable, to which a party may be entitled, so that the common law courts can award any form of equitable remedy, and the Chancery court can award damages or other legal form of remedy.

SYSTEM OF APPEALS

A great leap forward was made in the creation of a common court of appeal as part of the Supreme Court. This court, which consists of judges drawn from all divisions of the High Court, is the least specialised and the most hardworked court in the land. It hears appeals from all the divisions of the High Court, from the county courts[43] and from many tribunals. Appeals to the Court of Appeal are a matter of right in relation to final orders and judgments given at trial, but only with leave from interlocutory orders. Appeals to the House of Lords lie only with leave of the Court of Appeal or the House of Lords.[43a]

SYSTEM OF ENFORCEMENT OF JUDGMENTS

The most important change in the system of the enforcement of judgments has been the abolition of imprisonment for civil debt, except in relation to maintenance orders and Crown debts and rates and the introduction of the system of the attachment of earnings which is administered by the county courts.[44] These developments have taken place by way of implementing the recommendations of the Committee on the Enforcement of Judgment Debts but the other main recommendations of the Committee still await full implementation, such as the creation of an enforcement office, the distribution of the assets of the debtor *pari passu* with all the creditors, the extension of administration orders and so on.

42. See *Ward* v. *James* [1966] 1 Q.B. 273.
43. The system of appeals to the Divisional Court of the Q.B.D. was abolished in 1933.
43a. Under the Administration of Justice Act 1969, ss. 12 & 13, appeal may lie direct from the High Court to the House of Lords, thus by-passing or " leap-frogging " the Court of Appeal.
44. See Administration of Justice Act 1970, s.11.

SYSTEM OF COSTS AND LEGAL AID

The most important development in this field has been the introduction of legal aid in all civil cases under the Legal Aid and Advice
Act 1949, and its amending Acts. This has done a great deal to make
access to the courts more available to those in need and to remove the
jibe of one law for the rich and another for the poor. But still there remains a considerable area of unmet needs which have still to be provided
for.

PROSPECTS FOR THE FUTURE

Although from the point of view of the third quarter of the twentieth
century we seem to have made great strides in the progress of civil
procedural law, that is no justification for indulging in self-righteous
satisfaction and still less in complacency. On the contrary, it should infuse
us with the determination to improve our present system. There are
fortunately a number of bodies whose objectives are to keep up the
impetus for changes in procedure.[45] We need to keep continually in mind
the task of reforming the law to meet the needs of modern society. Perhaps
we should learn from the epitaph on the tomb of David Dudley Field:

" He devoted his life to the reform of the law;
To codifying the common law;
To simplifying legal procedure;
To substitute arbitration for war;
To bring justice within the reach of all men. "

It is the last sentence—" to bring justice within the reach of all men "—
which should remain our guiding star, an ideal, a practical task to which
it is necessary to bring dedication and enthusiasm in which none will
suffer and all will gain.

45. These include the Institute of Judicial Administration of Birmingham University;
the Socio-Legal Centre at Oxford; Justice; and the Legal Action Group.

IX

Professions

From Laissez-Faire to Discipline

TOM HARPER

INVITED, as I am, to write about the legal profession as it was in 1799 and
as it is today, I feel like a student again, faced with one of those examination questions that begin: " Compare and contrast .... " These are of
course not merely distinct but mutually exclusive operations, in the
sense that the less there is to compare, the more there is to contrast, and
vice versa. In the case of the legal profession then and now, there is
scarcely anything to compare, simply because in virtually every respect
the condition of the profession as it is today differs fundamentally from
what it was in 1799. Moreover, even the origins of those processes of
change which were to shape the profession we now know, then belonged
for the most part only to the future. Certainly that is true if, in speaking
of processes of change, one has in mind positively constructive movements, as opposed to the processes merely of obsolescence and decay,
whereby old institutions pass away and in doing so leave *vacua* which
new institutions come in due course to fill. It is true of course that the
decline of the Inns of Chancery and the emergence of the professional
institutions that took their place may be seen as aspects of one and the
same process of change. The connection is, I think, episodic rather than
causal. Certainly it was the emergence of the new institutions that was
crucial in determining the structure of the profession in this century.
To that, however, I shall return later.

THE AGE OF REFORM

When in 1799–1800 Steven Sweet and Alexander Maxwell launched
their separate business ventures and so initiated what was to become a
new era in legal publishing, an era had just ended in English history,
and inevitably in legal history also. On the other hand, the era that
succeeded it had not as yet begun. For in between was what Trevelyan
in his *English Social History* calls " Cobbett's England." It stretched from
the French Revolution to the Reform Bill and was dominated by the
war between this country and France that ended at Waterloo. Other than
that it fell within the long reign of George III, Cobbett's England had
little in common with, on the one hand, " the classical world of the
eighteenth century, with its self-esteem and self-content," though it was
by no means lacking in liberal, humanitarian aspirations, and, on the
other hand, the " restless England of Peterloo and the rick-burnings,"

191

in which many of those liberal, humanitarian aspirations were given practical expression, with the result that the period between 1825 and 1885 is remembered today as " The Age of Reform," not merely because of what changed in social and political contexts, but also for the legal reforms that came about during it.

The contrast between the eighteenth and nineteenth centuries, and the significance of the former as, in many respects, the finale to an era that stretched back in legal history over many centuries, is encapsulated in the fate of Blackstone's *Commentaries*. Originally published in 1765–69, they have been described as the greatest work of legal scholarship since Bracton's *De Legibus*. Like it, the *Commentaries* exposed and defined the essential principles of English law as they had developed up to Blackstone's own times. The contemporary importance of his work is apparent from the fact that eight editions had appeared by his death in 1780, and further editions prepared by various editors continued to come out at regular intervals thereafter. But whereas Bracton's work had continued to be used by many generations of lawyers, either directly or through its derivatives, because of the essential stability of the law at that period, the historical accident which gave the *Commentaries* added significance at the time of their publication also made the term of their practical usefulness as a restatement of English law a very short one.

That historical accident, closely related to all that characterised " The Age of Reform," was the shift away from judge-made law—the law not only of the courts but of the abridgement-writers and reporters also— towards the law made by Parliament as a more reliable and speedier way of attaining reformist aspirations by constitutional means. This was, as I have said, far more than " the England of Peterloo and the rick-burnings." As the stabilising base for such a revolutionary develop- ment in legal creativity, the exposition of long-established legal principles provided in the *Commentaries* was of inestimable value (ironically so, for Blackstone himself was no revoluntionary, but, according to Edward Gibbon, of the *Decline and Fall*, " a pious son " anxious only to " conceal the infirmities of his parent "). However, it was the same shift away from judge-made law that made it impossible to adapt the *Commentaries* to the new order, and already the editor of their fifteenth edition was writing within a few years of Blackstone's death that they were in the nature of " a national property . . . which no man of proper feeling will meddle with inconsiderately." Stephen's attempt at a radical recasting—a " rearranging . . . from top to bottom " was Dicey's description—failed altogether and was not repeated.

The shift away from a régime under which the law had for centuries been shaped almost entirely by lawyers to a system under which Parlia- ment assumed an increasingly significant influence in the law-making process profoundly affected the professional life-style of practitioners in both branches. In general, the law propounded by judges spoke for itself, but then, as now, the law enacted by Parliament called for considerable interpretation before it spoke clearly at all. It therefore greatly increased the dependence of ordinary people on their lawyer and, as the scope of Parliament's interventions widened, the number of those who became conscious of that dependence also increased. This greatly benefited the solicitors and attorneys who were the link-men between the public and the legal system. But it also gave a new dimension to taking counsel's opinion. Already, it had been possible for Lord Kenyon, who died in 1802, to make 3,000 guineas in a single year from fees for opinions alone. No doubt, merely because this instance is on record at all, it may be taken that it was exceptional, but it is all the same an illustration of a general phenomenon. It cannot moreover have been mere accident that by 1800 the solicitors and attorneys had succeeded in establishing that they alone should have direct contact with lay clients and that the Bar should act only through their intermediacy. In relation to the initiation of litigation, that process had been begun by statute as far back as 1729 (though for a long time afterwards it was frustrated by the courts).

GENTLEMAN PRACTISERS

The twofold significance of this and succeeding parliamentary interventions did not escape the attorneys. On the one hand, they naturally rejoiced at this statutory protection for their interests. On the other hand, they saw the dangers in the fact that that protection came from outside and implied parliamentary restraint no less than parliamentary patronage. As officers of the courts, they were already subject to judicial control. So they were moved to discover what they could do to safeguard their interests, using their own resources. It is surely significant that they formed their first professional institution, the Society of Gentlemen Practisers, as early as 1739 and that its influence was carefully nurtured by a judicious blend of identification with the established order and sabre-rattling against its less welcome manifestations. Indeed, if this is expressed in terms of the functions of a governing body and those of a trade union, the conception the Society of Gentlemen Practisers had of its role was surprisingly advanced in its resemblances to that of its successor, the present Law Society, which assumed its mantle in 1823. Meanwhile, however, the Gentlemen Practisers had, in 1804, established the solicitors' and attorneys' monopoly of conveyancing throughout the country, as a result of a deal with the younger Pitt, under which the Exchequer benefited in return, in the shape of increased stamp duties on practising certificates and articles of clerkship. The attorneys had already ousted the scriveners of the City of London from the conveyancing scene in an epic encounter in the courts some forty years previously.

It would be unfair to imply that the Gentlemen Practisers were motivated solely by mercenary considerations. The Founding Fathers in 1739 accorded the rooting out of malpractice a high priority among their stated objectives and, within the limitations of their powers and jurisdiction, they did not shirk their responsibilities in that respect. On the other hand, it is quite true that, in the circumstances of the eighteenth century, as it is true also of today, the exclusion of disreputable conduct by its members, and not merely conduct unbecoming in a specifically professional respect, was not an entirely disinterested aspiration. The public reputation of solicitors and more particularly of attorneys was not an enviable one at the end of the eighteenth century, and their progress would undoubtedly have been greatly impeded on that account but for the fact that they were needed to handle the land transactions and financial dealings, the wills and the settlements, by which private wealth was preserved and increased and at the appropriate moment passed on to the appointed beneficiaries. Moreover, the age of the factory industrialist was superseding that of the cottage industrialist, the amalgamation of smallholdings was spawning large-scale farming enterprises, and extensive road-building and, a little later, the advent of the railways, all combined to create new wealth (exports which in the 1780s amounted to £12 million a year had risen by 1799 to over £30 million), and therefore fresh work for solicitors and attorneys. Inventions were another area from which lawyers could benefit; the number of new patents taken out annually doubled between the 1780s and 1790s. To ensure that their claim on these increased opportunities was firmly staked out against encroachments by old foes and new ones alike, the profession had to establish a reputation, which it certainly could not assume ready-made. An emphasis on the rooting out of sin is never to be confused with the pursuit of holiness, but at least in the case of the Gentlemen Practisers it could be argued that the establishment of exclusive monopoly rights in certain areas helped to give the profession a clear identity and to distinguish the sheep, whose misdeeds could (and frequently were) visited with painful consequences, from the goats who were not, by definition, amenable to professional disciplining (" broken tradesmen and other loose and disorderly persons "—to quote one of many contemporary resolutions on the subject of the Society of Gentlemen Practisers).

REMUNERATION IN THE EARLY YEARS

Solicitors' remuneration for all non-contentious business, conveyancing included, was made up of item charges, determined according to " the custom of the trade " and the amounts allowed by the courts on taxations of such bills as were from time to time taken to taxation. Not until 1883 were *ad valorem* scale charges introduced for the first time, the main purpose of this change being to reinforce the effect of the Law of Property Act 1881 in reducing the length of the documents used in property transactions. Their length had been the yardstick by which solicitors were previously paid. *Ad valorem* scales were intended, in the words of the Law Society, " to remove any incentive to prolixity on the part of solicitors." In this respect at least, then and now may be compared, as opposed to contrasted, for scale charges are largely no more again. Meanwhile, however, long usage of standard forms has stifled the talent for prolixity—or so one may hope.

Even as far back as the fifteenth century, solicitors' and attorneys' litigation charges were regulated by rule of court and the scope of that judicial control was progressively widened, by virtue of the fact that the recipients of the charges were officers of the courts. Then, in 1729, Parliament intervened and gave clients a statutory right to have their bills taxed. This left ultimate control with the courts still, but the transfer of the initiative to the client was a significant change, even though statistically its impact was not very great.

By the end of the eighteenth century, both the reputations and the fortunes of solicitors were in the ascendant. The war with France, according to Trevelyan, " proved a source of increased wealth to the landed gentry " and of " prolonged calamity to the wage earner." For the " middling orders," on the other hand, the situation was " a gamble " and it was from the " middling orders " that solicitors predominantly came. For them, collectively and in many cases individually also, the gamble paid off. The Bar, on the other hand, still came in the main from the higher strata of society, and while the access to private means which that implied softened the undoubted rigours of the early years of practice (supplemented, in some cases, with earnings from other pursuits, some of which—like writing for newspapers for reward—upset the Benchers) it was the patronage which the relatively well-connected could enlist, whereas the " middling orders " still could not, which ultimately determined, more than wealth as such, whether a member of the Bar went far, or perhaps whether he went at all, at any rate in private practice. There were of course a few exceptions, like Charles Abbott (1762–1832) a wig-maker's son who, as Lord Tenterden, rose to be Chief Justice of the King's Bench. For the rest there were, as an alternative to private practice, a vast galaxy of public offices associated with the courts (and in particular the Court of Chancery) which were open to purchase because they ranked as the freehold of the incumbent for the time being, and, when that time ended, his to dispose of to the highest bidder. The resultant problems of title and transfer even led to litigation from time to time. The emoluments in the shape of court fees that went with such offices were considerable, especially since the work for which the fees were paid was actually performed by flunkeys who were given very little out of the proceeds for their pains. A handsome balance thus remained in the hands of the office-holder. In 1799 such offices still provided an attractive alternative to private practice for those so inclined and with the necessary capital. The various commissions that investigated the system, exposed its iniquities and so paved the way for its dismantling belonged to the early years of the nineteenth century. The whole episode is exhaustively reported in Holdsworth's *History*.

THE BAR

Although in 1799 the Bar was a unified profession, it had within it different ranks and orders which, even if they were merely sub-species, like the civilians of Doctors' Commons, nevertheless had a sense of being separate which counted for a great deal more then than it would today. Certainly, these ranks and orders created divisions and even conflicts within the Bar which sometimes went as deep in their effects and the bitterness they provoked as the division between the Bar and the solicitors and attorneys. In fact, the exclusion of the latter from the Inns of Court was not formally established for another quarter of a century, although it had already been achieved for all practical purposes in the 1790s by decrees of the Benchers requiring any solicitor who aspired to membership of an Inn to have first abandoned practice for at least two years. As Martial Charrier once remarked in another context, " Le difficulté n'est pas de faire un syndicat mais de vivre ensemble." The making of " syndicats " belongs more to the professional ethos of this century, even though occasional difficulties of " vivre ensemble " still remain. They were very much in evidence however in 1799 and one of the causes of this situation (apart from the demarcation and other rivalries I have already referred to) was the substitution of equity pleaders' and conveyancers' offices for those of solicitors as the preferred breaking-in ground for future barristers. As long as this responsibility was with solicitors, their former protégés were unlikely to turn and bite the hand that had, in professional terms, fed them.

Within the ranks of the Bar itself, the most famous separatist group was that of the Serjeants-at-Law. From very early times they had enjoyed an exclusive right of audience in the Court of Common Pleas and common law judges were appointed exclusively from their ranks. In their heyday they enjoyed great prestige because the judges belonged to the Serjeants' Inns and it was in them that disputed issues of law were thrashed out. The Serjeants had two inns, one of which had, by 1799, already ceased to exist. The other lingered on, like the Serjeants, and was finally disposed of in the 1870s. By then the Serjeants had, by statutory intervention, lost their exclusive right of audience to the general body of the

Bar, and their claim to provide the judges for the common law courts was defeated simply by the appointment of those who in the Serjeants' eyes did not qualify.

THE INNS OF COURT

By the end of the eighteenth century, effective power had passed to the Benchers of the Inns of Court and to the judges who, because they were not Benchers themselves, sat as a review body to whom members of the Inns, aggrieved by decisions of the Benchers, could and did appeal, particularly student members excluded from call by the Benchers in the exercise of their absolute discretion (Mansfield held in 1780 in *King* v. *Benchers of Gray's Inn* that the courts had no jurisdiction in regard to call). Even the right of recourse to the judicial review body was held in *King* v. *Benchers of Lincoln's Inn* (1812) to belong only to *members* of the Inn, and not therefore to a prospective student refused admission.

Coke described the Inns as " the most famous university " not only for the study of law but also that of " any one human science that is in the world." Contradicting Coke does not come easily to me, but this was of course a ridiculous claim. Nevertheless the Inns did enjoy a great, reputation as centres of learning, prior to the late seventeenth century, although even in 1854, at the time of the Commission on the Inns of Court, the glory that once was was still remembered, in that they were then described as " a university in a state of decay." By the end of the eighteenth century the Inns had adopted mutually consistent conditions for call, among which only the most oblique reference was made to academic standing. Pride of place was given to " actually keeping commons in ye Hall twelve terms," including being in place for grace before and still there for grace after.

LEGAL EDUCATION

In an earlier reference to the institution of the Society of Gentlemen Practisers, I said that its Founding Fathers gave high priority among its objectives to the rooting out of professional malpractice. They gave equal priority however to the advancement of legal education which on their side of the profession had at this juncture suffered the by no means crippling loss, but the loss nevertheless, of the Inns of Chancery and of the historic association of the " lower branch " with the Inns of Court. To continue the story it is necessary first to advance to the present day. Though the Ormrod Report on Legal Education (1971) has done much to gain recognition for academic instruction as an authentic part of the training of future practitioners, the profession's commitment to the dichotomy of legal learning into academic and professional has not yet been seriously shaken. That dichotomy is not peculiar to this country, except that here it has amounted to an article of faith, and faith in the inherent merits of the status quo is always suspect where, as has often happened in legal affairs, practices and institutional arrangements become established largely through historical accident, rather than by a conscious and informed choice between available alternatives.

The common law originated in this country and came to maturity as a complete system of municipal law, distinct from and independent of the Civil law systems of the Continent. The withdrawal from continental influences which as a result the common law system enjoyed (or suffered) was not however shared by the universities of Oxford and Cambridge where the law that was taught and written about was, as with other branches of learning, shared by and with legal scholars all over the Continent. The law that was taught and written about at Oxford and Cambridge was therefore Civil law and it was taught and written about as an integral part of a European scholarship. It is to this fact, rather than, or at any rate as much as, to any conscious urge among medieval practitioners to establish professional bodies for their own sakes that the emergence of the Inns of Court is attributable. Certainly they appeared on the scene primarily as institutions for the training of future barristers, in parallel with the largely dependent Inns of Chancery for solicitors and attorneys. However, long before Steven Sweet and Alexander Maxwell appeared on the scene in 1799, both the Inns of Court and the Inns of Chancery had ceased to be effective law schools. In their day, the teaching at them had been given by practitioners and it is said that its ultimate decline was brought about by a lack of practitioners able or willing to give their time to teaching. This may well have been true of the Inns of Court. The Inns of Chancery also withered away, but the causes of their decline were different and more complex, reflecting structural changes in the " lower branch " of the profession, rather than merely the need for a different approach to legal education. Whereas therefore, after the " mootings, boltings and other learned exercises " had ceased, the four Inns of Court continued as the centres of professional activity they are today. the Inns of Chancery soon became moribund. Without student members, they lasted for a while as the convivial haunts of solicitors and attorneys, until finally they were wound up and their premises disposed of. In 1799, the premises of virtually all the Inns of Chancery in existence in Coke's time were still intact. The last of them, Clifford's Inn, withstood the inevitable until the mid–1930s.

Already, in 1729, apprenticeship had been made compulsory by Act of Parliament for solicitors and attorneys and the system of pupillage was at that date well established at the Bar. At the universities also the old order had been yielding to new. At Oxford, a chair of English Law—the Vinerian Professorship—was created in 1758, with Blackstone as the first incumbent. At Cambridge, the Downing Professorship was founded in 1800. The significance of these foundations was that they were chairs of English law (common law) by contrast with the long-established chairs of Civil law. Chairs were established at University College, London in 1826 and at King's College, London, in 1831. For all that, a Commons Select Committee appointed in 1846 reported that " there was virtually no institutional law teaching of any kind in England," even at that late date. At Oxford the lectures in English law Blackstone had started still continued, but there was no degree in common law for those who attended them. There was a degree in Civil law but the Regius Professor had ceased to lecture because he had no students to lecture to. At Cambridge the Downing Professor had met with the same fate. Degrees in English law arrived at Oxford in 1852 and at Cambridge three years later.

At the Inns of Court, the pupil paid his money (a £100 deposit and £10 a year), ate his dinners, and took what training his master chose to give him. Whether that was much or nothing, no one else was ever likely to discover, for there was no examination before call. For aspiring solicitors, lecture courses were introduced in 1833, under the auspices of the Law Society. Bar students waited more than another decade for any comparable advantage. As with pupillage, the quality of the training provided under articles of clerkship to intending solicitors was a pure lottery. The pre-admission examination conducted by the judges was made obligatory by rule of court in 1836 and by statute from 1843, but it was, in the words of the 1845 Select Committee, " merely . . . a guarantee against absolute incompetency." It was not until 1877 that the profession wrested the examining of aspiring entrants to its ranks from the judiciary. A Bar final first introduced in the 1850s (but only for those who had *not* attended lectures) was not made obligatory for all until 1872. It is of interest that whereas all the Law Society's efforts were directed at this period towards establishing an effective examination system, the Inns' overriding objective was to resist the institution of any examinations at all.

Inevitably the impact between the immovable mountain of the conservatism of the professional institutions (notably the Inns, and the Inner Temple above all) and the irresistible forces that characterised " The Age of Reform " produced changes; but they were changes that reinforced the dualistic pattern of legal education—academic here and professional there—that was already established, rather than directed it in the reverse direction. In 1799, the changes of a less fundamental kind which I have already described all belonged to the future. Only the introduction of compulsory apprenticeship for future solicitors and attorneys distinguished their education from what, in all essentials, it had been since the Middle Ages. That did not mean however that Steven Sweet and Alexander Maxwell and those of their contemporaries who bothered to inquire would necessarily have concluded that that would be the position for ever. By 1799 the campaign for changes in the legal education system, such as it then was, had started, and Blackstone had already, forty years earlier, lent it his powerful support in the inaugural lecture he delivered as Vinerian Professor and which he included as a prologue to the published *Commentaries*. But against the " conservatism of a powerful profession " incurably addicted to " the old method of office apprenticeship "—Blackstone's description—the reform movement followed a circular course. As a result, on most fundamental issues, there is more common ground between the views Blackstone had expressed in the 1750s about the relationship between the academic and the professional teaching of law and the views officially endorsed by the profession today than at any period in the intervening two and a quarter centuries.

Blackstone, however, looked forward also to a time, which has not arrived even today, when " a competent knowledge of the laws of that society in which we live " would be recognised as the " proper accomplishment " of any normally educated person, not only or primarily for the practical usefulness of such an accomplishment, but also because it is, as he emphasised, on the law that the rights and obligations that are the very lifeblood of civilised social existence depend, so that the ordinary citizen ought on that account alone to be instructed in that law. In 1974, the relationship between an understanding of the law and the needs of ordinary men and women is by no means a matter of academic concern. Blackstone would surely have been horrified to find that elementary law is still not taught in our schools and above all that law has no place in the Open University's curriculum.[1]

1. I acknowledge the help I have derived in the preparation of this essay from the following works: Sir William Holdsworth, *A History of English Law* (Methuen and Sweet & Maxwell, 1956); G. M. Trevelyan, *English Social History* (Longmans, 1946); Dorothy Marshall, *Industrial England 1776–1851* (Routledge & Kegan Paul, 1973); Report of Committee on Legal Education (The " Ormrod Report "), Cmnd. 4595/ 1971 (H.M.S.O., 1971); Brian Abel-Smith and Robert Stevens, *Lawyers and the Courts* (Heinemann, 1967); Michael Birks, *Gentlemen of the Law* (Stevens, 1960); Sir Robert Megarry, *Inns Ancient and Modern* (Selden Society, 1972); W. J. Reader, *Professional Men* (Weidenfeld & Nicolson, 1966).

X

Property and Equity

Property and Equity

EDWARD F. GEORGE

By the year 1800 the law of real property had not been subject to radical alteration for a long time. Almost the only statutes of importance to conveyancers were the Statute of Uses 1535, the Statute of Enrolments 1535 and the Statute of Frauds 1540. The owner of property was still very much concerned with the doctrine of tenure; save on rare occasions today copyholds are merely a subject of historical interest. There was a multiplicity of legal estates of a complex nature,[1] so that quite often it was impossible to acquire a fee simple, not because of unwillingness to sell but inability to do so. Apart from life interests under settlements, there were estates tail, tenancy by the curtesy, dower and so on. Wills of realty not merely came on to the title but did not have to be proved in court—it will be remembered that they had to be attested by three or four credible witnesses—and intestacy with its varying rules must have been a nightmare for conveyancers. Only the lease can still be recognised; a solicitor today has no more difficulty in construing an old lease than he does one granted a year or two ago.

Consider the position of the purchaser's solicitor. When he received the draft contract, all the conditions were set out in full, and he wrote what today would be called preliminary inquiries in the margin, first having made a complete copy of the draft. On exchange of contracts he received an abstract of title going back some sixty years (against the modern fifteen) and on to that title came all the settlements, mortgages, wills, intestacies and the like. He had no land charges register to help him and the doctrine of notice made life very difficult for him. When it came to drawing the conveyance he was still using the lease and release. He did not cut short his covenants for title or indeed any other part of the conveyance, and had no incentive to do so. When scale fees, designed to make conveyancing more efficient—and they succeeded—were introduced at the end of the last century, they were opposed by solicitors, as the return to the old system was a year or two ago. The vendor and purchaser summons, which settled so many points at the end of last century and the beginning of this, was a thing of the future but it is clear that the parties avoided actions like the plague, because of the appalling inefficiency and expense of litigation, particularly in Chancery. It was said[2] that

---

1. Witness *Fearne on Contingent Remainders*.
2. John Williams in the House of Commons in 1824.

" the law affecting the transfer of real property was reserved for the consideration and profit of a select few, removed from the general practice of the profession, ' whose ways were past finding out,' "

but whether there were many conveyancing transactions which were not carried through without undue difficulty it is difficult to say.

Lord Eldon was Lord Chancellor for a quarter of a century from 1801 onwards and completed the settlement and systematisation of equity so that after him there was little scope for expansion. The one great substantive contribution of equity in the nineteenth century was the evolution of the restrictive covenant as an interest in land. It was in the realm of procedure and the fusion of the administration of law and equity that reforms were to come. Nepotism in the administration of justice was rife.[3] The delays were appalling: cases were still unheard not merely for months but sometimes for more than ten years after setting down. Lord Eldon opposed all reform but it went through. Since the last war equity has been showing some signs of activity which are noted below, not always with entirely happy results.

Changes in the law of property were to be brought about principally through legislation. The rapid expansion of England as a result of the Industrial Revolution was not particularly related to land so that the changes were not at first fast or particularly radical, but eventually it dawned on the community that Mark Twain summed up the position accurately when he said that the best commodity for an investor to put his money in was land because " they are not making it any more " and so the impetus to modernise grew and our land law and conveyancing practice bears little relation to those of 1939 let alone 1800.

REGISTRATION OF TITLE

It has always been accepted that titles to land in England are so complex that a vendor is not to be held liable for damages for loss of bargain if he cannot prove title.[4] Deeds Registries proved to be a conveyancing cul-de-sac, but the system of registration of title was probably the most important Victorian contribution to conveyancing. Getting off to a slow start its real impact has been felt only during the last quarter of a century. Today every practitioner has to think in registered land terms. It was conceived as a system of recording and guaranteeing the state of a title at a given time so that on any new transaction the title would merely be brought up to date: the purchaser would not have to wander outside the

3. This continued at least down to 1865 when Lord Westbury had to resign from the Lord Chancellorship because of the flagrancy of his conduct.

    The age of meritocracy is modern; Sir John Harding was a law officer while " under care as a lunatic without prospect of recovery " in 1862.

    4. *Bain* v. *Fothergill* (1873) L.R. 7 H.L.C. 158. The rule is not to be extended; *Wroth* v. *Tyler* [1973] 2 W.L.R. 405. It is believed that the Law Commission question the justification for the rule today.

recorded title. It was recognised that there would be some matters—adverse possession, short tenancies, prescription and the like—which would not appear on the register, but it was hoped that these would be easily discoverable by inspection. In the result, it has been brought home to practitioners that the system of registration of title does not merely deal with the machinery of conveyancing but has affected substantive rights and there are still traps which are not necessarily discernible even by the wary.

Let us look at some of the differences in law and practice:

1. It is well settled in the case of unregistered land that a person who acquires a title by squatting does not obtain the former owner's title but an entirely new one which merely bars the right of the former owner.[5] Although in the case of registered land it has been denied that the effect is different,[6] it must be because the registered proprietor after the requisite period holds his title in trust for the squatter and the squatter can apply to be registered in his place.[7] Assuming that the squatter could have some sort of inferior title, not discernible from the Land Registration Act, when he transfers to a third party how can the third party or anyone else possibly tell the provenance of the title without going behind the register?

2. Merger will not be brought about automatically in the case of registered land. Unity of seisin will not cause a right of way to disappear if the benefit is noted in the register,[8] for when the dominant tenement is sold the transferee will automatically acquire the right because it is on the register. A registered lease will similarly not merge until the leasehold title is closed on request.

3. When a company is the registered proprietor of land a transferee is not affected by a floating charge not noted on the register even though duly registered under the Companies Act.

4. In the case of unregistered land an option to purchase or renew a lease must always be registered under the Land Charges Act if it is to bind the purchaser of a legal estate,[9] but in the case of registered land if the option is contained in a lease which is an overriding interest [10] it binds a purchaser even though not noted in the register.[11] Nor is it any answer to say that the lessee will be in possession, for he may well not be. A reversionary lease or one to commence in the future may well be an overriding interest. On the other hand some land charges are not regis-

---

5. *Fairweather* v. *St. Marylebone Property Co. Ltd.* [1963] A.C. 510.
6. *e.g. Palace Court Garages (Hampstead) Ltd.* v. *Steiner* (1953) 108 L.J. 274.
7. Land Registration Act 1925, s. 75.
8. It may or may not be, depending on the origin of the right and the application made to the registry.
9. Law of Property Act 1925, s. 199 (1).
10. And this may be a lease exceeding 21 years: see next paragraph.
11. *Webb* v. *Pollmount* [1966] Ch. 584.

trable at all in the case of registered land, *e.g.* an agreement affecting all
the land acquired or to be acquired by the person granting the right,[12]
and others operate in a different manner, because a land charge in the
case of unregistered land is registered against a name and it matters not
that the person registered against is only a lessee though the charge affects
a freehold.

5. In the case of unregistered land a purchaser is in theory bound by
the rights of an occupier save so far as not disclosed on inquiry, but in
practice he is bound by very little because since 1925 he is not affected
by any rights which are registrable but in fact not registered.[13] In the
case of registered land the purchaser is exposed to much greater risk.
The relevant overriding interest is: "The rights of every person in actual
occupation of the land or in receipt of the rents and profits thereof, save
where inquiry is made of such person and the rights are not disclosed."
It is not always easy to tell who is in occupation. If a husband, wife and
children are living in a house and the son is the registered proprietor, on
the face of it he is the only person in occupation,[14] but if he has procured
a transfer to himself by fraud committed against his father, the father is
still in occupation and may be entitled to set aside the transfer against an
innocent purchaser from the son.[15] The extension of the definition to
cover receipt of rents and profits is quite unwarranted. If premises are
empty but a lessee pays rent to someone in respect of them, how on earth
can a purchaser discover this? The breadth of the overriding interest is
considerable. A is the lessee under an unregistered lease. If he is in
possession he is protected and, as we have just seen, the lease may contain
further rights such as an option to purchase.[16]

6. In the case of registered land positive covenants can effectively be
made to run with the land by means of a restriction preventing transfer
without the consent of the person entitled to the restriction. It must be
added that in practice this machinery tends to break down through the
sheer inertia of the person entitled to the benefit in failing to see that the
restriction is renewed on transfer. The entry of a restriction can be used
to secure the effectiveness of other rights of a purely personal nature.[17]

7. Once registration has been effected, nearly all dealings with registered land must be by registered disposition, so that, for example, if an
easement is granted over registered land the grant must be noted against
the title of the servient tenement if it is to bind transferees for value. It is

12. *Turley* v. *Mackay* [1944] Ch. 37.
13. *Hunt* v. *Luck* [1902] Ch. 428; Law of Property Act 1925, s. 199 (1).
14. *National Provincial Bank Ltd.* v. *Ainsworth* [1965] A.C. 1175.
15. *Hodgson* v. *Marks* [1971] Ch. 892.
16. Or the lease may have been varied by correspondence: *Dovto Properties Ltd.* v.
Astell (1964) 28 *Conveyancer* (N.S.) 270.
17. *e.g.* a right of pre-emption if it is correct that it is not an interest in land: *Murray* v.
Two Strokes Ltd. [1973] 1 W.L.R. 823.

to be regretted, therefore, that the Court of Appeal in *Re Dances Way*[18] held that an easement granted by a deed prior to first registration does not have to be noted on the register of the servient land with the result that in theory it is never safe to part with pre-registration deeds.

8. The position of a transferee between transfer and registration is an example of the blurring of the border between law and equity that has been observable for some time. It probably does not matter in that it is the question of priority that is of importance.

9. One of the superiorities of registered over unregistered land is the guarantee of title. Someone may obtain title under a forged transfer. Of course two persons cannot own the same land adversely to one another but one of them will keep the land and the other get compensation.[19]

COVENANTS

Tulk v. *Moxhay*[20] is usually regarded as a revolutionary decision. Everyone knows of it but how many have read it? The whole report is only about five pages. The Lord Chancellor did not even call on the respondent's counsel. His reasons go back to the roots of equity:

" It is said that, the covenant being one which does not run with the land, this court cannot enforce it but the question is, not whether the covenant runs with the land, but whether a party shall be permitted to use the land in a manner inconsistent with the contract entered into by his vendor, and with notice of which he purchased. Of course, the price would be affected by the covenant, and nothing could be more inequitable than that the original purchaser should be able to sell the property the next day for a greater price, in consideration of the assignee being allowed to escape from the liability which he had himself undertaken."

The purchaser's conscience was affected by the obligation and he was not going to be allowed to reap an uncovenanted benefit by avoiding it. We shall see that this principle underlies many post-war decisions establishing " the new equity."

In *Morland* v. *Cook*[21] parties to a deed covenanted to contribute to the expenses of maintaining a sea wall which was for the benefit of all their lands. It is held that the covenant was enforceable by and against the successors in title of the original parties to the deed. Unfortunately, however, it subsequently became settled law that the burden of only restrictive covenants would run with the land.[22] This was in keeping with nineteenth century philosophy generally that criminal and civil obligations (other than those in contract) should merely be negative in nature, a view which has only been changing slowly helped by a different legislative philosophy. Last century a man could allow thistles to grow on his land

---

18. [1962] Ch. 490.
19. *Re 139 Deptford High Street* [1951] Ch. 884 is a good example.
20. (1848) 2 Ph. 774.
21. (1868) L.R. 6 Eq. 253.
22. *Austerberry* v. *Oldham Corporation* (1885) 29 Ch.D. 750.

with impunity; today he cannot escape liability in nuisance by saying that the trees constituting the nuisance were self-sown. There are many laws today imposing positive obligations on owners and occupiers of land.

Practitioners have nevertheless continued to insert positive covenants in conveyances and, although they have been assured by the academics that positive covenants could not be made to run, practitioners were not surprised at the decision in *Halsall* v. *Brizell*[23] that where A is granted an easement subject to contribution to maintenance expenses his successor can only exercise the easement so long as he is prepared to contribute to the expenses. Positive covenants can also be annexed to rentcharges. The technical problem of making positive covenants run with the land has been the major difficulty in connection with the sale of flats but, so confident were practitioners that the law was as it was found to be in *Halsall* v. *Brizell*, that the device there decided to be valid was used in flat schemes for some years prior to that decision.

Parliament has never felt any difficulty over making positive covenants enforceable, and in section 62 of the Pastoral Measure 1968 they simply provided that in conveyances under the Measure, for the purposes of enforcement, positive covenants should be treated as if they were negative. Under the Leasehold Reform Act 1967 the court has power to approve schemes containing positive covenants. No doubt after the usual legislative gestation period positive covenants generally will be put on the same footing as restrictive covenants.

FUSION OF LAW AND EQUITY

It is trite theory that the Judicature Acts merely fused the administration of law and equity, but it is becoming increasingly apparent that the border between the two systems is becoming more and more blurred. Indeed, technically there is no reason why there should not be fusion; the Statute of Uses did it once before—and then some of the anachronistic rules from which we suffer, particularly those relating to consideration, third parties to contracts and deeds, might disappear. It is largely the operation of the rules of notice that determine whether a particular interest is binding or not. A general equitable charge, a puisne mortgage, a deposit of a land certificate: all these depend for their efficacy against third parties on registration. A conveyance of land in a compulsory area ceases to have effect at law unless application for registration is made within a given time. A lease exceeding twenty-one years where the lessor's title is registered does not bind unless noted against the lessor's title but becomes binding as soon as the lessee goes into occupation.

23. [1957] Ch. 169; approved by the Court of Appeal in *Ives* v. *High* [1967] 2 Q.B. 379.

FORMALISM

Although a great deal of formalism has gone out of our land law, from time to time archaisms rear their heads to cause trouble to conveyancers. Often the courts do not seem to understand the problems of practitioners. In *Hollington Bros. Ltd.* v. *Rhodes* [24] Harman J. (as he then was) stated the practice on the grant of a lease in impeccable terms:

" It is a commonplace that in many, indeed, in most cases, where a lease is to be granted everything remains in negotiation until the lease and its counterpart are finally exchanged between the parties. . . . It is said [that the execution of the lease and counterpart] ratified the terms settled by the solicitors and so created a contract. In my judgment such a contract cannot be spelled out of this state of things. There was, I think, no intention on either side to be bound by the course which negotiations took until the lease was exchanged with the counterpart, and this was never done."

It has been settled law for many years that a deed operates on signing, sealing and delivery by one party, notwithstanding that some other party has not executed and indeed may never execute the deed,[25] though it is true that the delivery may be as an escrow and not take effect until some condition is fulfilled, *e.g.* execution by another party, payment of the purchase money, etc. When the condition is fulfilled the operation relates back to the time of execution. This is, of course, manifest nonsense in practice and ignored by everyone.[25a] On completion the conveyance or lease is dated on that day and thereafter the presumption applies that that is the date of execution. It apparently never occurred to the legal advisers in *Beesly* v. *Hallwood Estates Ltd.*[26] that the law differed from the practice as stated by Harman J., but after the conclusion of the evidence and some legal argument, it was suggested that though the lease and counterpart had not been exchanged, as the lessors had impressed their seal the lease was already in operation, and so it was held.

These technicalities were taken to an extreme in *D'Silva* v. *Lister House Development Ltd.*[27] where the underlease there in question would have been in breach of the headlease and was sealed in error. Nevertheless it was held that the underlessors had executed the lease and could not hold it back. The fact that it was sealed without authority was held to be irrelevant because section 74 of the Law of Property Act 1925 says it was

24. [1951] 2 T.L.R. 691, 694.
25. *Naas* v. *Westminster Bank Ltd.* [1940] A.C. 366.
25a. In *Re Nichols, deceased* [1974] 1 W.L.R. 296 a conveyance and lease were both executed on June 15, 1955, but dated respectively June 24 and July 16. The court held that they were not contemporaneous but " took effect " from their respective dates.
26. [1961] Ch. 105.
27. [1971] Ch. 17. Had there merely been an agreement for a lease or a lease under hand only, specific performance would not have been ordered and the principle of *Walsh* v. *Lonsdale* (1882) 21 Ch.D. 9 would not apply: *Warmington* v. *Miller* [1973] 2 W.L.R. 654.

deemed to be properly executed because it purported to have been executed in the presence of a director and secretary. Up till then practitioners thought that this was an evidentiary rule only. The cases cited are only the tip of the iceberg. In *Vincent* v. *Premo Enterprises (Voucher Sales) Ltd.*[28] Winn L. J. made a strong plea for the modernisation of the law.

To ensure that the ancient lore is not lost, in *Chelsea and Walham Green B.S.* v. *Armstrong*[29] the court considered carefully the distinctions between deeds poll and other deeds and held that a transfer of registered land, if not a deed poll, at any rate was not a deed *inter partes*, so that a third party could sue on it.

Two rules which have an inhibiting effect on commercial and property transactions are those which stipulate that a simple contract must be supported by consideration and that a third party cannot as a general rule sue on a contract, and it was a great disappointment that the House of Lords felt unable to follow the Court of Appeal and give to section 56 of the Law of Property Act 1925 (third parties taking under instruments) its natural meaning and instead tied its construction to earlier enactments with narrower wording.[30]

In *Shiloh Spinners* v. *Harding*[31] Lord Wilberforce expressed the view that the section dealing with registrable land charges should be given a plain and ordinary interpretation.

" It is a section which involves day to day operation by solicitors doing conveyancing work: they should be able to take decisions and advise their clients upon a straightforward interpretation. . . ."

Alas, not by any means all the decisions reflect such a solicitude for conveyancers. If an option holder fails to register his option so that it does not bind third parties, he can nevertheless sue the person who granted him the option.[32] As one solicitor bitterly commented, the courts expect a vendor's solicitor to search in the Land Charges Registry against his own client before sending out a draft contract. And in *Barclays Bank Ltd.* v. *Taylor*[33] Goulding J. held that a chargee of registered land was not protected because he got the note of his interest in the wrong part of the register, though fortunately for borrowers from banks the Court of Appeal disagreed with him. However, in *Murray* v. *Two Strokes Ltd.*[34] the court held that a right of pre-emption can be defeated unless protected in the right part of the register.

28. [1969] 2 W.L.R. 1256.
29. [1951] Ch. 853.
30. *Beswick* v. *Beswick* [1968] A.C. 58.
31. [1973] 2 W.L.R. 518.
32. *Wright* v. *Dean* [1948] Ch. 686.
33. [1973] 2 W.L.R. 293.
34. [1973] 1 W.L.R. 823.

THE NEW EQUITY

Remedies

Although the sobriquet " the New Equity " has been given to certain aspects only of recent case law development, it is perhaps not too fanciful to detect a determination by the judges to see that their law is fitted for, and suits the requirements of, contemporary conditions. For example, immediately after the war motor-car manufacturers, seeking to ensure that a black or grey market in new cars did not arise, took covenants from buyers not to sub-sell above list prices. When they sought to enforce the covenants it was argued that they had suffered no damage and it was improper to grant an injunction in relation to an ordinary mercantile transaction. Had this argument been accepted it would have meant that in some areas of law valid contracts would have been virtually unenforceable. Injunctions were granted and these cases were the forerunners of a series of cases in which the courts expanded the use to which equitable remedies could be put.

It is impossible to sell flats unless someone is responsible for the main structure. If the obligation to repair is not carried out and the flat-owners merely left to a claim for damages, they would not have an effective remedy. The court in such a case will grant specific performance.[35] If a licence to enter land is granted in an appropriate case the court will enforce that right and not leave the licensee to an action at common law.[36] Sometimes an equitable remedy is not appropriate: every judge knows that no kitchen has ever been built big enough to contain two cooks.[37] If parties get together to frustrate a solus agreement it is useless to argue that because a conveyance has taken place the court is powerless: it can order the land to be conveyed back.[38] Indeed, in one case the court granted an injunction to prevent an employer dismissing his employee.[39]

The most important of the decisions on equitable remedies for many years is *Beswick* v. *Beswick*.[40] It had been held in *Re Miller's Agreement*[41] that, where A contracts with B for a payment to C, in the ordinary course of events C cannot sue B. This was in fact a decision welcomed by many widows and dependants, for if C was A's widow and the payments had to commence on A's death the payments escaped estate duty and many pension schemes have been drawn with this decision in mind. But, of course, if B seeks to evade payment this may produce a great injustice.

35. *Jeune* v. *Queens Cross Properties Ltd.* [1973] 3 W.L.R. 738.
36. *London Borough of Hounslow* v. *Twickenham Garden Developments* [1971] Ch. 237.
37. *Cf. Thompson* v. *Park* [1944] 1 K.B. 408.
38. *Esso Petroleum Co. Ltd.* v. *Kingswood Motors (Addlestone) Ltd.* [1973] 3 W.L.R. 780.
39. *Hill* v. *C. A. Parsons & Co.* [1971] 3 W.L.R. 995.
40. [1968] A.C. 58.
41. [1947] Ch. 615.

If A sells his goodwill to B in return for an annuity commencing after A's death payable to C and B refuses to pay, and he cannot be compelled to pay, he gets the goodwill for nothing. And that is precisely what B tried to do in *Beswick* v. *Beswick*. He said that equity never granted specific performance of a contract to pay money and if A's estate sued the damages would be nominal. Not surprisingly, the House of Lords would not be a party to such a denial of justice. If damages were not an adequate remedy, as manifestly they were not, and if A's personal representative cared to sue, as she did, she could have specific performance. It will not need a great deal to persuade the court to order the personal representative to sue if he is unwilling to do so. Then there will not be much left of the common law rule that a third party cannot sue on a contract.

Estoppel

One of the objects of the 1925 legislation was to see that as many third party rights as possible were registered in the Land Charges Registry or the Land Registry, as the case may be. As land becomes more and more valuable every right over it, however apparently trivial, tends to increase its worth and, as a result, every method has been used to establish rights. Section 62 of the Law of Property Act 1925 (general words) seems to be fairly innocuous but consider the position. A lessee of a building asks his lessor for permission to park his car on the latter's adjoining yard and permission is given. The lease is renewed. A assigns his lease to B and B purchases the freehold reversion. To his surprise he finds he has now got a legal easement to park his car. Faltering now and again,[42] the law of easements has been steadily expanded to cover modern conditions.

One line of approach, by no means fully exploited, to further rights is the doctrine of non-derogation from grant. The doctrine is likely to have a good deal of importance in relation to sales of flats. The vendor will not be able to deal with unsold flats contrary to the terms of the flat scheme, express or implied,[43] or to diminish amenities over the grounds by increasing the number of persons entitled to use them, as by granting rights over the driveways. The obligation imposed by the doctrine does not have to be registered, but binds successors in title to the burdened land regardless of notice.[44]

Another line of approach which has been flourishing to greater effect is estoppel both legal and equitable. Again, registration is irrelevant so that if the estoppel is legal a successor in title is bound regardless of notice. A good example is *Hopgood* v. *Brown*[45]: an owner of land agreed

42. *e.g. Phipps* v. *Pears* [1965] 1 Q.B. 76 (no easement of shelter—the decision was certainly right, the denial of any such easement retrograde and contrary to principle); *Kwiatkowski* v. *Cox* (1969) 213 E.G. 34 (no easement to enter adjoining premises to repair a downpipe lawfully erected).
43. *Newman* v. *Real Estate Development Corporation* [1940] 1 All E.R. 131.
44. *Cable* v. *Bryant* [1908] 1 Ch. 259, 264.
45. [1955] 1 W.L.R. 213.

his boundary with his neighbour and contracted with the neighbour that the latter would build a garage on the owner's land. In fact the garage encroached on the neighbour's land. It was held that the neighbour's successor in title could not require the garage to be taken down. Merely to do nothing cannot constitute an estoppel.

In *Ives* v. *High*[46] an owner built a block of flats and his footings trespassed on his neighbour's land. The neighbour agreed to acquiesce in the encroachment provided the owner of the block permitted him to take his car across the yard of the block. The neighbour could not have a legal easement because there was no grant and prescription was impossible as user was with consent. The block of flats changed hands and the new owner sought (one might have thought ill-advisedly) to prevent the neighbour using the yard for access to his garage. It was held that there was an equitable estoppel and as the successor had notice of the right he was bound. (If he had not had notice how would he have resisted an injunction to remove his encroaching footings?[47])

" Licences "

There is another line of cases somewhat similar to the estoppel cases. An owner of land permits someone to incur expenditure on the owner's land and to use the land under the arrangement. He is not then permitted to go back on the arrangement. This line may be traced back to *Dillwyn* v. *Llewellyn*,[48] a decision of Lord Westbury, and *Plimmer* v. *Wellington Corporation*,[49] one of the Privy Council, so that it has a respectable parentage. These are not cases of contract. A good deal of fuss has been made of the decision of the Court of Appeal in *Errington* v. *Errington*.[50] In that case, a father-in-law permitted his son-in-law and daughter to occupy land so long as they kept down the mortgage instalments and agreed to convey the house to them when the debt was paid off. The successor of the father-in-law on his death sought to oust the son-in-law and daughter and failed. As the successor was not a purchaser for value, one might be pardoned for thinking that this was a simple case of contract.

Of much more interest is *Inwards* v. *Baker*[51] where there was no question of a contract. There a father permitted his son-in-law to expend money on a bungalow on the father's land and to live there. Here there was no question of the parties' intending that the land should be conveyed to the son, but he was permitted to stay there as long as he wished. Although, again, the plaintiff was a successor in title who did not give value it is clear that the son's equity would bind a purchaser of the legal estate for

46. [1967] 2 Q.B. 379.
47. *Halsall* v. *Brizell* [1957] Ch. 169.
48. (1862) 4 De G.F. & J. 517.
49. (1884) 9 App.Cas. 699.
50. [1952] 1 K.B. 290.
51. [1965] 2 Q.B. 29.

value with notice as well and, as the son's equity was not registrable, whether the land was registered or unregistered, a purchaser would be bound to have notice by reason of the son's occupation.

In their enthusiasm for protecting deserted wives the courts built up a large judicial structure, the effect of which was that a third party, whether purchaser, chargee or trustee in bankruptcy, was bound by their somewhat ill-defined rights. This jerry-built structure fell to the ground in *National Provincial Bank* v. *Ainsworth*.[52] Third parties, even purchasers for value with notice, are bound only by rights " which have the quality of being capable of enduring through different ownerships of the land, according to the normal conceptions of the title to real property."

The mere fact that a purchaser buys subject to a right of a third party does not mean that he is bound by that right, even if he paid less for the land by reason of that fact.[53] An ordinary commercial licence does not bind purchasers of the legal estate for value even with notice: *King* v. *David Allen & Sons*.[54] One might have thought that this authority of the House of Lords would conclude the matter, but he would be a rash person who would assume that this is so. Although it is reasonable to assume that a licence cannot bind a purchaser where an equitable remedy is not available, either because damages would be an adequate remedy or for any other reason,[55] a solicitor acting for a purchaser is bound to assume that the courts might hold that some licences will bind the purchaser. One cannot help wondering whether the licences to run trains over the tracks of other railway companies would not have bound purchasers with notice.

There is a tendency to assume that today all trusts of land are either settled land or trusts for sale,[56] but this is clearly incorrect. If an owner is under an equitable obligation to reconvey land to another, he holds as trustee for that other. In *Binions* v. *Evans*,[57] Evans had worked all his life for a landowner and after his death his widow, the defendant, was permitted to occupy a cottage on the estate as long as she wished. The landowner sold the property subject to the " tenancy " to the plaintiffs at a lower price than he would have realised if the defendant had not got a right of occupation. The facts were clearly within the reasoning of *Tulk* v. *Moxhay*[58] and bear a close similarity to *Beswick* v. *Beswick*.[59] Obviously what the landowner was saying was: " I will sell you this land if you will

52. [1965] A.C. 1175.
53. *Hollington Brothers* v. *Rhodes* [1951] 2 T.L.R. 691.
54. [1916] 2 A.C. 54.
55. *e.g.* as in *Thompson* v. *Park* [1944] 1 K.B. 408.
56. See *Bull* v. *Bull* [1955] 1 Q.B. 234.
57. [1972] 2 All E.R. 70.
58. *Ante*, p. 184.
59. *Ante*, p. 184.

agree that Mrs. Evans shall have the right to continue to occupy it." Can there be any doubt that if the contract had been phrased in this way the landowner could have got specific performance of the contract for the benefit of Mrs. Evans? But the landowner was not a party to the proceedings. The court referred to a constructive trust, but is it not more correct to say that on a fair construction of the contract the purchaser agreed to hold the property on trust to permit Mrs. Evans to continue to reside there? If the court was not entirely clear why the purchaser was bound by the widow's rights, it had no doubt that he was.

DEFECTIVE PREMISES

The days when a judge could say that, " fraud apart, there is no law against letting a tumble-down house "[60] have long since departed. The Public Health and Housing Acts have put various obligations on owners of property so as to ensure that dwelling houses are fit for occupation, principally in relation to poorer properties. Section 32 of the Housing Act 1961 went much further and imposed an obligation on landlords of dwelling houses generally where premises are let for a term of less than seven years to keep the structure, exterior parts and service installations in repair. Although these statutory obligations are important in ensuring that tenants do not live in conditions which are no longer acceptable to the community, they do not touch on the standards of construction of houses.

A limited remedy for poor construction was given in contract to a purchaser of a house which was not completed at the time of the contract. The vendor impliedly warranted that the builder would do his work in a good and workmanlike manner, would supply good and proper materials and that the house would be reasonably fit for human habitation.[61] This warranty operated erratically and could be expressly or implicitly excluded, in whole or in part,[62] nor did the warranty help third parties such as successors in title to the original purchaser, though they might[63] have a limited remedy in negligence against the builder where he was different from the original vendor.[64]

At this point of the development in the law came the decision in *Dutton* v. *Bognor Regis U.D.C.*[65] where a successor in title to an original purchaser sued a local authority whose surveyor had negligently passed the foundations of a house and the Court of Appeal held that, whether or not the builder was liable, the local authority was.

Going back to 1937, the National House-Builders Registration Coun-

60. Erle C.J. in *Robbins* v. *Jones* (1863) 18 C.B. 221 at 240.
61. *Miller* v. *Cannon Hill Estates Ltd.* [1931] 2 K.B. 113.
62. *Lynch* v. *Thorne* [1956] 1 W.L.R. 303.
63. See *Travers* v. *Gloucester Corporation* [1947] K.B. 71.
64. *Sharpe* v. *Sweeting* [1963] 1 W.L.R. 665.
65. [1972] 1 Q.B. 373.

cil, a rather weakly child of the building industry, was born and was given official status by a pre-war Building Societies Act. The Council certified buildings and the builder entered into a contract to rectify defects. The current form of contract also contains a guarantee by the Council against major defects which remains in force for ten years and is assignable. So important has the Council become that many building societies and local authorities refuse to lend money on a modern house unless the Council's certificate was issued in respect of it. Against this background the Defective Premises Act 1972 was passed. The common law implied warranty was made statutory and liability cannot be excluded and any person having a legal or equitable interest in the building can sue on the statutory warranty. Where, however, the developer is registered with the Council and a certificate is issued and Council's contract entered into, the obligation under the contract takes the place of the statutory warranty.

At the same time, the Occupiers' Liability Act 1957 was extended so that a landlord under an obligation to repair or having a right to repair was put under an obligation of care to all persons who might reasonably be expected to be affected by defects resulting from his failure to carry out his obligations.

MODERN CONVEYANCING PRACTICE

One of the principal objects of the 1925 legislation was to simplify conveyancing and to make it expeditious. Solicitors' remuneration reflected the then fact that investigation of title to unregistered land was still complex, but with the reduction of title to fifteen years the work involved in unregistered conveyancing is not materially different from that in registered. Quite often the root of title is the only document of title and may be on one side of a sheet of quarto. But conveyancing is not simple, expeditious or cheap. What has gone wrong with the dream?

Assume the simplest possible transaction. A vendor agrees to sell a freehold dwelling-house, subject to no restrictions, to a purchaser at the price of £15,000, completion in a month's time. The contract is short and incorporates a standard set of conditions. Printed preliminary inquiries, local searches, and standard additional inquiries are put in. A short conveyance is prepared and a land charge search made against the vendor. The vendor might well think that nothing could go wrong. If the purchaser were to default the vendor would forfeit the deposit.[66] *Wroth* v. *Tyler* [67] shows that there may be other snares in his path. There the vendor's wife, after contracts had been entered into, caused notice of her rights of occupation under the Matrimonial Homes Act 1967 to be registered, with the result that the vendor could not complete. The sale price

66. Even this is not necessarily simple: see *Re Engall's Agreement* [1953] 1 W.L.R. 97.
67. [1973] 2 W.L.R. 405.

was £6,000 but the purchaser was awarded £5,500 damages. The vendor's solicitor may be asked to advise on the question of liability to tax on the profit made on the sale and this may by no means be an easy question to answer. It may be the vendor's second home; he may not have resided throughout his period of ownership; he may have bought with a view to realising a gain; he may have used part of the premises as a doctor's surgery; if he is about to emigrate he may be well advised to postpone the sale until he has ceased to be resident here and then one will have to consider the exchange control permission.

So far as the purchaser is concerned the planning permission will have to be considered. If the house was recently erected the planning permission will have to be examined and even in the case of an older house, there may have been alterations. A garage will not usually require planning permission but sometimes it does. Although the four-year time bar applies to construction without planning permission, it does not bar the enforcement of conditions. Then, if the purchaser is married the question, whether the house should be put in the joint names of the husband and wife, must be considered and today it is becoming commoner for them to take as tenants in common, though the cynical may think that until the Court of Appeal have ruled on the matter no-one can be quite sure what the effect will be.[68] In the case of unregistered land the investigation of title will not throw up land charge entries against the land from 1925 to the root of title, possibly in 1960. The purchaser will be bound though he may get compensation under section 25 of the Law of Property Act 1969. If the vendor has the benefit of an NHBRC agreement it should be assigned to the purchaser.

The truth of the matter is that land has appreciated in value to a much greater degree than almost any other asset. The necessity of having a roof over one's head and the opportunity of making considerable unearned, and often untaxed, gains have combined to ensure that some purchasers will take unwarranted risks and some vendors will act in an unscrupulous manner. Every technical point will be taken: a husband will deny the authority of his wife to enter into a contract; a vendor will argue that specific performance cannot be granted in the case of an exercise of an option because the consideration for the option is nominal; a purchaser will seek to enforce an oral contract evidenced by correspondence between solicitors trying to agree a formal contract; and so on. When things go wrong, some clients, with the help of legal aid, sue their solicitors, sometimes successfully, sometimes not. In recent years solicitors have been sued for failing to exchange contracts quickly enough, even though they have not received their local land charge search cer-

---

68. In *Bedson* v. *Bedson* [1965] 2 Q.B. 666, the Court of Appeal, without allowing the wife to be heard, granted an unasked injunction preventing her from severing a joint tenancy and thus compelling her to let her husband have her share on her death.

tificates back through no fault of theirs; for failing to deter their clients from entering into contracts before they have arranged their finances; for failing to apply in time for a new lease under the Landlord and Tenant Act 1954, Part II; for failing to advise that an entail should be barred; for failing to advise that consent to a change of user under a lease could be refused unreasonably; for failing to advise that restrictive covenants were binding even though the client did not tell his solicitor what he wanted to do with the land. The courts exact a high, but not impossible, standard from solicitors. Unfortunately when liability is established the amount of damages may bear little relation to the amount of consideration involved.

We said earlier that the one instrument of 1800 that is easily comprehensible today is the lease. The long lease of residential premises has not changed very much, although the death knell was sounded by the Leasehold Reform Act 1967, after a preliminary warning bell had been sounded by inflation. If a lessee can expropriate his landlord for compensation well below the market value, what developer is going to use the long lease? The short lease of residential property had been scotched somewhat earlier by the Rent Acts. The one residential lease of importance today is the long lease used in the sale of flats. It requires careful drafting because it lays down rules for a community for nearly a century. If a mistake is made it is difficult, if not impossible, to rectify it.[69] Where developers have sold flats in this way, such experience as we have—and it does not really go back a quarter of a century yet—shows that the leases are successful and the flats maintain their value in line with other residential property. The few decisions of the courts have been helpful, which is more than can be said for parliamentary interest in the subject which has so far confined itself to the provisions of sections 90 and 91 of the Housing Finance Act 1972 (relating to accounts) which totally ignore standard practice. It is probably the practice of selling flats that has led to the popularity of the absolute leasehold title, so that the practitioner is beginning to look on the good leasehold title with suspicion. Flat sales are never simple but it is a curious fact that the direct lease by the developer to the flat-owner without a management company is still the most successful. The lessor has his obligations for which the lessee pays and the firmer the administration the better the flat maintains its value.

Part II of the Landlord and Tenant Act 1954 is one of the most successful pieces of modern legislation because it put into statutory form good estate management practice. The tenant of business premises gets security of tenure except where the landlord wants the premises back for

---

69. See *Re Davstone's Estates Ltd's Lease* [1969] 2 Ch. 378: no one responsible for remedying a structural defect.

himself to occupy or wishes to redevelop.[70] The market is not distorted because the rent is readjusted on each renewal to the proper commercial rent. Indeed, renewals today will normally include a rent review clause every five years. The timetable of the Act concentrates the minds of the parties and though many actions are started the parties nearly always reach agreement. The Act has, however, led to certain eccentricities. A landlord lets a garage under an oral agreement for £1 a week and thinks no more about it. The tenant uses the garage for business purposes. The Act applies and not only will the landlord have to give six months' notice, but he cannot get his tenant out except on one of the statutory grounds. Landlords do not like subtenancies because they may find on renewal that the subtenant is entitled to a headlease of part of the premises originally demised. User clauses tend to be rigid. On renewal the court must have regard to the terms of the existing lease so that a landlord tends to draw his original lease as tightly as possible.

*   *   *

Conveyancing is a way of life. If a root of title consisting of an Act for the Restoration of the Blood does not stir the practitioner's interest he is in the wrong branch of the law. We remember one pedantic legal executive who insisted on seeing the original charter showing title to land and was very upset when the charter was produced—in Latin. Conveyancing is concerned with human beings, helping to turn houses into homes, tradesmen into merchants. Today's activities are tomorrow's history and the conveyancer is the chronicler; the details and methods change but the profession continues. The " stark simplicity " of a transfer of registered land has at any rate produced a professor of poetry at Oxford.

---

70. There are other grounds for refusing a new lease but these two cover the overwhelming majority of cases.